Playwrights throughout history have used the emotion of wonder to explore the relation between feeling and knowing in the theatre. In *Shakespeare and the Theatre of Wonder*, T. G. Bishop argues that wonder provides a turbulent space, rich at once in emotion and self-consciousness, where the nature and value of knowing is brought into question. Bishop compares the treatment of wonder in classical philosophy and drama, and goes on to examine English cycle-plays, charting wonder's ambivalent relation to dogma and sacrament in the medieval religious theatre. Through extended readings of three of Shakespeare's plays – *The Comedy of Errors, Pericles*, and *The Winter's Tale* – Bishop argues that Shakespeare uses wonder as a key component of his dialectic between affirmation and critique. Wonder is shown as vital to the characteristic self-consciousness of Shakespeare's plays as acts of narrative inquiry and renovation.

Cambridge Studies in Renaissance Literature and Culture 9

Shakespeare and the theatre of wonder

Cambridge Studies in Renaissance Literature and Culture

General editor
STEPHEN ORGEL
Jackson Eli Reynolds Professor of Humanities, Stanford University

Editorial board
Anne Barton, *University of Cambridge*
Jonathan Dollimore, *University of Sussex*
Marjorie Garber, *Harvard University*
Jonathan Goldberg, *The Johns Hopkins University*
Nancy Vickers, *University of Southern California*

The last twenty years have seen a broad and vital reinterpretation of the nature of literary texts, a move away from formalism to a sense of literature as an aspect of social, economic, political, and cultural history. While the earliest New Historicist work was criticized for a narrow and anecdotal view of history, it also served as an important stimulus for post-structuralist, feminist, Marxist, and psychoanalytical work, which in turn has increasingly informed and redirected it. Recent writing on the nature of representation, the historical construction of gender, and of the concept of identity itself, on theatre as a political and economic phenomenon and on the ideologies of art generally, reveals the breadth of the field. "Cambridge Studies in Renaissance Literature and Culture" is designed to offer historically oriented studies of Renaissance literature and theatre which make use of the insights afforded by theoretical perspectives. The view of history envisioned is above all a view of our own history, a reading of the Renaissance for and from our own time.

Drama and the market in the age of Shakespeare
DOUGLAS BRUSTER, University of Chicago

The Renaissance dialogue: literary dialogue in its social and political contexts, Castiglione to Galileo
VIRGINIA COX, University College London

Spenser's secret career
RICHARD RAMBUSS, Tulane University

Shakespeare and the geography of difference
JOHN GILLIES, La Trobe University

Men in women's clothing: anti-theatricality and effeminization, 1579–1642
LAURA LEVINE, Wellesley College

The reformation of the subject: Spenser, Milton, and the English Protestant epic
LINDA GREGERSON, University of Michigan

Voyages in print: English travel to America, 1576–1624
MARY C. FULLER, Massachusetts Institute of Technology

Subject and object in Renaissance culture
edited by MARGRETA DE GRAZIA, MAUREEN QUILLIGAN,
PETER STALLYBRASS, University of Pennsylvania

Shakespeare and the theatre of wonder
T. G. BISHOP, Case Western Reserve University

Anxious masculinity in early modern England
MARK BREITENBERG

Seizures of the will in early modern English drama
FRANK WHIGHAM, University of Texas at Austin

Shakespeare
and the theatre of wonder

T. G. Bishop

Case Western Reserve University

CAMBRIDGE
UNIVERSITY PRESS

Published by the Press Syndicate of the University of Cambridge
The Pitt Building, Trumpington Street, Cambridge CB2 1RP
40 West 20th Street, New York, NY 10011–4211, USA
10 Stamford Road, Oakleigh, Melbourne 3166, Australia

First published 1996

Printed in Great Britain at the University Press, Cambridge

A catalogue record for this book is available from the British library

Library of Congress cataloguing in publication data

Bishop, T. G.
   Shakespeare and the theatre of wonder / T. G. Bishop.
      p.   cm. – (Cambridge studies in Renaissance literature and culture; 9)
   Includes bibliographical references
   ISBN 0 521 55086 6 (hardback)
1. Shakespeare, William, 1564–1616 – Criticism and interpretation.
2. Wonder in literature.
3. Knowledge, Theory of, in literature.
4. Shakespeare, William, 1564–1616. Comedy of errors.
5. Shakespeare, William, 1564–1616. Pericles.
6. Shakespeare, William, 1564–1616. Winter's tale.
7. Mysteries and miracle-plays, English – History and criticism.
I. Title.   II. Series.
PR3069.W65B57 1996
822.3'3–dc20   95–15644 CIP

ISBN 0 521 55086 6 hardback

CE

for my teachers

There is a tender empiricism that identifies with its subject-matter and only through that becomes a theory.

Goethe

My contribution is to ask for a paradox to be accepted and tolerated and respected, and for it not to be resolved. By flight to split-off intellectual functioning it is possible to resolve the paradox, but the price of this is the loss of the value of the paradox itself.

D. W. Winnicott

Contents

Acknowledgments   *page* xi
List of abbreviations   xiii

Introduction   1

1   Theory of wonder; theatre of wonder   17

2   Vision and vocation in the theatre of God   42

3   Compounding "*Errors*"   63

4   *Pericles*; or, the past as fate and miracle   93

5   *The Winter's Tale*; or, filling up the graves   125

Conclusion   176

Notes   178
Bibliography   211
Index   219

Acknowledgments

As with all such undertakings, versions of this study have passed through many helping hands. I want here to offer my thanks to some that have been especially generous with their time and assistance. When shaping its earliest avatar as a doctoral dissertation at Yale, I was especially fortunate in my advisors, George Hunter and John Hollander, both of whom gave unstintingly, as they have done since, of their knowledge and judgment. Professor Hollander also read and commented carefully on a late draft of the entire manuscript. Larry Manley and Lars Engle invited me to try out early versions of Chapter Four on their lecture classes, and both offered helpful advice and comments. In addition, Lars Engle graciously allowed me to use for my own argument a significant discovery he had made. Paul Fry and Heinrich von Staden fielded questions on classical matters with good humor and acuity. The comments on the final dissertation of Professors Fry and Manley, together with those of Professor George Lord, were helpful in reorganizing the work at a critical stage. Alice Miskimin also offered important advice at a crucial stage.

Other friends, teachers and colleagues have also been instrumental, either in encouraging early explorations or in weighing later, more concrete results. Howard Felperin and Mary Dove led seminars at the University of Melbourne that introduced me to many of the materials I have taken up here. Peter Holbrook, Imre Salusinszky, Hugh Craig, Nancy Wright and others at the University of Newcastle, Australia invited me on separate occasions to deliver versions of Chapters Two and Three and discussed them with me fruitfully. The comments of Ken Gross and Suzanne Wofford on part of Chapter Five in an SAA seminar chaired by Paul Yachnin sharpened my perception of several points, and Anthony Dawson generously allowed me to read some of his ongoing work presented there. Those who attended the 1994 Ohio Shakespeare Conference were also generous in their comments on selections from that chapter. Andrew Ford also kindly allowed me to quote from a forthcoming paper.

In Cleveland Martin Helzle and Colin McLarty read and discussed Chapter One with me, as did David Evett with the greater part of the manuscript. My colleagues in the English Department at Case Western Reserve University, and in particular Gary Stonum and Suzanne Ferguson, have my thanks for supporting my work at a difficult time. Kristin Dunkle gave me material assistance when my computer tried to give up the ghost, as did Nathan Price from further afield. Dennis Bye magically produced some vital software out of thin air. Kristen Olson gave invaluable help with proofreading and indexing.

Most recently I have also had the great good fortune to have Stephen Orgel read and edit my work. Others who have worked with him will know how unfailingly generous, acute, and improving I have found his insights. This work would have been very much the poorer without his careful and genial sifting. I am deeply indebted to him. What lapses remain in knowledge, care, or insight are mine alone.

I have been fortunate also in the institutions that have assisted me in my work. The librarians at Sterling Memorial Library at Yale, the Folger Shakespeare Library and Freiberger Library at CWRU found answers to all the questions I had wit enough to ask them. I am grateful to the Mrs. Giles Whiting Foundation, the National Endowment for the Humanities and the W. P. Jones Fund at CWRU for grants and fellowships in support of my work. The Shakespeare Centre Library in Stratford-on-Avon kindly assisted me in securing the cover illustration. At Cambridge University Press, Josie Dixon and Rosemary Morris have been models of professional grace.

My wife Laura contributed to and somehow survived all the versions of this project, in days both fair and foul. The real wonder to me is the forbearance and good humor with which she did so.

Abbreviations

AJP	*American Journal of Philology*
EETS es	Early English Text Society – extra series
EETS ss	Early English Text Society – supplementary series
ELH	*English Literary History*
ELN	*English Language Notes*
MP	*Modern Philology*
PMLA	*Publications of the Modern Languages Association*
PQ	*Philological Quarterly*
SEL	*Studies in English Literature*
STC	*Short Title Catalogue of English Books, 1475–1640*, second edition
YES	*Yearbook of English Studies*

Introduction

... ut Hymettia sole
cera remollescit tractataque pollice multas
flectitur in facies ipsoque fit utilis usu.

Ovid

This self-encounter which I consider the major source of the potency
and success of beneficent fictions may be defined also as imaginative
identification. Things are then not merely happening *before* us; they
are happening, by the power and force of imaginative identification,
to us.

Chinua Achebe

When we go to the theatre, we make a deliberate surrender. As a vital
part of what theatre is, we agree to let the play control in large measure
the tempo and terrain of our experience for the next two hours' traffic. In
this, drama differs from poetry or prose narrative. We cannot, no matter
how we might wish to, speed up, slow, review, reject, or skip. We cannot
shut the book and wait for the right mood to return; we cannot tame an
evil or ecstatic moment by avoidance or repetition or some other readerly
strategy. And though in this theatrical performance is like other arts that
unfold in real time, such as film or music, it is unlike these in that it acts
at once in two different moments. One is the remote moment of the story
being told, to which the audience (and the actors) are only ever admitted
by the fact of a common fiction. The other, more specific to the theatre, is
that real, immediate, and vulnerable moment where the performers put
together the play by word and gesture in the audience's presence. From
this latter moment actors can appeal directly to their watchers, and vice
versa, at times both planned and unplanned, as no film character can do.
A musician is only ever here, a film actor only there, but a stage actor
moves between here and there, and takes us willingly along. The deepest
work of theatrical representation is to make spectators see and feel these
two moments in mutual implication.[1]

The theatre takes vivid advantage of us, has us so much at its mercy.
And yet not entirely: it must at the same time convince us to be convinced.

If audiences are overwhelmed by what they witness, their vulnerability is an election they themselves have made and make. When children scream and hide under the seats at the evil, grasping forest in *Snow White*, they are acknowledging their terrible powerlessness before what they have themselves chosen, and a deep part of the affront is their own implication in producing the dreadful fantasy. Much the same can be said of the blinding of Gloucester, with its unparalleled power to make adult audiences flinch away at the very moment the old Earl is deprived of sight. We may close our eyes, even, *in extremis*, walk out or try to interrupt the show. But if we do, then we acknowledge that what we had agreed to at first we have now abrogated and perhaps failed to live up to. There is only one way to intervene in a dramatic fiction, and that is to enter it oneself as a performer. If for instance, following the Folio text of the play, the servants who relieve Gloucester were absent from a production, it might be possible to rise from the audience and play their lines to register a protest. But nothing short of this would reach the character. Anything else would count only as interfering with the actor's work.

Such desperate measures are rare and their very extremity indicates to what extent they are abnormal, but they make their point. If the Gloucester example has us, as a last resort, interceding directly, there is an important sense in which that move only makes explicit the way the theatre always invites us to be and act. Though Dr. Johnson was right to insist that theatre audiences are always in their right senses, they are often in translated or troped versions of those senses, and the relations between a plain and a figured sense can be very complex. Almost all audiences, even of children, are quite sophisticated about this in practice, and negotiate their way back and forth with a skill the more remarkable for being mostly unreflective. But the theatre plays its strangest and most powerful tricks across just this boundary.

I

This book is about some occasions on which plays desire and expect audiences to be "overwhelmed" by what they hear and see. Such fraught moments have a way of making us feel a curious mixture of pain and elation, whether their circumstance be happy or sad. Where categorical boundaries dissolve and extremes of plenitude or emptiness shade into one another, we may resort to oxymoronic formulae, such as "tragic joy" or "sweet sorrow," or note, like the First Gentleman in *The Winter's Tale*, that "the wisest beholder ... could not say if th'importance were joy or sorrow."[2] From this point of view it is more the fact of the intense emotive response than its direction that counts for me, and if I have chosen for the most part to focus on scenes of recovery and rejoicing, that is partly because they have been less attended to than the work of trauma and tears, and partly because my ultimate objects of study, Shakespeare's plays, seem to me on balance more deeply inclined towards joy than sorrow, and to shape much of their sorrow out of the failure of what might have made for joy. What happens at such moments, for those within the fiction, those on the stage and those in the audience, and especially what happens to the relations *between* these constituencies, where the central work of the theatre takes place, is my subject.

This "between" is the preposition *par excellence* of the theatrical. Drama, as I noted above, unfolds between stage and audience as well as between here and not here. In one sense, theatre shares this condition with every perception that unfolds between observer and world, yet the theatre deliberately doubles that transaction, and this sustained doubling sets it apart. We see what is not in what is, a fabling link the more insistent in that so much of the material out of which theatrical fiction is made is demonstrably real material: real bodies, real objects, words really uttered. Seeing, feeling, and knowing are peculiarly framed and directed at themselves, and the various ways from sense to its objects and back are opened to exploration. Perception is liable at any moment to become the theatre's subject, so that theatre is always about to suggest a theory of itself, just as at the same time it points beyond itself to an imagined "regular" world. Again, it is in the relation between the two inquiries, into itself and into the world, that the theatre performs its poetic work.

The emotion known as wonder is a characteristic and heightened experience of this "between" quality of theatricality. Wonder particularly raises the question of the theatre's interest in the emotions it generates through its characteristic creation of a dynamic space of flux and intermediacy – between stage and audience, between the real and the impossible, between belief and skepticism, between reason and feeling. Into this space the audience lets itself be pulled. It is one of the most peculiar, and most welcomed, returns on our engaged attention, a feature regularly expected and applauded. Nor is this merely a matter of seeing strange and unusual sights in costume or staging, though these can be one source of theatrical wonder. More particularly, as Aristotle observes, wonder is an emotional response to certain events framed for inspection in the theatre as a particular action – events placed under a particular "pressure" towards the revelation of significance.

Some combination of force, indeterminacy, and detachment has been a feature of wonder in many accounts from the earliest times. For both Plato and Aristotle wonder occupied the ground between ordinary thought and philosophical inquiry. Plato called the feeling "the mark of the philosopher," where "mark" [*pathos*] has an almost totemic feel. Aristotle made the experience of wonder at once a goal of poetry and a prelude to philosophy, hence implicitly a bridge between them. In turn, Albertus Magnus and Thomas Aquinas spoke of it as a middle-marker on the path to knowledge, and Descartes called it "the first of the passions," the point where mind and world collided. In each of these thinkers, the discussion of wonder becomes an occasion to articulate the particular goal of a self-aware and philosophical knowledge lying beyond the emotion. In order for knowledge to appear, reason must be purged of its contamination by delusional emotion within the magic circle of wonder. Disciplined, wonder becomes the conduit of truth; left to resonate in itself, it is a locus of captivity. This impulse to purge wonder of its excess emotive charge is frequently associated by the philosophers with a chastening or rejection of false knowledges, and especially that of poetry.

If the theatre shares philosophy's impulse to frame acts of human perception in a critical and self-conscious way, it differs from the philosophical eye in wishing to incorporate the emotional dynamisms that mark perception into its investigations. Wonder is an especially potent gift in the theatre's pharmacopoeia for the very reason that it foregrounds the difficulty under extreme conditions of framing, and still more of distinguishing, a subject and an object of perception. In that labile moment, the intimate interrelations of emotion and reason are explored, and wonder becomes a kind of high-level "switchpoint" for transactions between emotional and rational responses. It is not the purging or conversion of wonder into something else that theatre seeks, but the placement of that emotion in relation to an audience's understanding of the action. In particular, wonder registers not the audience's analysis of the action, but something more like their sense of its significance. Wonder, that is, is less directed to the acquisition of knowledge than to the perception of meaning.

II

The emotional power of poetry has been a constant topic of critical commentary. When Plato imagined his ideal community, he exiled poetry from it out of a conviction that the power of its appeal to the emotions was too unpredictable, too difficult to regulate within the bounds of reason and good order. Our surrender to the elaboration of collective fantasy, our being overwhelmed by the action, these were precisely what Plato wished to prevent. The emotions generated by poetry were badly trained, or trained on the wrong objects. In his turn, Aristotle claimed that fictions provided opportunities to discern and judge processes of cause and effect in human action. He insisted that poetic *mimesis* was a fully proper and human activity, an aspect of knowledge and reason, and that those plays were best where the activity of reason was most clearly vindicated. He may also have believed that intellectual perception of the formal structure of an action was a kind of net or governor for the management of the unruly emotions prompted by the enormity of dramatic events. But no matter what specific relations he imagined between reason and emotion, Aristotle conceded that the emotion roused by tragedy needed to be managed or neutralized. His term for this process, *katharsis*, has occasioned an immense commentary since the sixteenth century, one that shows no sign of abating.[3] In addition to the famous "pity and fear [and] such emotions" on which *katharsis* is said to work, Aristotle insisted that wonder was part of the proper end of tragedy, and he attached it consistently to an audience's perception of the logical structure of interrelations between events. Indeed, wonder was the characteristic emotion elicited by the key event of Aristotle's best kind of action, the recognition. What connection there might be between *katharsis* and wonder he does not, however, say.

Another way of addressing the intense emotionality of poetry can be found in Longinus' treatise "Of the Sublime." A rhetorician and critic rather than a philosopher, Longinus was interested in the power resident in language under certain circumstances vividly to mold the experience of its hearers and thereby compel their assent. Without pronouncing on the moral value of such surrenders, he investigated above all the emotional force that language can bring to bear on its users and auditors, and particularly evoked the relation of that force to images of extremity, struggle, and threat. Instead of denying, as Aristotle seems implicitly to do, Plato's claim that there is too much unruly emotion in poetry, Longinus sought to refute his assertion that such emotion is necessarily a bad thing.[4] For Longinus, the overwhelming "force" in words needed to be acknowledged, since it could not be commanded away. His argument is the more striking in that he turns against Plato himself certain aspects of the latter's own work, shrewdly finding examples of the force and struggle of poetic authority particularly in Plato's own relations with Homer.[5]

A dichotomy thus presents itself for interpreting our emotional response to plays between how, on the one hand, we are overwhelmed and surrender to the power of the theatre's fictions to implicate us and how, on the other, we find our way through emotion to eventual detachment and judgment of the play's phenomena as relevant (or not) to our experience of the world. Awareness of this dichotomy emerges repeatedly when these classical commentators consider wonder as an element in poetry. On the one side we find Aristotle's "thinking and reasoning out" and on the other Longinus' "force and flight." What boundary is being negotiated here? And what, if any, is the relation between this dichotomy and the double moment of a dramatic performance at once controlled by actors and audience in the present and free to unfold in another moment through the theatricality of that present?

III

The relation between force and knowledge in wonder, at least for the philosopher, can be initially clarified by examining Descartes's analysis of "l'admiration" from his *Les Passions de l'Ame* of 1649. Descartes makes "l'admiration" one of his six "primary emotions," and gives it pre-eminence as "the first emotion of all."[6] Setting aside his physiological account of emotion as "the agitation by which the [cerebral] spirits move the small gland in the middle of the brain," the phenomenological impressions he records give a good sense of the variety of impulses involved. In particular, he displays an odd mixture of celebration and mistrust.

First of all, wonder is the emotion particular to the mind's first, pre-evaluative contact with phenomena that appear "novel or strongly different from what we knew beforehand." Descartes insists on the primacy of this emotion; hence it is the mark of the mind's apprehension of its own operations as a consciousness that knows or can know. Other emotions such as "Veneration and Disdain" or "Love and Hate" follow appropriately as cognition and evaluation proceed in sundry directions from their occasion, but wonder raises the question of representation at the primary level of perception: "What is it that is presenting itself to me?" Uniquely, wonder is an emotion that concerns knowledge alone, so that "there is no change in the heart or in the blood with this emotion."[7]

The circumscription of wonder to the register of knowledge nevertheless "doesn't prevent it having a great deal of force" through "the sudden and unexpected arrival of the impression." Descartes continues his account in images of impact and violence that give a quite literal feel to his usual vocabulary of mental "impressions," as though it were a question of direct and threatening contact between mind and object. Descartes's shielded mental organs suddenly seem infinitely tender, like the eyes of snails. In response to this vulnerability, knowledge itself emerges as a defensive "callusing" of the mind, its way of adjusting to a chronic discomfort:

It is also certain that objects new to the senses touch the brain in certain parts where it is not used to being touched, and that, these parts being more tender or less firm than those which frequent agitation has hardened, this increases the effect of the movements which they excite there. This is hardly incredible if one considers that a comparable reason determines that, the soles of our feet being accustomed to fairly rough touching through the weight of the body they bear, we feel only very little that touching when we walk; whereas another much lesser and softer [touching], as when they are tickled, is almost unbearable to us, only because it is not normal for us.[8]

Wonder is, it seems, the mental equivalent of the hand's flinch at the touch of a flame. It registers threat, and calls the mind to itself to inspect the damage. But it is Descartes's image of the sole of the foot that gives his most acute sense of knowledge as a kind of developed response to the world's unfriendly toughness, a defensive hardening of the mental apparatus in its daily dealings with the unyielding world of objects and events. Thinking is like walking – a naturally human activity that gets us about in the world deliberately, with a measured and even instinctive tread. Knowledge is what we develop to walk the world in, and real thought toughens the soul.

If wonder helps us develop knowledge, however, it is not necessarily welcome. It is not unlike pain; and like pain it can overwhelm and damage. Even as he gives primacy to wonder as that which alerts us that protective knowledge is missing in this spot and works to "keep this impression" for further study, Descartes also fears wonder's power to disable us and restrict our mental mobility. In extreme cases, it can paralyze us altogether, turning us into a thing frozen and hard with the hardness of the very world it seeks to warn us against. This petrified state Descartes calls Astonishment ("l'Estonnement"), "which makes the whole body stand still like a statue, so that one can see only the first aspect of the object which presented itself, and as a result one can acquire no more particular knowledge of it."[9] The trauma is so great it is no longer even perceived as trauma and we become deadened in turn. Our mental paralysis registers as physical immobility, stuck face to face with the astonishing impression, and all other function ceases. A delicate, vital economy between outside and inside has been disrupted.

According to Descartes, one can make too much of a habit of such dangerous pleasures, becoming addicted to rapture over unworthy things, and "this can completely remove or pervert the use of reason." Though wonder's initiatory force is important, even from the earliest times of our life, in attaching us to the world as our sphere of action "since it disposes us to acquire knowledge," nevertheless "we ought always to strive afterwards to deliver ourselves from it as much as possible."[10] Like "dull and stupid people," those who cannot deliver themselves fail in the task of reason, a fate particularly reserved for those who "don't have a great opinion of their capacity." It is as though nature had built a device into the mind to prevent it aspiring too high, so that only "the ablest" through their exceptional mental fight can advance past a barrier by turns traumatic and narcotic. For those who fail to win through, there remains a kind of stupefaction in which the mind learns to limit itself by

a habit, which disposes the soul to stop in the same way before all the other objects which present themselves. ... And this is what prolongs the disorder of those who are blindly curious, that is to say, who seek for rare things only to wonder at them, and not at all to know them.[11]

Too much wonder can blind us. Descartes has now moved notably from an analytic to a moralizing stance. His tone is that of someone who has himself confronted this trial and won through it, showing himself one of "the ablest," his eyes intact and his mental economy uncompromised. Wonder is a rough magic, which the true philosopher can tame and convert to his own uses.

Descartes's account of the experience whose role in drama is the subject of this study has itself a curiously narrative and dramatic quality: wonder is the portal, weirdly guarded and dangerously beset, through which we pass into new knowledge. It is almost as though wonder is in part the enemy of knowledge, an internal governor set to prevent us from knowing too much. Against its own powers of astonishment, the philosophic mind, self-divided, struggles towards mastery, like a knight battling against some Medusa, or passing through a door of fire on a romance quest.

Descartes's famous philosophical skepticism in the *Meditations on First Philosophy* appears in this light as the introjection of wonder into the field of traditional authority, where it is used to imagine a clear and distinct break with past entanglements. All sensual data and all received opinion are examined anew as if they were so many objects of wonder to be interrogated and overcome. This break cleanses wonder of lesser occasions, allowing Descartes eventually and triumphantly to reclaim it when he proves the existence and vindicates the goodness of God, towards whom Descartes can turn secure in having a proper object for the wondering suspension of his struggle: "I should like to pause here and spend some time on the contemplation of God; to reflect on his attributes, and to gaze with wonder and adoration on the beauty of this immense light, so far as the eye of my darkened intellect can bear it."[12] In the end, Descartes wishes to save wonder for philosophy, to mark off a space where it can be legitimately exercised without fear of the illusionary paralyses inflicted on knowledge by "the deceiver," whom Descartes has bested.[13]

This will to move beyond the pathos of appearances and to challenge mutability itself through mental rigor can be read in one final example in which wonder plays a significant, if tacit, role – Descartes's famous encounter by his evening fire with a piece of wax:

> Let us take, for example, this wax. It has been taken very recently from the comb. It has not yet lost all the savor of its honey. It retains some of the scent of the flowers from which it has been collected. Its color, shape, and size are manifest. It is hard, cold, easily touched, and if you hit it with a knuckle it will emit a sound. And so all those things are present which seem needed for a body to be known most distinctly. But look! While I am talking, it is moved towards the fire: the remnants of savor are purged off, the scent blows away, the color is changed, the shape is taken away, the size grows, it becomes fluid, hot, it can hardly be touched, and if you hit it it will no longer emit a sound. Does it still remain the same wax?[14]

Descartes's experiment confronts Dame Mutabilitie in her minute sensual particulars. Despite the air of scruple and observational neutrality, it is hard not to hear in this passage an elegiac plangency, more obvious if we bear Prospero or Spenser in mind. Reading the passage we watch the senses one by one withdrawn from a world of pleasures. Yet Descartes does not linger: he seeks a substantial truth and persistent recognition beneath disguises. The Knight of Knowledge rejects the Gardens of Mediation: Descartes is a kind of anti-Prospero, whom the melting into air cannot touch with its intimations of mortality. He performs his magic trick for us, he conjures the wax away   and then shows how it was not magic at all: the wax is still there. Or rather, what is still there is Descartes's unmoved mind, which scorns mere mutability. The challenge is to follow him through our wonder and out the other side into philosophy.

The wax passage produces through a kind of *kenosis* a strange sense of challenge as we watch Descartes enforcing his own liberation from delusion. The will to lose these sweets ranges and measures itself against their power to conjure our nostalgic attachment. Though the prose is calm, there is within it the sense of a struggle to let nothing escape self-conscious attention. Under this pressure, the details emerge as though Descartes were exorcising nine demons from the wax: demons of appearance, theatrical demons. His battle with the wax, that is, evinces a narrative and emotional structure similar to that of his account of "the first emotion" – past the blocking of an enthrallment to mere appearance to the assertion of himself as among "the ablest." He is a more subtle aspirer, a better Icarus – one who can live through what fire does to wax.[15]

Through our emotional involvement with the passage we can feel how astringent is the quality of Descartes's mental constancy, not unlike the fire in which the sensual immediacy of wax is being tried to deliver up its substantial sameness. Against the erotic Ovid of mourning and metamorphosis, for whom the mutability of the wax is a kind of emblematic allusion, Descartes opposes his own stern fable of a mind that knows the world as a persistent presence. His final question, "Does it still remain the same wax?" asks about more than mere identity of substance. It is also a question about the work done in the passage itself, with its complex emotional and allusive transformations. Only by purging the possibility of certain kinds of response to the exemplary wax can Descartes's particular philosophical project get underway. To have chosen for his work the very material of Daedalus' invention and Ovid's poetics signals his intention to take up "the matter of wax" in a new way, leaving the traces of its old savor to dissolve away.

Particularly striking about the scene of Descartes by his fire is its dramatic feel, its invitation to "us" ("Sumamus") to enter, watch, and take part. And as a scene, it is especially notable how much its general framework resembles Aristotle's dramatic prescriptions. We have a careful intellectual inquiry, a certain emotion, and a specific purgation of that emotion from the medium (like the "saporis reliquiae") by the rigor of our intellectual attention. The whole process concludes with a sense of transformation and surprise, which recognizes finally an object in which we can hardly believe: "the same wax." The complex emotional and rhetorical texture of Descartes's apparently nonce example brings us back to the interinvolvement of wonder with inquiry and with *katharsis*.

Indeed, what Descartes achieves here bears a remarkable resemblance to what Andrew Ford has recently argued Aristotle does by invoking *katharsis* to render drama up to philosophical analysis. Ford argues that by confining the unruly emotional effects of drama under the heading of *katharsis*, Aristotle is able to shift his attention to the best methods of achieving this highly desirable outcome through careful control of narrative structure. Refusing *katharsis* fuller treatment in the *Poetics* thus "performs a lustration on a field of inquiry and makes possible a new literary genre – the theory of literature."[16] Though Descartes presumably did not have the *Poetics* in mind, his care at the outset of his own philosophy to effect a purgation of emotive and intertextual distractions before confronting the issue of knowability has a similar design.

IV

Descartes and Aristotle wished to exorcise or circumscribe emotion in order to enable analysis; the theatre does not. It relies on emotional engagement as a major mode of coupling between the audience and the fiction through the actions of the performers. At the same time, it is always within the performers' repertory of strategies to alter that engagement by reminding the audience pointedly of the mutually constructed nature of their enterprise, to underline the figurative switchpoints of the transaction. When, for instance, the actor playing Richard of Gloucester comes down the stage towards us in his assumed role of villainous chorus to announce that "Now is the winter of our discontent / Made glorious summer by this sun of York," the work of theatre hangs on the cardinal words "Now" and "our," with their complex gesturing through him at once out to us and back to Yorkist England. The senses of exultation, glee, and hability criss-cross in the speech so that we connect an engagement with performer to one with character, and this determines the tenor of our involvement with Richard for much of the play to come. But the vocabulary of "involvement" needs careful management here. It consists of a continuum of implications and emotional postures, and is by no means a simple or automatic process. We may easily entertain different modes of "involvement" with different characters or sections of a single play – with Falstaff or Hotspur, Mak or the Angel. Thus when Ford comments of the *Poetics* that "the role of structure is simply to drive us more surely into involvement with the experience" he is skirting over difficult matters, as, he contends, was Aristotle himself.[17] It would be fairer to say that a complex set of modulations is constantly going on between engagement and detachment, or, more accurately still, between theatrical actions perceived as referring at the same time variously here to us and not here, to somewhere else.

This "back and forth" of reference across itself is where our keenest engagement with the theatre unfolds, is what leads us to speak of its "magic." And just as reference is always split in this way (though not always so pointedly as Richard Gloucester makes it), so also the emotional engagements we are drawn into by theatrical representation have their provisionality always at hand. Whatever else Aristotle, or any later theorist, may mean by *katharsis*, the central fact to be accounted for is that theatre audiences do not run in fear or intercede in pity. The theatre wants emotion, but wants it also "placed" in relation to a fictional structure well recognized by all concerned, and used by all concerned as a foil and a frame (both surround and skeleton) for emotion. When wonder enfolds into itself, as we shall see it does, an emotional maximum and an access of metadramatic and figurative self-consciousness, this dialectic of engagement and detachment reaches an extreme of development in which the potential of theatre itself as a mode of human inquiry is in question, and from which emotions are not and cannot be hygienically exiled. How is it that we thus plumb the significance of our emotions even as we have them? This study will attempt to give an account of the complex acts of self-consciousness that some plays invite players and audiences to engage in even as they are profoundly moved by the felt resonances of their commitment.

V

It would have been possible to have adopted a more consistently historicist approach to the question of wonder in early modern drama. The claim would have run broadly that in an historical moment so charged with transition, upheaval, and the reorganization of regimes of both knowledge and social practice, it is only to be expected that public fictions like plays would reflect and reflect on wider social and intellectual narratives of newness. As the emotion proper to "everything that can seem rarest and strangest," wonder was ideal for confronting and coming to terms with the early modern Shock of the New, and a general evocation of a European "culture of wonder" could well form the foundation for a thesis in cultural poetics ranging widely across disciplines and cultural practices for evidence of instability – theorized, interrogated, and confirmed especially in the public arena of the Shakespearean stage. Something much like this has recently been done for the New World discoveries by Stephen Greenblatt in his *Marvelous Possessions*, which collates around a short passage from the voyage diaries of Christopher Columbus the history both of European colonialism and of Renaissance aesthetic theory.[18]

Such a thesis is attractive, neat, and perhaps even correct. A version of it will in fact be sketched in Chapter Three in order to place Shakespeare's attitude to his own developing dramatic narratives. Yet it does not quite satisfy me, largely because of the very scope of the generalizations it must make, and I have not in the end structured this study around it for a number of reasons. The first is a sense that I do not now have the resources to undertake such an extended project of historical and cultural analysis. A much larger work than I can offer here would be required. Even Greenblatt's suggestive meditation presents something more like a set of possibilities than a fully worked-out study, and some of his connections are, at the very least, rather loose. Making large claims for some crucial transition in the "history of subjectivity" on the basis of a poem or two and a documentary extract is threatening to become a habit of criticism.

A deeper reason for resisting such an historicist path has been my strong sense that complex verbal artifacts such as plays demand and deserve treatment of an answering patience and complexity, one that is not always easy to achieve, least of all where one eye must be kept on the pursuit of a large historical thesis. My principal interest is in the transactions that occur between the stage and its audience, influenced though these must be by a whole range of cultural conditions and assumptions on both sides. This has led me to return to a more formalist analytic stance than has recently been popular in Renaissance studies, though I would also insist that the recent polemic separation between formal and historical methods of address is in the end a false and largely invidious dichotomy, what Blake would have called a "cloven fiction." Concentrated attention to either the formal articulation or the historical provenance of the language of a text inevitably demands inquiry and yields insight into its counterpart. Here, for instance, it has proved impossible to account for the recurrence of images of linearity in *The Comedy of Errors* without eventually facing the question of the play's economies of reproduction, and hence its view of gender. The kind of close attention I have here paid to rhetorical organization and movement – though now associated with an Old Criticism – has thus inevitably led me to conclusions about the historicity of Shakespeare's language and his particular assumptions about time, history, and human being. I draw some comfort in this double game from the belief that such a dialectic operates between writer and historical moment in the act of composition itself, so that neither history nor text can be reduced to a mere effect of the other.

This book therefore has what may appear to be a split focus. On the one hand, it is an attempt to describe the complexities of a certain recurrent theatrical experience called "wonder," and especially to investigate how various plays have included that experience in their emotional and intellectual textures. The main assumption in treating drama has been the Aristotelian one that drama is a form of human knowledge comparable with other forms, and that therefore it has an interest in investigating and seeking to represent its own nature and status as a form of knowledge. In order to place the particular resources drama has for generating and interrogating wonder, I have had to spend time exploring the latter's treatment by the competing promise of philosophy. At the same time, the discussion of particular kinds of drama has necessitated examining the social occasions within which they arise and represent themselves. If a kind of experience we call wonder seems recurrent across (at least) certain European cultures, the terms available to understand or evoke that experience vary historically and cannot be fully understood without taking into account both the verbal and social universes in which wonder emerges, and which it seeks to address.[19] This study therefore necessarily has an historical dimension, and moves from a set of more or less theoretical co-ordinates towards an attempt to analyze the recurrent evocation of wonder in the cycle-plays of late-medieval England, and thence in the work of Shakespeare, in terms of how aspects of the evocation are framed at particular historical and dramatic moments.

In the first chapter, I investigate the deployment of wonder by Plato and Aristotle in their accounts of the work of philosophy, at once its adjunct and its antagonist. Wonder as a prelude to philosophic reason is welcomed and championed by these writers, but wonder as an emotional power is regarded with a more cautious eye. To explore this latter power further, I turn to Longinus with his ear for the dynamisms of threat, the "hydraulics" of emotive energy in poetry and rhetoric. In turn I connect the latter's concern with how "the sublime" destabilizes boundaries between speaker and hearer, literal and figurative, to aspects of the audience's experience of a double orientation on the theatrical action. In a final section of the chapter, I resume briefly the place of wonder in the voluminous literary arguments that grew out of the Renaissance redis-covery of classical theory, and in particular of the *Poetics*. Here I find a provisional context for Shakespeare's practice in Italian discussions of the playwright's power over the audience through his manipulation of spectacle and of emotion.

The second chapter examines the medieval cycle-plays as a theatre committed to presentation of the miraculous history of God's design for humanity and time. I examine the tension in selected plays between the desire to represent miracle through a kind of theatrical "incarnation" with the same general structure as the eucharistic Sacrament, and a counterdesire to police or control representation by encapsulating miracle within a stable and known order of Celestial design which it can cite or refer to, but not embody. For instance, in the York "Fall of Lucifer," I show how the runaway dramatic and rhetorical energies of Lucifer that threaten to break through the envelope of the stage are reined in by a secret citation of Scripture that the falling angel does not recognize. The chapter concludes with an analysis of the "Appearance to Mary Magdalene" section of the N-Town "Resurrection" sequence, showing how that play dramatizes the power of Christ's voice to rename his follower, yet locates that voice in some way "outside" dramatic mimesis.

Three chapters on plays of Shakespeare follow – on *The Comedy of*

Errors, Pericles, Prince of Tyre, and *The Winter's Tale*. Each reading develops terms for addressing the eruption of wonder at the play's end out of the overall action. The first chapter begins by proposing a model of "dynamic conservatism" for Shakespeare's relation to the narrative and dramatic traditions of the theatre he worked in. It then reads *The Comedy of Errors* as an experiment in transformative *contaminatio* between a romantic drama of wandering, Plautine dramatic linearity and Pauline models of sacramental community. Wonder emerges as the emotional effect of the "recovery" of a habitable world, whose availability attracts a retooled language of sacramental embodiment.

The chapter on *Pericles* addresses that play as an exploration of the problem of transmission – biological, political, and cultural. Again the outbreak of wonder in the final scenes is linked to the experience of "recovery" which I argue includes the sense of the play's relation to the traditions of dramatic and poetic story-telling it absorbs and transmits. The key to this process is the paradoxical figure of Marina, who fuses in herself a scrupulousness about the literality of words and an opening out into the figurative, a conjunction which echoes the double activity of the performance itself.

In the discussion of *The Winter's Tale* that concludes, I attempt to put together the two recent approaches to the play that seem to me to have generated the most powerful insights, but which rarely contact one another: that which investigates the operation of networks of knowledge and sexual fantasy, for which the central figure is Leontes, and that which concerns itself with the play's recurrent worrying of the "art/nature" debate, where the key is the statue of Hermione. It seems to me that the play cannot be fully elucidated or responded to without seeing these two great Shakespearean topics in intimate relation to each other.

The latter chapters on Shakespeare thus address the ways he reworked within his public and commercial theatre a dramaturgy of wonder that spoke directly to his inheritance of a multiple tradition, in the service of what I will call a "poetics of incarnation." This idea of Shakespeare's work as a consistent seeking of the world, using the force of wonder to register both the difficulty and the promise of that quest, sees him running counter to the strong transcendentalizing use of wonder and the sublime which dominated the medieval dramaturgy. Here there might be another historical thesis about a "turn towards the world" in Shakespeare and his moment, a thesis which would engage both Descartes and the question of "the Renaissance" from a different direction. Yet this turn in Shakespeare does not have the world-freezing sobriety of the Cartesian eye, even if the latter gesture is included in the range of stances presented in his work, for instance in Leontes. On the contrary, Shakespeare's dramas of wonder evoke more frequently a therapeutic magic *against* the freezing of the world. They are instinct above all with a desire to restore or refurbish a world that has somehow gone wrong, that has resisted or refused the touch of our need. Wonder in such terms is a mark not of subjection but of an overcoming and satisfaction that "delivers" us into the world (the term is a favorite of Shakespeare's) – at once like a message, a captive, and a child.

Susan Sontag called thirty years ago for the replacement of hermeneutics with "an erotics of art."[20] Since that time, something of what she called for has been begun. Yet even the investigation of "desire in narrative" has come sometimes to seem an abstract matter, hardly in touch with the pulse. We still labor to speak of how art involves our deeper emotional needs along with our colder understanding, and it is not clear to me that anger is a more liberating posture for the work of interpretation than love – though love has its own blindnesses. I have loved these works as I could, and that love has led me to speak of what I saw in them, and therefore necessarily to change it and them. Insofar as the turbulent dynamics of wonder I explore here are in some ways not unlike those of love, insofar as it is possible to entertain the idea of loving poetry and the theatre and what can live in them and in us in them, I hope this study makes a contribution to answering Sontag's call.

1   Theory of wonder; theatre of wonder

There is an effort of the mind when it would describe what it cannot satisfy itself with the description of, to reconcile opposites and to leave a middle state of mind more strictly appropriate to the imagination than any other when it is hovering between two images: as soon as it is fixed on one it becomes understanding; and when it is waving between them attaching itself to neither, it is imagination.

Coleridge, *Lectures of 1811–1812*

"The highest a man can attain," said Goethe on this occasion, "is wonder, and when the primordial phenomenon [*Urphänomen*] makes him wonder he should be content; it can give him nothing higher, and he should not look for anything beyond it; here is the boundary. But the sight of a primordial phenomenon is not generally enough for men; they think there must be more in back of it, like children who, having looked into a mirror, turn it around to see what is on the other side."

Eckermann, *Conversations with Goethe*

I begin with Plato and Aristotle because in them, first of all, philosophy and poetry or drama find themselves intertwined. Even when Plato speaks harshly of poetry (and he does not always do so), his harshness is born of a deep sense of its appeal and strength as an alternative source of knowledge. Recognition of the cognitive claims of drama forms the principal ground of Aristotle's account of it in the *Poetics*. Though neither of them gives a full account of how poetry accomplishes its effects, both are deeply responsive to its power to work on our emotions, and both locate the emotion of wonder in particular at the juncture between what poetry does and what philosophy does.

I

References to "the wonderful" (τὸ θαυμαστόν) and "the astounding" (τὸ ἐκπληκτικόν) in both epic and tragedy are scattered throughout Aristotle's *Poetics*, and appear recurrently where the principal elements of

17

poetry are discussed. It is unfortunately typical of the treatise that a term which occurs in so many crucial contexts is not examined independently. The long debate over *katharsis*, an effect perhaps closely linked to wonder, should be a warning not to do more than locate the general environment in which "the wonderful" arises.[1] To look at "the wonderful" as part of the "proper pleasure" of drama, we must first examine the fleeting but strategic occurrences in the *Poetics* of the term and its companion, the emotional effect Aristotle calls *ekplexis*, or "astonishment."[2]

Wonder first appears in Chapter 9 of the *Poetics*, where it concludes a discussion of the composition of plots as chains of events linked through "likelihood" and "necessity." Here wonder stands at the juncture of the emotive and logical criteria that good tragic plots must fulfill:

Yet the imitation is not only of a complete action, but also of fearsome and piteous incidents, and incidents come to be most fearsome and piteous, or more so, when they arise because of one another [sc. according to probability and necessity] and yet are contrary to what would seem to follow [παρὰ τὴν δόξαν δι' ἄλληλα]. For the wondrous [τὸ γὰρ θαυμαστὸν] will be more wondrous if it arises in this way than if it comes to be through chance or fortune, since even incidents that come to be through fortune seem to be most wondrous [θαυμασιώτατα] to the extent that they appear to arise purposely [ὥσπερ ἐπίτηδες φαίνεται γενομέναι]. (1452a.1–7)

A plot constructed only from, as it were, "ordinary" likelihoods would not be a proper tragic plot. A tension, if not a contradiction, arises between a need for "intelligibility" in events and one for a special affective power enhanced by events that are "contrary to what would seem to follow." Wonder is the outcome when both of these conditions are met at once – that is, when what seems inexplicable (even terrifyingly so) is made available to rational inspection. In the example offered of the statue of Mitys crushing the man who caused his death, wonder arises from the interaction in it of two possible explanatory regimes: one in which this is a terrible accident, the other in which "such incidents do not seem to arise without plan."

It remains the major problem of Aristotle's treatise that cognitive pleasure at tracing orders of events in a "worthy and complete action" (Chapter 6) is never satisfactorily coordinated with the affective pleasure of these events "achieving through pity and fear a *katharsis* of such affections." A recurrent difficulty of reading phrases such as "the end of poetry" or the "proper pleasure" is deciding which of these two major foci is in question at a particular moment. The problem persists right up to the end of the treatise, appearing as late as the end of Chapter 26 (1462b.14), of which D. W. Lucas comments that "it is not specified whether this pleasure arises from the stimulation of pity and fear and also, presumably, from their *katharsis*, or whether it is the kind of pleasure ... produced by formal unity."[3] *Katharsis* has been the place where commentators have traditionally attempted to reduce the dilemma.[4] Yet the term that stands most frequently between the formal and the affective axes of Aristotle's commentary, despite its absence from the Chapter 6 definition, is not *katharsis*, but wonder, which apparently had both an affective and a cognitive valence in ancient Greek as it does in modern English.

This mediating or liminal character of wonder is a recurrent feature of its deployment. In Chapter 14, Aristotle considers the various co-ordinations of act and recognition for protagonists:

Better still, is to do [the intended act] in ignorance and to recognize [sc. friendship] upon doing it. For there is nothing repulsive [μιαρὸν] here and the recognition is astounding [ἐκπληκτικόν]. (1454a.2–4)

Again astonishment mediates directly between the emotive magnitude of the act and its recognition and integration within a graspable logic of events. Though Aristotle does not say so explicitly, it would seem that his emphasis on the importance of these moments of personal recognition grows from their figurative relation to our own cognition of the entire structure, so that our knowledge and that of the characters reach out to one another through the double moment of the performance. Aristotle insists that the successful achievement of such recognitions, whether before or after disaster, is marked by a characteristic and desirable emotional response. The passage makes it clear that when Aristotle speaks of wonder, he is not merely referring to the propensity of tragedies to concern mythological events of an extreme or superhuman character – maenads bending trees, Hercules wrestling Death and so forth. Rather, he thinks of wonder as intimately integrated with the business of "learning and reasoning out" that is at the heart of mimesis.

Chapter 16 continues to associate wonder with recognition: "But of all forms of recognition the best is that which arises from the incidents themselves, the astonishment coming to pass through likelihoods [τῆς ἐκλήξεως γιγνομένης δι᾽ εἰκότων, 1455a.16–17]." Lucas comments that "the article suggests that *ekplexis* is the emotion that an *anagnorisis* naturally evokes" (p. 27). Terrible events are not in themselves wonderful simply because they move us. But when those events unfold through a plot that reveals their intelligibility as processes of cause and effect (though the example of the Mitys statue suggests these can be moral or supernatural processes), then intellectual and emotional pleasures meet in a critical moment felt as *ekplexis*. Cognition is charged with emotion, which in turn is contained or allayed by cognition. The images of mutual force that arise here are ways of registering the turbulence of the moment.

This cognitive valence of emotion responds implicitly to Plato's charge against tragedy in the *Republic* that, as Francis Sparshott paraphrases it, "by their vicarious grief at tragic performances the spectators get into the habit of indulging their emotions, so that the effect of being emotionally moved in the theatre is to make one a more emotional and therefore a less rational person."[5] Aristotle's attention to wonder is in this regard part of his general attempt to demonstrate that some kinds of emotion are, as it were, philosophically inclined, and that tragedy can be a valuable activity in encouraging engagement with questions of virtue, moral choice, and happiness.

But the very force and excess associated with "astonishment" in the above passages carries with it a less easily contained side, with which Aristotle contends in Chapters 24 and 25. Here emotionally charged events appear more like a flaw in the smooth machinery of narrative inference:

Now while the poet ought to produce the wondrous [τὸ θαυμαστόν] in tragedy, the unreasonable [τὸ ἄλογον] (through which the wondrous most often happens) may be produced more easily in epic-making because what is done is not seen. For the incidents concerning the pursuit of Hektor would appear ludicrous on the stage with the Greeks standing still and not pursuing and Achilleus waving them back, but in epics this is overlooked. And the wondrous is pleasant [τὸ δὲ θαυμαστὸν ἡδύ]. (1460a.11–18)

If the poet has produced impossibilities [ἀδύνατα], then he has made a mistake, but rightly so if this happens to serve the end [τοῦ τέλους] of poetic science (for this end has been mentioned) and thus makes this or any other part more astounding [ἐκπληκτικώτερον]. An example of this is the pursuit of Hektor. (1460b.22–26)

If the wondrous most often happens through the unreasonable, the margin for "the best" tragedy that links wonder and reason shrinks markedly. Yet wonder is made most available to tragedy as it becomes manageable, in the process of its evaporation into understanding (cf. *Poetics*, Chapter 4). If dramatic action thus liberates the wild only in order to domesticate it the more firmly, at the same time the unruliness of the emotion seems to trouble the clarity of Aristotle's model, and he repeatedly locates it either at or beyond the borders of what is allowable in poetry.

The *Poetics* itself does not address this apparent contradiction between wonder as force and wonder as thought. Such a doubleness in wonder that both enables and blocks our knowledge turns out to be characteristic of its relation to the project of philosophy in both Aristotle and Plato, and to form part of both philosophers' reservations about the value of emotion and of poetry.[6]

II

Plato's discussion and evocation of "wonder" throughout his work is as divided on its significance and value as is Aristotle's deployment of it in the *Poetics*. Most often it plays the role of a switchpoint belonging at once to emotive and cognitive faculties. Its appearance can be rough or smooth, alarming or exhilarating, epiphanic or destructive – and it may disrupt even these neat pairs. Two modes of wonder – we could call them "commensurable" and "incommensurable" – often cohabit, intermingle, or are played off against one another as alternative paths to understanding. They correspond to the conjugation of wonder respectively with "recognition" and "the unreasonable" in the *Poetics*.

In the first place, wonder forms part of the prehistory of philosophy, as the genetic moment of the philosophical impulse. In the *Theaetetus*, for example, we find the following:

THEAETETUS No, indeed it is extraordinary [ὑπερφυῶς ὡς θαυμάζω] how [such puzzles] set me wondering what they can mean. Sometimes I get quite dizzy with thinking of them.

SOCRATES That shows that Theodorus was not wrong in his estimate of your nature. This sense is the mark of the philosopher [μαλα γάρ φιλοσόφου τοῦτο τὸ πάθος]. Philosophy indeed has no other origin, and he was a good genealogist [sc. Hesiod] who made Iris the daughter of Thaumas. (*Theaetetus*, 155d)[7]

Socrates describes for Theaetetus a transition from wonder (as yet) unresolved, which leaves the ephebe confounded in the search for meaning, with no secure resting-place, to a wonder resolved into questioning and hence into a process and habit of philosophizing. The first condition is thus a constitutive part of the philosophical search, annexed to the radical impulse to doubt that afflicts the true philosopher. To attain philosophic knowledge of something is always to have experienced this doubt about one's knowledge, to have seen some thing under an alien and unmasterable aspect. Philosophy begins in a characteristic *pathos* of dizzy confusion, and to philosophize is, according to Socrates, to be returned consistently to this state.

Wonder can be a misleading portal to philosophy, however, if its *pathos* is exploited to obtain power over the mind. This is a principal ground on which Plato opposes poetry in the *Republic*. The philosopher-as-charlatan is humorously displayed in the *Euthydemus*, where ἔκπληξις or ἐκπλήττειν occur thrice, and forms of θαῦμα twelve times in ironic amazement at the Chian mountebanks.[8] The pseudo-philosophy of the know-all brothers aims to enslave hearers by an unending production of wonders, but they are unable (and do not wish) to convince Clinias to "love wisdom and practice virtue" as Socrates urges. Plato perhaps lays such stress on the abuse of wonder here precisely because he believes it a crucial element in the impulse to philosophy.[9]

The more difficult task is to find some way out of Theaetetus' labyrinth. Two possible pathways are explored in different moments of Plato's writings: the Socratic dialectic, and the blessing of divine enlightenment. In the *Theaetetus*, it is dialectic which is pursued, but the Hesiodic genealogy of Thaumas and Iris suggests an alternative specifically associated with poetry: theophanic persuasion through the mediating power of a divine emissary. Of course there is always the chance that this latter too is a trick, an illusion designed for our subjection. Hence the recurrent suspicion of verbal artifice. But the existence of idols does not disprove divinity, and Plato remains committed to the possibility of theophany.

Accordingly, Plato at other times directly invokes the power of wonder and attempts to depict its impact. At such times, there is a shift in the tone and function of the writing and a powerful impulse to celebrate, prolong, and recreate in its texture and movement the turbulence of the experience as a high and ecstatic path to the knowledge a less inspired philosophy strives to win through dialectic. Striking evocations of *ekplexis* as the emotion proper to divine mediation are important elements in several of Plato's works, and they throw a light on the dynamics of the experience that formal analysis would not achieve. The most complex of these passages have to do with love, Plato's paramount "ekplectic" emotion. The value of the analogy between this erotic astonishment and that which Iris mediates for philosophy in the *Theaetetus* emerges in a passage from the *Phaedrus* justly famous for its vividness and metaphoric energy:

And now that he [the beloved] has come to welcome his lover and to take pleasure in his company and converse, it comes home to him what a depth of kindliness he has found, and he is filled with amazement [ἐκπλήττει], for he perceives that all his other friends and kinsmen have nothing to offer in comparison with this friend in whom there dwells a god [τὸν ἔνθεον φίλον]. So as he continues in this converse and society, and comes close to his lover in the gymnasium and elsewhere, that flowing stream which Zeus, as the lover of Ganymede, called the "flood of passion" pours in upon the lover. And part of it is absorbed within him, but when he can contain no more the rest flows away from him, and as a breath of wind or an echo, rebounding from a smooth, hard surface, goes back to its place of origin [καὶ οἷον πνεῦμα ἤ τις ἠχὼ ἀπὸ λείων τε καὶ στερεῶν ἁλλομένη πάλιν ὅθεν ὡρμήθη φέρεται], even so the stream of beauty [τοῦ κάλλους ῥεῦμα] turns back and re-enters the eyes of the fair beloved. And so by the natural channel it reaches his Soul and gives it fresh vigor, watering the roots of the wings and quickening them to growth. So he loves, yet knows not what he loves; he does not understand, he cannot tell what has come upon him; like one that has caught a disease of the eye from another, he cannot account for it, not realizing that his lover is as it were a mirror in which he beholds himself [ὥσπερ δ᾽ ἐν κατόπτρῳ ἐν τῷ ἐρῶντι ἑαυτὸν ὁρῶν λέληθεν]. (*Phaedrus*, 255b.3–d.6)

This is the climax of Socrates' account of the exiled soul in its struggle back towards supernatural communion, and describes the disorienting amazement of love which prepares the soul for apprehension of the divine. The variety of metaphors Plato generates to represent the force of the revelation ("stream," "flood," "breath," "sound," "disease," "mirror") seems deliberately designed to impede exposition and analysis in order to retain at once motility and difficulty at the level of reading. The metaphors have in common a sense of being in an overwhelming medium – a fluid, an air – which carries some sort of communication, even if only "a disease." There is an aspect of casting about to the style which leads it into sudden changes, alternations, and negations, and this restless energy is a principal source of its evocative power. Plato seeks to prolong the description, adding to its variety and vividness by, as Coleridge remarks of another fluctuating description of love, "hovering between images."[10]

To fend off as long as possible the collapse of this heightened emotion into any definite recognition, Plato's metaphors concentrate on the evocation of deflections and reversals of flow, of going back along the trail. The momentum of the passage is retarded even while its imaginative force is built up through the images of reversal, deferring the necessity for Plato to state what it is that is "really" in question. Proroguing, deferring, supplementing with further metaphor, piling up anaphora, he retards progress as long as possible, at the level both of syntax and of representation. This back-and-forth cannot be sustained indefinitely, but an image of such persistence appears as the mirror in which the beloved unknowingly beholds himself. In our recognition of his non-recognition lies both the paradox and the humor of the passage: the endless propagation of images can be sustained only as long as they remain unfamiliar and mysterious. We will see that such an arrest of temporal flow into contemplation of a visual scene, coupled with an uncertainty as to the boundaries of what is seen (here or there, mine or his?) is a characteristic textual response to wonder that is also strategically deployed in drama.[11]

If the image of the mirror cannot finally be omitted, the recognition scene it points to is never quite presented in this passage, so that moment when wonder is transformed into some procedure of philosophic enquiry is deliberately withheld. Though the main thrust of the passage is celebratory and prepares the way for a divine vision, Plato seems at the same time to harbor some doubt about the feelings of divine participation he describes so evocatively: he refers to them as a contagious "disease of the eye" which prevents the truth from being recognized. To retain this beautiful love, it seems the beloved must remain ignorant about the truth of his experience: the renewed cognition of himself in the soul's recovery of its divine power. Plato attempts to convey the imaginative experience by "hovering between images" as extensively as possible, to suggest and also to endorse the very different modality of experience peculiar to that state, in which evanescence, deferral, and a peculiar disorientation play important roles. Above all, it is a state in which one waits for explanation to come, with a sense that every moment is pregnant with meaning. But the philosophic writer himself, in order to represent this state of participation, must stand outside it, must have already deciphered the mirror. There is, as with Descartes and the wax, the suggestion of a kind of loss, if one willingly suffered, in taking up philosophy.

Plato continues in other works to celebrate the thaumaturgic power of the erotic and its apparent twinship with what philosophy seeks. The similarity of the daimonic Eros to the philosopher is made explicit in Socrates' talk with Diotima in the *Symposium*:

- And now, she said, haven't I proved that you're one of the people who don't believe in the divinity of Love?
- Yes, but what can he be, then? I asked her. A mortal?
- Not by any means.
- Well, what then?
- What I told you before: halfway between mortal and immortal.
- And what do you mean by that, Diotima?
- A very powerful spirit [Δαίμων μέγας], Socrates, and spirits, you know are halfway between god and man.
- What powers have they then? I asked.
- They are the interpreters and envoys that ply between gods and men [ἑρμηνεῦον καὶ διαπορθμεῦον θεοῖς τὰ παρ᾽ ἀνθρώπων καὶ ἀνθρώποις τὰ παρὰ θεῶν], flying upward with our worship and our prayers and descending with the heavenly answers and commandments, and since they are between the two estates they weld both sides together and merge them into one great whole. (*Symposium*, 202d.9–e.12)

Love is a commerce between ignorance and understanding, the discovery of a passage from "Desire and Lack" on the one hand to "the wondrous, beautiful in its nature" (τι θαυμαστὸν τὴν φύσιν καλόν, 210e.6). Love here plays the role of mediation taken by Iris, the daughter of Thaumas, in the *Theaetetus* passage.

The crisis of selfhood imagined in the unrecognized mirror-image in the *Phaedrus* appears also in the *Symposium* in Aristophanes' magnificent comic speech, where erotic passion stems from a meeting between the two halves of a cloven organism. Non-recognition is again the necessary condition of the expectant but endless deferral of significance which characterizes desire:

And so when this boy lover – or any other lover, for that matter – is fortunate enough to meet his other half, they are both so intoxicated with affection, with friendship and with love, [τότε καὶ θαυμαστὰ ἐκπλήττονται φιλίᾳ τε καὶ οἰκειότητι καὶ ἔρωτι] that they cannot bear to let each other out of sight for a single instant.... The fact is that both their souls are longing for a something else – a something to which they can neither of them put a name, and which they can only give an inkling of in cryptic sayings and riddles. (192b.4–c.2, c.6–d.2)

As in the *Phaedrus*, the intensity of emotion depends on the absence of a name. The proposal of Hephaistos miraculously to unite the lovers and bring about a literal identity marks the end of the restless casting-about for "reasons" which has destabilized psychological and semiotic orientation alike. Aristophanes' reference to the apparently compulsive production of "cryptic sayings and riddles," assuaging but not allaying the distress, suggests that we are also in the presence of a genetic scene of figurative language. Aristophanes characterizes this inability as comic, deluded, and mechanical, and his "cryptic sayings and riddles" are like the lies of the poets. The slyness of Plato's masking as Aristophanes here is that among these "riddles" we may have to count both Socrates' tale of Diotima and the eddying metaphors of the *Phaedrus*: the *Symposium* is Plato's craftiest work.

We find in Plato two ways of approaching wonder, cognate with the alternatives we discerned in the *Poetics* but more clearly specified. One sees it as the forecourt of a process which leads to philosophy proper, the other as an experience *sui generis* which cannot be entirely contained or accounted for only as preparation for something else. This latter way Plato both celebrates and is inclined to suspect. In the *Republic*, such uncontained emotion produced by the poets is the object of severe censure. What is at stake is in the end apparently a question of power and subjection: wonder is the gift of a god, to whom we must submit (one should not underestimate Plato's feeling for the gods), but the power of poetry is in the hands of men and therefore to be rejected if it cannot be disciplined to do us good. That discipline was to be philosophy, of which in his *Letter VII* Plato speaks as something requiring long and careful labor. Yet the theophanic quality of philosophy, both in

Plato's experience and in his text (Plato himself makes the distinction in the same letter) remains crucial to it, is no mere prolegomenon, and to that quality wonder remains intrinsic.

III

In his own account of the genesis of philosophy in the first book of the *Metaphysics*, Aristotle too adverts to the possibility of an uncontrollable element of *pathos* in the quest for knowledge, but he categorically rules out the threat. The passage requires quotation in full:

It is through wonder that men now begin and originally began to philosophize; wondering in the first place at obvious perplexities, and then by gradual progression raising questions about the greater matters too.... Now he who wonders and is perplexed feels that he is ignorant (thus the myth-lover is in a sense a philosopher, since myths are composed of wonders); therefore if it was to escape ignorance that men studied philosophy, it is obvious that they pursued science for the sake of knowledge, and not for any practical utility.... Clearly then it is for no extrinsic advantage that we seek this knowledge; for just as we call a man independent who exists for himself and not for another, so we call this the only independent science, since it alone exists for itself.

   For this reason its acquisition might justly be supposed to be beyond human power, since in many respects human nature is servile; in which case, as Simonides says, "God alone can have this privilege," and man should only seek the knowledge which is within his reach. Indeed if the poets are right and the Deity is by nature jealous, it is probable that in this case He would be particularly jealous, and all those who excel in knowledge unfortunate. But it is impossible for the Deity to be jealous (indeed, as the proverb says, "poets tell many a lie"), nor must we suppose that any other form of knowledge is more precious than this; for what is most divine is most precious. Now there are two ways only in which it can be divine. A science is divine if it is peculiarly the possession of God, or if it is concerned with divine matters. And this science alone fulfills both these conditions; for (a) all believe that God is one of the causes and a kind of principle, and (b) God is the sole or chief possessor of this sort of knowledge. Accordingly, although all other sciences are more useful than this, none is more excellent. (*Metaphysics,* 1.ii.982b.11–983a.20)

Wonder is once more a mediating and enabling moment whose value is to point us down the path to knowledge. As Aristotle describes it, the process is neat and ordered: we begin in wonder, perhaps pass through an intermediate stage of "myth" which is a kind of pseudo-philosophy, and emerge finally into a knowledge that has dissipated the original feeling for the strange. The sequence has the clarity of Aristotle's own account of narrative. But as he begins his inquiry into fundamental and primary knowledge, an interesting obstruction arises which specifically suggests another narrative. For this brief, digressive doubt, Aristotle turns to a language of power, subjection, violence and tragic *pathos*.

Along with the peculiar excellence and rarity of metaphysics, Aristotle must confront its difficulty and remoteness, that it "might justly be supposed to be beyond human power." Such an objection would be devastating to the intellectual self-legitimation of the philosopher, who would be revealed as deluded "since in many respects human nature is servile." Servility supposes a master, and a dominating power appears pat as a jealous guardian of knowledge (καὶ πέφυκε φθονεῖν τὸ θεῖον). We have long known this god to punish *hubris* with a heavy hand, making "all those who excel in knowledge unfortunate" (δυστυχεῖς εἶναι πάντας τοὺς περιττούς). The alarming possibility arises, in the very transition from wonder to knowledge, that the philosopher might meet with disaster.

One can discern in this small agonistic fiction the traces of a certain kind of tragic narrative, something like that of Sophocles' *Oedipus*, with its turbulent dismembering of the "independent man" and its demonstration of how at the very point of his most powerful self-assertion he is felled by an ancient, half-forgotten wound to his integrity. Rather than Aristotle's open story of systematic advancement, the story of Oedipus doubles back upon itself over and over, fragmenting Oedipus' history into a pattern of astonishing repetitions that hammer home only how deeply dependent he is. This sense of the taboo, the dangerous or the impossible in human knowledge, is imperiously resisted by Aristotle, who here, in contrast to the *Poetics*, stands soberly against the poets and the entire discourse of tragedy. Aristotle advances himself and us with him towards enlightenment by human reason alone, leaving superstitious and poetic amazement behind as lies and mystification. The gods have given us the means to share their knowledge. In asking us to cower before their image of a jealous deity, "poets tell many a lie." Philosophy transmutes and tames wonder, so that it becomes the housepet of the man who has "the knowledge of many things that are wonders" (ἔστι δ᾽ ἡ σοφία πολλῶν καὶ θαυμαστῶν ἐπιστήμη, *Rhetoric*, I.xi. 1371b.33). Wonders, that is, to non-philosophers.

The language and scenery of tragedy continue to appear when Aristotle speaks of wonder and learning. In the *Rhetoric*, for instance, we find the following:

And learning and wondering are as a rule pleasant; for wondering implies the desire to learn, so that what causes wonder is to be desired, and learning implies a return to the normal.... And since learning and wondering are pleasant, all things connected with them must also be pleasant; for instance, a work of imitation, such as painting, sculpture, poetry, and all that is well imitated, even if the object of imitation is not pleasant; for it is not this that causes pleasure or the reverse, but the inference that the imitation and the object imitated are identical, so that the result is that we learn something. The same may be said of sudden changes and narrow escapes from danger; for all these things are wonders [καὶ αἱ περιπέτειαι καὶ τὸ παρὰ μικρὸν σώζεσθαι ἐκ τῶν κινδύνων πάντα γὰρ θαυμαστὰ ταῦτα]. (*Rhet.* I.xi. 1371a.36–40, b.3–12)

As in *Poetics* 4, a "work of imitation" gives pleasure because it offers us the opportunity to exercise our reasoning in recognizing the relation of synthesis and reconstruction between the *mimesis* and the familiar world. We follow a narrative both *by* piecing together and *in order to* piece together the events in relation to one another (relations of the necessary, the probable and, sometimes, the amazing). In so doing we gain knowledge of the various conditions of human actions. In this sense an audience is always involved with "wondering" as an activity of intellectual inquiry in which imaginative participation plays an important role, and which is intellectually pleasurable and satisfying. Aristotle's account of the link between wonder and learning has, accordingly, the structure of a recognition scene ("Oh, I see, this is like that," 1448b.16), and his preferred dramatic structure is a narrative form of his theory of the cognitive work of mimetic production.[12]

This is all well and good, but what has it to do with the final reference to "sudden changes and narrow escapes from danger"? Here once more a cognitive vocabulary gets mixed up with an emotive one. In this latter, more difficult pleasure, learning would seem less adjacent than fear, "the impression of an imminent evil that causes destruction or pain" (*Rhet.* II.iv.5. 1382a.25–7). If there is wonder attached to this moment of difficulty, danger, and struggle, it requires a language of power and peril otherwise foreign to the passage. Suppose it were this thrill-pleasure that those in search of wonder were seeking? What would this do to *mimesis* and its nice syllogisms?

Both the *Metaphysics* and the *Rhetoric* suggest again that wonder collapses together two contrary intimations. For if wonder-as-learning "implies a return to the normal," the normal must already have been left behind, and yet it is precisely wonder that marks the departure. J. V. Cunningham reproduces this difficulty when he comments that "the relationship of wonder and pleasure is that wonder is pleasurable. It is pleasurable in itself. It is pleasurable also in that it is the occasion and motive for learning." And later: "[wonder] corresponds to the displacement, large or small, that initiates internal movement: with respect to the intellect, inference, the processes of logic, and learning; with respect to the irrational part of the soul, feeling and emotion." There are two movements here and the problem is that Aristotle's theory of pleasure requires that the former be unpleasurable.[13] We need a separate account of the pleasure of that initial "displacement," what Cunningham here calls the "pleasurable in itself." This pleasure is unexplored in Aristotle's work, which is at pains to discuss "resemblance," "probability" and "learning" rather than the "alien," "impossibility," and "danger."[14]

IV

What is needed to explain the gap in both philosophers' accounts of the disorienting, alien, and anxious straits of *ekplexis*, where the world seems for a moment to fear and thrive on unreason [τὸ ἄλογον], is a psychology of wonder. Such an account is implicit in the *Phaedrus,* but is more easily apprehended in the explicitly literary commentary of Longinus on what he calls "height" [ὕψος], where the language of struggle, force, and threat comes to the fore to account for the quality of trial and risk in imaginative experience.

It must be admitted that the ground shared between Plato, Aristotle, and Longinus is somewhat shifting. While there are some conformities between Plato's sense of the soul as "aspiring" and Longinus' insistence on the power of poetry to "elevate," Longinus fits his account of the psychology of rhetoric into no overall philosophical context. On the other hand, the very absence of the systematic from this point of view allows Longinus to consider more fully what Plato, perhaps from his very sense of its potency, tends either to co-opt into his text or to dismiss. Compared to Aristotle, Longinus is mainly concerned with discussions of local rhetorical moments manifesting in brilliant flashes the inexplicable, daimonic force of poetic "magnanimity." As his tradition is essentially rhetorical, his interest in narrative is severely limited. But again, this very circumspection gives the advantage of a narrow focus on an aspect of poetry that seems only to embarrass Aristotle by destabilizing his distinctions. One way to understand "the wonderful" is to see it as that moment where the powerful dynamic of imaginative coercion and consent that is Longinus' subject impinges on Aristotle's more orderly apparatus of narrative persuasion.

One immediately striking aspect of Longinus' choice of "height" for his principal metaphor, particularly for the discussion of drama, is its insistence on putting the matter in terms of spatial relations, suggesting the difficulty of determining orientation in the field of "the sublime." Is "height" a quality of the work? The poet? The audience? Longinus' most famous formulation stresses above all its transitive nature: "as if instinctively, our soul is uplifted by the true sublime; it takes a proud flight, and is filled with joy and vaunting, as though it had itself produced what it had heard" (7.2).[15] The plasticity and openness to metaphor of this formulation is especially notable, and we are invited to see "height" as a dynamic and labile force felt in this very ability to blur boundaries. The sense of disorientation recalls the *Phaedrus*, but this time figures of power and of space are strategically linked: disorientation is the sign of some forcible sweeping away or rarefying of limits. We have no choice, we are taken "as if instinctively," and though Longinus emphasizes the successful recuperation of such an assault as self-generated empowerment, there is again a darker way of putting the matter in which we confront potential violence and loss. Throughout his treatise, Longinus is particularly drawn to imagery of danger, aggression and imminent death (in Chapter 10, for instance) in a way that suggests these examples have a figurative relation to the central subject of his treatise.[16] The dynamism of this power, that is, is ethically quite indifferent to us: for blessing or maim, poem reaches out for reader, spectacle for spectator. And in the process, it attacks the ordinary boundaries that keep cognitive and social worlds stable. Longinus, as William Wimsatt complained, is all fluidity; when he says "there!" one never quite knows where he is pointing. But this is the very aspect of the quality that he wishes to stress. As Paul Fry insists: "it is much the same, though never wholly the same, whether one speaks of nature or art, author or audience; or whether one speaks ... of unconsciously or consciously imposed form."[17] Distinctions between the affective and the tropological are similarly jeopardized, so that Longinus can collapse verbal and emotive aspects of rhetoric together also: shifts of word become themselves shifts of feeling.

The connection between Longinus' vocabularies of space and violence, themselves the poles of a dialectic, and the vocabulary the *Poetics* uses for wonder becomes clearer if we examine the etymological substrate in the central terms. Digging out the metaphors confirms the conjunction of a spatial with a traumatic vocabulary, and moves us back towards the description of theatrical experience, allowing an access to some powerful currents in dramatic examples that neither Longinus nor Aristotle can address.[18]

The basic orientation of θαῦμα seems to be spatial, and to involve spectacle: a "wonder" is an object or event which is gazed upon by a beholder. In epic diction the word is always singular, suggesting a sudden and unitary force to the experience.[19] Its ultimate etymological roots are with the Indo-European *dha-w* group meaning "see," "show." The word is thus related to θέαμα = "a sight, spectacle," to θεάομαι = "gaze at, behold, view as spectators," and hence to θέατρον = "a place for seeing, a theatre."[20] Links between wonder and the spectacular, marked in the language of visualization in some descriptions of the experience, are thus reinforced by etymology. The relation of this to the visual element in theatrical action will need further exploration.[21]

The main thrust of ἔκπληξις on the other hand is of a blow, an act of violence. It is related to πληγή "a blow," and derived from the root *plea = "strike, beat" (cf. Lat. plango, Eng. flog). Greek occurrences in such a literal meaning are comparatively rare. More common is a derivative of consternation or amazement which "strikes," as in English, with metaphoric and psychological violence. The occasion can be extreme fear (cf. Eng. "panic-stricken"), but also "any sudden overpowering passion" (Liddell and Scott). Here one is not simply an arrested spectator of a compelling but spatially remote spectacle, but rather one is actively solicited, touched, somehow under attack. This derivation inscribes into the word itself a perception of struggle and violence, suggesting a deep phenomenological responsiveness to threat.

Between the observing distance of θαῦμα and the vulnerable proximity of ἔκπληξις, the Longinian preoccupation with fluidity of relation reappears in the very vocabulary of wonder.[22] In this respect, we should note that accounts of "wonder" often seem incapable of resisting a figuration of writer or reader as polarized, doubled, or caught in a reflection. Longinus offers the image of a new and empowered self that finds itself producing the text, or vice versa, where this very exaltation may be a defensive strategy against the greater threat of an intimate attack. In Plato, some inadequacy ("a disease of the eyes") precludes the beloved recognizing a specular reflexiveness explicitly asserted by the text. And in Aristotle's *Metaphysics*, the tale of the abject sufferer is hidden inside that of the "independent man," as though the two were secretly twins. Metaphors of spatial displacement combine with those of self-division to produce these doubling effects. Neil Hertz has suggested in a discussion of the sublime in Romantic poetry that the writer's need in similar moments to produce images and spectral doubles of the inquirer is a controlling defense against a more threatening dissolution: "[T]he self cannot simply think but must read the confirmation of its own integrity, which is only legible in a specular structure, a structure in which the self can perform that supererogatory identification with the blocking agent."[23] Here the very assertion that an act of reading rather than thinking is required suggests a need for some act of distancing or "reflection" on the process of identification whereby this integrity of knowledge is secured.

What I would suggest is that it is the self's relation to the origins, force, and significance of its knowledge of the world that is at stake in these moments. The spatialization of wonder rendered in etymology as metaphors of the visual is part of a dialectical dynamic in which distance becomes a defensive projection which keeps threat *away*. The "remoteness" of the threatening knowledge, "out there," buys time against its power and lies about its alarming intimacy.[24] In the theatre, such a distancing is immediately available as a spatial separation from the action which doubles and tropes an ontological "break" with the fiction and can provide for emotional relief from its invasiveness.[25] To collapse this specular distance is to accept both wounding and knowledge at once. Oedipus puts out his eyes to express as much his acceptance of knowledge as its refusal. But the arresting distance of theatrical spectacle is only temporarily effective. At the same time, visual distancing is entwined with evocations of the aural, with their implicitly vocative and "penetrative" aspect, though even here the dialectic of recognition and deferral may continue, since aural figures can also be made to proliferate and echo in a way that suggests, without ever achieving, infinity.

V

When Aristotle in the *Metaphysics* speaks of wonder retrospectively as the necessary middle of a completable and completed story, he is telling us only half the tale, equably purged of its strain and violence. This stance emphasizes the temporality of the experience and its openness to inspection. Wonder will have been the pregnancy and plenitude of significance as the mind rushed victoriously toward it. So put, we can allay any awkward anxieties by ignoring the possibility that the meeting with knowledge might be a fatal or apocalyptic one which bereaves even as it exalts. The latter intuition "as if instinctively" attempts to avoid the moment of recognition by doubling it, dissolving it in metaphor, breaking up its narrative progress. Its language is of force, pain, and power. The exhilaration of wonder is the promise that we can survive and incorporate this new "way of seeing," the bereavement is the sense that we can*not*, that it must destroy us. The former expects a recognition scene, the latter a scene of violence.

Aristotle's resistance to anti-narrative impulses within theatrical experience narrows his responsiveness to those aspects of the dramatic presentation that are most part of the dynamic of wonder. As we might expect, his treatment of the visual spectacle (ὄψις) and of acts of violence in the *Poetics* is especially unsatisfactory. Though spectacle is first in Aristotle's list of the six principal parts of tragedy (ὄψεως κόσμος, Chapter 6 1449b.33), in the subsequent analytic treatment it is ranked last as "the most inartistic and least appropriate to poetic science" (ἀτεχνότατον δὲ καὶ ἥκιστα οἰκεῖον τῆς ποιητικῆς, 1450b.17–18) which "more authoritatively belongs to the costume-maker's art [τοῦ σκευοποιοῦ τέχνη] than ...

the poet's" (1450b.20).[26] Though the Greek tragic theatre was spectacular and kinetic, with sudden and co-ordinated movement in small and large groups and with impressive costumes, one gets little sense of it from Aristotle's treatise. Such visual devices as the changing fortunes of the crimson cloth in Aeschylus' *Oresteia* apparently escape his interest, and he objects to the use of properties in recognition in Chapter 16, preferring an internal logic as more satisfying and controllable. His preference is for an intellectual order, so much so that he claims that plays (or at least their plots) do much the same work when simply recounted or recited as when performed. In distinguishing between the *techne* of the poet and of the "designer," Aristotle neglects the important possibility that dramatists may deliberately include stage spectacle within the symbolic order of their narratives. The breaking of the prison in the *Bacchae*, the rising of Darius' ghost in *Persians* or the physical barrier of Alcestis' veil are good examples. As we have seen, wonder is both etymologically and by usage especially associated with an arresting emphasis on the visual. To account for the place of this visual power in wonder, a more sensitive approach to *opsis* is needed. Aristotle does acknowledge the power of spectacle as "attractive to the soul" (ψυχαγωγικὸν, 1450b.17), but does not explore the implications of this, and this limitation hampers him from noting the full complexity of the theatre's relations with its audience.[27]

The question of acts of violence in the theatre is likewise related to the dialectical structure of wonder we have been considering, as it is here that figures of our emotional trauma can be concentrated. The reluctance (though not refusal) of classical drama to display violence directly may be an aspect of this dialectic, a visual withdrawal to compensate for the extremity of the threat when affective "distance" across the footlights is at a minimum. It is on these occasions especially that boundaries are likely to waver, and audience and characters to wince at cognate and shared violences. A startling example of this occurs in the *Agamemnon* when, from within his palace, the warrior king utters a sudden, penetrating cry: "Ah, I am struck a deadly blow" ("ὤμοι, πέπληγμαι καιρίαν πληγὴν ἔσω," l. 1343). The blow strikes all in the theatre in the same instant: King, Chorus, and audience share in a linked *pathos* of agony and amazement.[28] The difference among the parties is as real yet as fragile as that between a literal and a figurative use of "I am struck" (πέπληγμαι: the relation to *ekplexis* is clear). Such moments of overpowering subjection in dramatic action can only be diluted in retrospective analysis, where the sense of immediacy and abolition of boundary is hard to recapture. Aristotle's account of them is not very satisfying: *pathos* is merely one of the parts (μέρη) of a tragic *mythos*, included but neglected. In *Poetics* 14 the portrayal of *pathos* is one method of producing the emotions proper to tragedy. There it appears that suffering in itself is a necessary but not sufficient condition for tragedy, and this gives rise in turn to a division and ranking of plots into four kinds, and so forth. But *pathos* is hardly scrutinized and the pleasure that is peculiar to it is a major unresolved problem in Aristotle's account.[29] There remains a core of turbulence and even contradiction at precisely that point where the "reasoning out" of our knowledge is supposed to reach its most philosophic fulfillment, and there Aristotle's language of progressive stages yields almost despite itself – even given the difficulties of interpreting the *Poetics* – to an alternative language that draws on more forcible or chaotic metaphoric energies not of reasoning but of power.

Theatrical performance is an ideal site to play out versions of the dialectic of knowledge and subjection we have been exploring, as its sensual resources offer the possibility of making literal or concrete this figurative interplay. With its insistently temporal dimension, performance correlates the time of the story and the time of the audience, and the availability of appeals to both eye and ear means that the visual and aural registers can be conjoined or opposed or otherwise counterpointed against each other. Theatre's unfolding in space allows various kinds and degrees of separation from the action to be mapped and enlivened directly by actual movement, approach, and withdrawal.

It is worth re-examining Aristotle's favorite exemplar, *Oedipus the King*, in this light. As Oedipus begins his forensic investigation, we are ahead of him, working backwards towards him in anticipation of the singular point at which our knowledge will be translated onto the stage and made public. As long as the solution is only ours, the plot will not conclude: there is as it were a semantic "charge potential" across the stage boundary, one which the frustrated rages of scenes like that with Teiresias exploit. Even as the plot moves forward, a crucial element remains static and in an important sense "external" to it. The unfolding of successive events in this respect merely returns us over and over to recalling what has not (yet) appeared, and – like Teiresias – we cherish a powerful reluctance to having our knowledge opened. Even as we watch Oedipus rushing towards it, and the inhuman *daimon* who is its sponsor poised to leap upon him (lines 1301, 1312), we wish to turn aside from that moment. Our contradictory desires in the narrative are expressed on stage in the contrast of Oedipus' fury for knowledge and Jocasta's desperate plea for silence. The value of knowledge itself is at stake. The closer the revelation steps, the more progress seems to be impeded, to impede itself, the greater the violence required to wrest it from darkness. The reluctance of the witnesses increases, as does the

savagery of Oedipus' desire, down to the last possible moment, where
the dialogue deliberately holds us back one last time, even as it gestures
onward:

HERDSMAN   Oh master please – I beg you, master, please don't ask me
                more.
OEDIPUS   You're a dead man if I ask you again.
HERDSMAN   It was one of the children of Laius.
OEDIPUS   A slave? Or born in wedlock?
HERDSMAN   Oh God, I am on the brink of frightful speech.
                [οἴμοι, πρὸς αὐτῶι γ᾽ εἰμὶ τῷ δεινῷ λέγειν.]
OEDIPUS   And I of frightful hearing. But I must hear.
                [κἄγωγ᾽ ἀκούειν ἀλλ᾽ ὅμως ἀκουστέον.] (lines 1165–70)[30]

With great subtlety, Sophocles plays on our desire both for revelation
and for deferral, to endure and not to have to endure the moment when
the opposite vectors of the plot, both of which we have been following,
collide in devastation. The play is as much a success story as a disaster,
and it is Oedipus' will to know, to be once more the King who delivers
Thebes, that drives the scene. And just here, before the triumph of both
knowledge and subjection, where both images of the *Metaphysics* are
about to be fulfilled at once, we find a last-minute diversion from the
onrush of the narrative. Herdsman and King take each a line in self-
conscious reflection to watch themselves in the act of deferring knowledge one last time. Abstracted, their sense of the closeness of disaster is
expressed as the pause before the power of "frightful speech." It is a
brilliant ploy, reinforcing the theatricality of the moment and the role of
reflection in it just as, for Oedipus, all ability to find an orderly place for
himself within his biography is about to disappear into the maelstrom of
violence which reveals the jealous, Olympian power. The Messenger's
speech that follows (lines 1186–223) insists on the extent to which all the
violent events of the story are brought together and are present at once in
Jocasta's bedroom, which Oedipus confronts as a dire spectacle revealed
through the wrenched doors. The smooth narrative of inquiry and
biography is compacted into a metaphoric, forceful sight that strikes in
an ekplectic instant.[31] A single lexical instance sums this up. When the
Messenger relates Oedipus' self-wounding with Jocasta's bodice-pins he
speaks not of the King's eyes, but of "the swivel-joints of his orbs" (line
1270).[32] This odd phrase points directly to the ancient piercing of
Oedipus' feet referred to with the same word (*arthra*) at lines 718 and
1032. The deliberately difficult locution couches the terror and violence
of the act in an analytic and rhetorical self-consciousness all the greater
for being narrated rather than seen. Yet the radical condensation of
separate moments of both text and biography in the echo also strikes

with an impact that foreruns analysis, like the blow at Agamemnon. We note the power of the figurative to compact biography into an instant of tremendous force, yet we are also distanced by its rhetorical oddity: it both is and is not available.

These examples show how carefully a dramatist may exploit the various "distances" between literal and figurative, actor and role, stage and audience, to manipulate an audience's implication in the world of a dramatic fiction. At extreme moments, involvement and detachment are carefully weighed against one another at multiple levels. Our attention is directed not only to the fiction as an event and place charged with significance, but at the same time to the dramatic medium that creates that fiction, rather like seeing one's reflection on the pane of glass through which one nevertheless looks at the world. The semiotic machinery of the theatre that delivers emotion to us is not ignored or transcended, but made a part of the substance of that at which we wonder. If, that is, we are in pain or in joy at such moments, we are invited at the same time to see the mechanism of that pain or joy, and hence to recognize our own involvement, or resistance, as something we elect as well as endure. The theatre becomes an allegory of itself, and of our participation in it.

VI

The post-classical centuries before the revival of interest in the *Poetics* in the 1540s produced little extended commentary about drama, and much of that was associated with patristic or iconoclastic denunciations.[33] Though the *Poetics* was known earlier, it did not become a general focus of commentary until the publication of Robortello's commentary in 1548. Thereafter, however, it generated an immense volume of discussion in Italian, and subsequently French, humanist theory and no commentator failed to develop his views in relation to an interpretation of Aristotle. In addition, the syncretic habit of humanist thinking sought fervently to reconcile Aristotelian pronouncements by careful interpretive maneuver with the Platonic remarks on poetry (larded with those of Neoplatonic commentators such as Proclus), and within the dominant context of Horatian and Ciceronian rhetorical theory. Two aspects of this body of theory are especially relevant to the present discussion: the treatment of *admiratio* as a goal of dramatic structure, and the debates surrounding *katharsis* as the principal moral and social justification for poetry. While the latter has notoriously continued to be a focus for debate, the former has largely dropped from the critical lexicon as a key

term. Nevertheless, Renaissance theory valued it highly, and often made
it the principal goal of poetic production.

In some significant ways, the cultural world of the Renaissance in
western Europe was especially primed to welcome an aesthetics of
admiratio. Wonder was sought after, deployed and cultivated all through
the period, variously and to various ends. Nicholas Cusanus evoked it in
his paradoxes to lead contemplation beyond itself and towards God.[34]
Descartes, as we have seen, called it "la premiere de toutes les passions,"
and wished to purge it of inferior distractions. Rulers alike of large and
small dominions sought to harness it, mounting spectacular exhibitions –
entries, masques, tournaments – to overwhelm witnesses both domestic
and foreign with the lavish strangeness of power. Between the efforts of
Columbus, Copernicus, and Bruno the dimensions of space expanded,
and travelers to undiscovered countries returned with news, words and
objects surpassing the dreams of merchants and monarchs – pepper,
canaries, comets, and gold. All Europe seemed hungry for amazement.

The emotional energies of wonder were particularly trained on the
recurrent Renaissance preoccupation with the figure of the hero, both in
life and art. It was especially here that power-politics sought to co-opt
wonder and to mobilize its intimations of force to practical ends. By
staging the ruler, whether Prince, Emperor, or Pope, as a being utterly
outside of common experience, endowed beyond the range of the
ordinary yet prepared to condescend, the magicians of Renaissance
diplomacy invested their masters with an aura of untouchability and
transcendence. These were not inconsiderable tools of public policy, and
though they carried no guarantee, their political efficacy was at times
remarkable. English monarchs from Henry VIII on sought to promote or
sustain policy in part by such marvelous means. Queen Elizabeth used
her summer progresses to display her royal person to her realm for
admiration and homage, and accounts of her passing by eye-witnesses
leave little doubt that her mere appearance in the common arena was a
powerful catalyst for loyalty. Her successor, King James, though less
inclined to public display, continued and enlarged this spectacular
politics in the masques and entertainments presented at his court.[35] In
this cultivation of *éclat*, the English monarchy was typical of its moment.
Heroes and their exploits were a recurrent preoccupation of political and
artistic image-makers alike, and great Hercules, not our modern
Oedipus, was the central mythological figure.[36]

Renaissance letters held wonder in a similarly high place. Baxter
Hathaway has shown to what extent it lay alongside, overlapped, and
competed for attention with the concepts of "imitation" and "the

commonplace" in Renaissance literary criticism, especially in the Italian critical scuffles of the sixteenth century.[37] *Admiratio* played a vital role in the influential aesthetic commentaries of Robortello, Minturno, Scaliger, and Cinthio.[38] At least one theorist, Franccsco Patrizi, made "la meraviglia" the cornerstone, indeed the entire substance, of a Neoplatonic and, refusing Aristotle's lead, anti-mimetic theory of poetry.[39] In England, where Aristotelianism's influence was much less, Sir Philip Sidney still shows his familiarity with the Italian commentaries in his dictum that tragedy ought to foster "a well-raised admiration."[40] The manifold uses to which the term was put, its application to questions of content and style, matter and execution, make it both a key and a quagmire in Renaissance poetics.

The difficulties in Aristotle's treatment of wonder outlined above were at once fruitful of discussion and frustrating for Renaissance commentators. Robortello's groundbreaking commentary is exemplary of the compromises into which any attempt to elucidate Aristotle systematically led the humanist scholar.[41] Robortello promotes *admiratio* as one of the three basic sources of pleasure in drama, the others being imitation and mastery of the difficult, a kind of *admiratio* directed to the skill of the poet rather than the action. Making admiration the chief source of pleasure, however, gives rise to a conflict with the criterion of credibility in imitation he has promoted elsewhere. Robortello deals with this by dividing the play into segments, each of which fulfills a different criterion for the proper pleasure. As Bernard Weinberg notes:

> The pleasures arising from imitation, from *difficulté vaincue*, and admiration are thus largely attached to parts of the poem different from those which produce utility.... This does not mean that the other "essential" parts of the poem do not give pleasure. It merely means that, in keeping with his analytical tendency, Robortello seeks as much as possible to find separate causes for the pleasure and the utility derived by the audience.[42]

Such a tension between the demand for the verisimilar and that for the marvelous bedevils much Italian commentary, and commentators resolve it in various ways, as Hathaway has shown in detail. Thus Tasso, for instance, makes the marvelous compatible with the verisimilar through the ingenious argument that the marvelous is the province of God and everything God does is credible.[43] Castelvetro, who has a poor opinion of the theatre audience's imaginative capacities, also makes admiration the principal source of pleasure – in effect he thinks of it as a shiny bauble to amuse the vulgar – and as a result has to intertwine it with the credible very dexterously to make drama work at all, radically narrowing the scope of the playwright.[44] In general, the attempt to follow Aristotle led consistently to such problems in the commentaries. Such scrupulousness about the letter of Aristotle's text, added to a general lack of critical method, can give a particularly dry emptiness to much of the debate.

At the same time, Renaissance theory joined stage practice in enormously expanding attention to the role of stage spectacle in creating wonder. Here Aristotle's comparative neglect left theorists with an opening that they fully exploited, and to the elaboration of "the poetics of spectacle" they brought other strands of humanist meditation on the visual, in particular Neoplatonic claims for the epiphanic power of images and Vitruvian writings on architecture and design. The Italian stage practice of inserting spectacular *intermezzi* between the acts of plays, culminating in Buontalenti's gigantic pageants in Florence at the end of the century (in their turn so important for shaping the theatre of Inigo Jones), was added incentive for Renaissance critics to move visual spectacle to the center of attention by linking it to Aristotle's demand for the marvelous, regardless of what their particular views were on other issues of poetics, or on wonder's relation to those issues.[45] Wonder was generally considered the central goal of the dramatist's art, the primary pleasure offered to the audience and a principal agent in effecting the much-discussed end of tragedy – the regulation of audience emotions through *katharsis*.

Katharsis was the crucial term for most Renaissance poetic theories after 1548. To the humanist scholar or poet, with his commitment to the educative functions of artistic and rhetorical expression, it seemed to offer an Aristotelian authority for poetry's moral and social utility which they could set against or use to soften Plato's well-known strictures. As Stephen Orgel puts it, "Catharsis tends to be the basis for any utilitarian claim that is made for theatre in the Renaissance."[46] At the same time, according to Baxter Hathaway, "The very brevity and mystery of Aristotle's references ... provided a challenge to the apologist for poetry and gave him free rein to apply his own cherished ideas in expanding upon what Aristotle had said."[47] As might be expected, theories of *katharsis* proliferated throughout the period and their variety can be bewildering. Orgel discerns three basic groupings: a homeopathic view in which only pity and fear are purged and – using an explicitly medical analogy – an allopathic model in which other antisocial passions are purged by the evocation of pity and fear (this usually preferred a mechanism of "ethical images"), and a little later a type of *éducation sentimentale* by way of "tempering all our passions through its vision of the pity and fear inherent in the uncertainties of great men's lives, thereby making our own ordinary unhappiness easier to bear."[48] There was also much back-and-forthing in the heat of debate and many commentators incorporate elements from all the models. It was the apparent promise that poetry might confer on its society a beneficent technology of the emotions that made discussion of *katharsis* such a promising line of enquiry. So important was this notion that it was quickly adapted from tragedy to cover other kinds of drama.[49] The ongoing debate concerned what kinds of emotions were involved, and just how they were mobilized and made over for the audience's improvement. Eclecticism and the desire to synthesize in order that no authoritative view be omitted also made certain that the requirement for *admiratio* and the mechanism of *katharsis* were eventually brought into contact with one another, since the former was widely understood to be one of drama's chief emotional pleasures and the latter the process that justified the evocation of emotion in the first place. The definition of poetry from Giason Denores' *Discorso* of 1586 nicely illustrates the kind of contact forged between the two:

Poetry, then, is an imitation of some human action, marvelous, complete, and sizeable, which has in itself a change of fortune either from prosperous to adverse or from adverse to prosperous, which is presented to the listeners through language in verse, either in narration or in dramatic form, in order to purge them by means of pleasure of the most important passions of the soul, and to direct them toward good living, toward the imitation of the virtuous, and toward the conservation of good republics.[50]

This is at once ample, admirably civic-minded, and vague. It shows clearly how *admiratio* and *katharsis* gravitated towards each other as aspects of the Renaissance critics' preoccupation with the management of emotions. Aristotle's concern with drama as a species of knowledge, as in fact a branch of logic, has almost completely disappeared. In its place is the pleasurable evocation of astonishment, through spectacle as much as through plot, and the manipulation of that pleasure in concert with other emotions in order to transform the audience into improved citizens.

Wonder thus became a "pharmaceutical" element in a form of ethical therapy. Though critics differed, sometimes sharply, about precisely how and on what faculties the operation was effected, and though there were some who dissented from the entire framework of *katharsis*, the general image of the playwright was as a technologist of virtue, whether through the intellect or the emotions, by example or by direct manipulation. The grab-bag formulation of Buonamici from his *Discorsi poetici* (1597) shows particularly well the variety of modes and functions *katharsis* could subsume by the end of the century:

the soul is purged by removing the excessive passions and correcting them with their contraries: melancholy, with music, with laughter; arrogance in the prosperous events of fortune with fear and with pity; with the example of good men, inviting us to virtue; with the example of bad men, turning us away from vice; with hymns and celebrations of the gods, sowing in our minds reverence toward God and piety. Comedy purges us with laughter, tragedy with pity, the epic with an example, the dithyramb with honors toward God, and all of them, finally, as it is written in the *Politics*, create pleasure – that pleasure which is according to nature, which consists in propriety.[51]

In this general schema, *admiratio* was a key element, both as a basic kind of aesthetic pleasure and as the site of a particularly powerful emotion to be harnessed to the betterment of the audience through their emotional involvement with the play.

It remains to be seen whether the practice of the theatre will in fact support such ventures of theory, especially in the case of Shakespeare who was, of all his contemporaries, among the least influenced by theoretical and learned speculation. It is for instance hardly true of his work to say that it is uninterested in drama as a species of knowledge, or that it neglects questions of cognition for those of emotion. On the contrary, the complex and manifold interrelations between knowledge and feeling are his chiefest subjects. *Macbeth*, for instance, might be described as an essay on a diabolical slippage between the two, and the whole of *Measure for Measure* could be unpacked from the puns on them available in English in the single word "sense."

Yet Shakespeare does fulfill the expectation of Renaissance theory that wonder and the final purpose of drama in emotional transformation of the audience will be intimately linked. For Shakespeare, as for the medieval drama that preceded him, wonder is neither a weapon for the domination of an audience (as it sometimes is in Marlowe), nor an additive for stimulating a certain kind of culinary pleasure, but a site for the complex modulation of audience identification and detachment, making the "between" of the theatrical performance a space of semiotic and psychological experiment, through which the audience, like the characters, must negotiate a way.

"Pass in, pass in," the angels say,
"In to the upper doors,
Nor count compartments of the floors,
But mount to paradise
By the stairway of surprise."

Emerson, "Merlin"

"But Satan, smitten with amazement, fell."

Milton, Paradise Regained

The great cycles of playlets performed in English towns in the later Middle Ages, strings of miraculous incidents depicting all or most of universal history, were committed by their architecture to evoking from their audience play by play an overarching wonder at the size, magic, and majesty of God's design. Into the interstices of this structure were fitted, like the gargoyles and roof-bosses on the great cathedrals, vignettes of contemporary life, bits of social commentary and popular stories about apocryphal figures. The cycles in turn took their place in an array of town ceremonies that celebrated at once a Church feast, usually Corpus Christi, and the secular order of the community in the hands of the town authorities under God.

Mervyn James has usefully described this wider Corpus Christi festival of liturgy, procession, and drama as a complex performance affirming the hierarchic structure and corporate character of the community.[1] James argues that, along with "enhancement of urban honor in the world at large, which most appealed to the urban magistracies," the festival was a "mechanism ... by which the tensions implicit in the diachronic rise and fall of occupational communities could be confronted and worked out. ... [so that], by means which were essentially informal, ... the implications of change could be given recognition and incorporated with a minimum of friction into the social body."[2] The semiotic and symbolic center which gave intellectual coherence to the whole festival complex was the Sacrament. Though the actual Host was not an especially prominent feature or theme of the cycle-plays, the Body of Christ and the fate of "bodies" generally is central to their action and meaning.

James's reading of the Corpus Christi festival as corporate ritual stresses that the plays were embedded in a suite of procedures for mapping social structure through shared, performed narratives. However, where the plays are concerned a gap remains between the visible acts of individual bodies on a "playing-place" and the central myth "incorporating" actors, guilds, and audience within the larger "body" of universal history. What needs to be spelled out is how the playing of the play "here" reaches for the community's knowledge of itself at and in the play in relation to the "there" of sacramental space and time. Such an account must pay particular attention to how experience of divine truth is acquired, conveyed, and signified, for it is there that the plays articulate historical and secular action with the ritual and the supra-historical.

Medieval theories of drama *per se* that might do this work are almost non-existent, since drama did not easily fit within any of the recognized intellectual disciplines. Global accounts of "the arts" consider dramatic performance only briefly, as a technical or mechanical activity that humans engage in, analogous to commerce, hunting, or armor-making. Hugh of St. Victor in his *Didascalion* and St. Bonaventura, following him, in *De Reductione Artium ad Theologiam* consider *theatrica* as a recreative activity contributing to mental hygiene and overall health, but make no attempt to reflect on drama as a specific cultural or performative practice.[3]

What consideration is given to drama is found largely in attacks on it, launched especially from patristic authority and Biblical injunctions against making "images." The most common defense against these was through analogies with more fully theorized "related" arts, such as painting or sculpture, allowing drama's defenders to co-opt the long and authoritative tradition of Church anti-iconoclastic teaching with only minimal adjustment for these "animate images."[4] This tactic is effective enough in polemic argument, but it sidesteps issues central to dramatic performance, above all the meaning of acts performed by human beings in a figurative or representational frame.[5]

Though for obvious reasons it was not relied on too openly in polemic contexts, the theology of the sacramental sign provides the needed bridge between the individual act or gesture and its figurative resonance, for this bridging was the essential function of the priest's "performance" of the Mass.[6] Aquinas defines a sacrament as "a sign of a sacred reality inasmuch as it has the property of sanctifying men," and more loosely as "a sign of some sacred reality pertaining to men" (3a.60.2).[7] He also suggests a more general semiotic and a connection with the rhetorical figures employed by Scripture:

Now it is connatural to men to arrive at a knowledge of intelligible realities through sensible ones, and a sign is something through which a person arrives at knowledge of some further thing beyond itself. Moreover the sacred realities signified by the sacraments are certain spiritual and intelligible goods by which man is sanctified. And the consequence of this fact is that the function of the sacrament as signifying is implemented by means of some sensible realities. The case here is similar to that in the holy Scriptures where, in order to describe spiritual realities to us, corresponding sensible realities are used to illustrate them. (*Summa* 3a.60.4)

This passage is as important for discussion of medieval drama as Aristotle's account of an audience "learning and reasoning out" when confronted with *mimesis* – indeed, the seeds of a theory of *mimesis* lurk in the vocabulary of "correspondence" here. Like Aristotle, Aquinas is concerned with "learning" about universal categories ("intelligible realities") through the material instance of the sign that greets our senses. He too orients us on the kind of cognitive activity performed by an audience seeking to understand and interpret what they see. It is especially important that Aquinas does not discount the sensible aspect of the sign, which "pertain[s] to the worship of the kingdom of God ... inasmuch as [it is a sign] of those spiritual realities in which the kingdom of God consists." The bringing together in the sacramental moment of a sensible and an insensible order is much like acting in the medieval theatre, which is sensible and "here" but points beyond the sensible and the present to an ultimate "there." The figure before us is at once a familiar townsman and a character revealed by God's dispensation through Scripture and Church. His character as our neighbor persists fully intact, yet he also participates and is caught up in the larger order of revelation.

While it could never be argued that the plays had officially the place or value of a sacramental reality in the Church order, Aquinas himself concedes that there are signs apart from the seven approved by the Church which, while they do not both signify and sanctify, nevertheless "signify a disposition to sanctity." "Sprinkling of holy water, consecration of altars" fall under this heading (3a.60.2), and so presumably do solemn processions of the Host on Corpus Christi day and other paraliturgical acts and performances. But once committed to viewing the material world as waiting, indeed longing, for transfiguration, it is hard to stop the search for correspondence. Only the imposition of an authority strictly arbitrary can prevent the process from running rampant out of the Church and into the community. Aquinas is quite explicit about the danger here, and about the need for the invocation of authority to control it: "just as it is for the judgment of the Holy Spirit to determine which figures are to be used in specific passages in the

Scriptures, so too the question of which things are to be chosen to act as signs in the case of any given sacrament must be determined by divine ordination" (3a.60.5). Miri Rubin has noted the results of this search for sacramentality in the period's gradual expansion of non-liturgical uses for the Host:

The Eucharist specifically created a link between the present and the moment in the past when power, and the access to it, was defined. The consecrated species was understood to effect a fundamental change in the nature of things: sickness into health, well-being into misfortune, the revelation of truth out of a mass of inconclusive facts in the working of ordeals.... From the very nature of its sacramental status, it belonged in every area of life, mediating between sacred and profane, supernatural and natural. [8]

Rubin goes on to detail attempts to regulate the economy of this symbolism against manifold pressures to expand it, noting that the authority of the Church "attempted to protect the design of its central symbol; it was willing to adjust and absorb readings and usages which were not fundamentally threatening." Any account of the plays needs to be alive to medieval suspicion of this sort of semiotic hypertrophy and enthusiasm for "boundlessness" in imaginations imbued with sacramentalizing thought.

The polemics that pursued dramatic performance through the medieval period made precisely this unauthorized generation of illicit "correspondences" one of their major points against dramatic representation of the sacred. The only substantial contemporary discussion extant on English medieval drama, a stern Lollard polemic entitled "A Tretise of Miraclis Pleyinge," gives pride of place in its attack to precisely this fear of blurred boundaries between authoritative and parasitic signs.[9] In so doing, the treatise demonstrates just how these boundaries had both a theological and a social dimension. The real danger in "miraclis pleyinge" is the anti-hierarchic moment which disrupts the normal ladder of authority and acts out parody and challenge:

A! Lord! syther an erthely servaunt dar not taken in pley and in bourde that that her erthely lord takith in ernest, muche more we shulden not maken oure pleye and bourde of tho myraclis and werkis that God so ernestfully wrouȝt to us; for sothely whan we so done, drede to synne is taken awey, as a servaunt whan he bourdith with his mayster leesith his drede to offendyn hym, namely, whanne he bourdith with his mayster in that and that his mayster takith in ernest.... thanne whanne we pley in his miraclis as men don nowe on dayes, God takith more venjaunce on us than a lord that sodaynly sleeth his servaunt for he pleyide to homely with hym; and riȝt as that lord thanne in dede seith to his servaunt, "pley not with me, but pley with thi pere," so whanne we taken in pley and in bourde the myraclis of God, he fro us takynge his grace seith more ernestfully to us than the forseid lord, "pley not with me, but pley with thi pere." Therefore sich emyraclis [sic] pleyinge reversith Crist.[10]

Unregulated or transgressive performance undermines authority's pre-rogative to define the appropriate range and context of actions. Here the authority of the polemicist asserts itself in a direct parroting of God's voice and in the image of a sudden, devastating violence that corrects too wayward or illicit a ludic drift.

To be sure, as communal undertakings by highly stratified and self-regulating groups, the cycle-plays were unlikely to produce radical departures. But their very striving to show how everyday boundaries between historical event and revelation had been and could be overcome, and to produce intensity of engaged devotion outside the established sacramental order, tends to push against neat hierarchic divisions.[11] Just how much sacrament and performance became integrated was a crucial issue for the drama itself, and has been so again for modern criticism. Into this environment of uncertain semiotic valence are drawn various tales of "mistakes" made by performers in taking the play for the real, the sign for the thing. Such misplaced literalism is a threat generated by all genuine sacramental thinking. Some commentators have responded to this uncertainty by claiming that the aim of the cycle-plays was to annihilate completely the distinctions between historical event and its enactment. Thus Anne Righter finds a naive sacramentalism or belief in some "real presence" in the mystery plays when she elaborates on the story of a spear-carrier who got overenthused and killed an actor playing Christ. And though her example comes from a 1631 moral tract, neither a neutral source nor reliable evidence, it seems to stem at least from a polemicist's shrewd reflection on the mode of thinking habitual to this drama.[12]

As an inevitable corollary of their parasitism on liturgy and sacra-mental representation, the plays suffer from a nagging doubt about how far the invocative activity of performance carries. Sacramental parody, literalization, and fraud emerge as key elements in the cycle-plays' self-consciousness. The joke-plot of Mak's sheep that doubles the Nativity in the Second Shepherds' Play is only the most famous instance. The consistent presentation of blustering tyrants is another, those roaring generators of a mix of wonder and fear at their pretensions to power who force their claims for attention and allegiance directly on the audience, as when the Coventry Shearmen and Taylors' Play instructs Herod to "rage in the pageant and in the street also." Such parodists of God's authority – Cain, Herod, Pilate, etc. – do not only dramatic but also metadramatic work, expressing and managing some of the plays' own concern with transgression and boundless ambition for representational control. And though we have no record of audience response to guide us in this, it is possible that the elaborate machinery of the pageant staging worked as much to foreground the distance between what humans could laboriously construct and what God could effortlessly bring to pass as it did to convince the audience of some magical reality unfolding before them unmediated.

The "space" of flux and translation where the materials and bodies before us seek, in Aquinas' terms, a signifying "correspondence" with "spiritual realities" is governed precisely by wonder. Righter's story of the spearman is a cautionary *exemplum* of engagement too fully embraced; the preacher's tale of the "mayster" who kills his servant evokes a jealous God not unlike the one Aristotle denied, who punished too close a scrutiny of his prerogative and privity. Wonder's dialectic of identification and defense maps closely the medieval impulses towards and away from a transparent sacramentalism in the plays. We saw in the last chapter how subtly vision and voice can operate in the dynamic of wonder – vision concrete but distanced, voice invisible yet penetrative – and how this interplay figures a crisis in the observer's sense of integrity. Though the cycle-plays differ radically from the drama Aristotle sought to describe, in this they share a dramaturgical strategy. The fusion of voice and substance is after all one way to express the mystery that underlies the entire sacramental order we have been discussing: "Verbum caro factum est." The cycle-plays – committed as they are to wonder as the message of God's universe – also fear that their staging of it will be unmanageable, unlawful, somehow too much.[13]

This doubt about the ramifications of the very emotions they set out to evoke leads to various strategies in the dramaturgy of the cycles whereby they at once command admiring involvement and still or defer it. In the brief readings that follow, I will show how emotional engagement and self-conscious reflection on that engagement intertwine with one another in three plays. In each play a carefully controlled moment occurs where the rhetorical and representational surface of the play is fractured to point away from itself. A sense results of the provisional status of representation as the site of revelation, and belief plays against a necessary and saving disbelief, in contrast to an often-observed naive or pictorial dramaturgy of simple investment. In the York Lucifer play, Scripture effects a pre-emptive attack to collapse Lucifer's hyperbolic self-assertion and sublime transgression into mere parasitism. In the York Transfiguration play, the competing claims of spectacle and voice are placed against one another in order to sharpen the audience's sense of the limits on their spectatorship. Finally the N-Town "Meeting in the

Garden" makes its recognition dependent upon God's call rather than the spectators' unmediated "open sight."

I

Each of the four extant cycles represents the Fall of Lucifer, either along with the Creation in the opening play or in the one following.[14] Suspicion about the representation of divine matters arises immediately in Lucifer's attempt to usurp God's prerogative. The Towneley, Chester, and N-Town plays show Lucifer attempting a literal usurpation by sitting on God's throne while He is out of the room. R. W. Hanning points out that in this original act of mimesis, Lucifer is simultaneously a dire threat and an enabling gesture for the dramatic project of the cycle-plays as a whole, which must thereafter carefully distinguish their own deferential mimesis of divinity from that of their primal mimic and parodist.

The York cycle-play, following Augustine, prefers to consider what lies behind the impulse to emulation in the first place. Augustine comments that "When the evil will abandons what is above itself, and turns to what is lower, it becomes evil – not because that is evil to which it turns but because the turning itself is wicked."[15] Rupture in the York play is subtler than mere mimicry, and has to do with hearing – or not hearing, or hearing awry, perhaps troping – a specific vocation. The lesson of the York play is in how to listen.

All four Fall plays begin with a speech by God alone "before" the creation of time, in which he emphasizes the infinite continuity, unity, and extension of his presence and will.[16] Division of any kind in the divine substance is explicitly denied (Towneley's God "may never twynned be;" Chester's "never shal be twyninge") and essential unity insisted on. The Towneley God announces the containment of the cycle within himself: "And all that evyr xall have beynge / it is closyd in my mende" (lines 6–7), so that Creation is a logical extension of his being. For the York God, too, naming and creating are one gesture, as is indicated by his word for the Creation of the world, "neuen" (line 25), which can mean both "fashion" and "name."[17]

Thus far all four cycles are in agreement, but with the appearance of the angels they diverge. Hanning points especially to the care with which modes of dramatic presentation evolve in the York play: from God's "declarative mode" with its rhetoric of pure authority, to "choric praise" from the angels, to "a kind of pre-dialogue" between angels and Lucifer "which only the audience, from its position of knowing the consequences of Lucifer's new voice, can evaluate properly," to finally, after the Fall, genuine dramatic interchange – in Hell as dispute and in Heaven as instruction.[18] The clarity of this development from exposition into drama suggests the unknown playwright's full awareness of the stakes. Notable in particular is the care with which the twinning of voices is articulated in the central section, where the collective speech of the angels and the galloping brashness of Lucifer alternate:

Tunc cantant angeli: Sanctus sanctus sanctus, dominus deus sabaoth.

6. Primus angelus seraphyn.
A! merciful maker, full mekill es the mighte,
That all this warke at a worde worthely has wroghte,
Ay loved be that lufly lorde of his lighte,
That vs thus mighty has made, that nowe was righte noghte;
In blys for to byde in hys blyssyng,
Ay lastande, in luf let vs lowte hym,
At beelde vs thus baynely abowete hym,
Of myrther neuermore to haue myssyng.

7. Primus angelus deficiens Lucifere.
All the myrth that es made es markide in me,
The bemes of my brighthode ar byrnande so bryghte,
And I so semely in syghte my selfe now I se,
For lyke a lorde am I lefte to lende in this lighte,
More fayrear be far than my feres,
In me is no poynte that may payre,
I fele me fetys and fayre,
My powar es passande my peres.

8. Ang. cherabyn.
Lord! wyth a lastande luf we loue the allone,
thou mightefull maker that markid vs and made vs,
And wroghte us thus worthely to wone in this wone,
Ther never felyng of fylth may full vs nor fade vs.
All blys es here beeldande a-boute vs,
To-whyls we are stabyll in thought
In the worschipp of hym that us wroghte
Of dere never thar vs more dowte vs.

9. Prim. ang. defic.
O! what I am fetys and fayre and fygyred full fytt!
The forme of all fayrehede apon me es feste,
All welth in my weelde es, I wete be my wytte,
The bemes of my brighthede are bygged with the beste.
My schewyng es schemerande and schynande,
So bygly to blys am I broghte,
Me nedes for to noy me righte noghte,
Here sall neuer payne me be pynande.   (lines 41–72)

The speech of the "cherabyn" echoes God's clearly and with hardly an alteration (compare lines 44 and 32; 46 and 24; 47 and 20–1, 35), fulfilling his charge to be "merour of my myghte." The lines are simple variants of God's own words, just as a mirror image or an echo depend on their originals; there is no troping or diversion to compete with God's authority. This is the play's way of registering the angels' consciousness as a continuous confirmation of God's unified self-presence, from which they themselves are hardly distinct.[19]

Lucifer's language strikes out in a radically different direction. His first line already shows an incipient self-consciousness: "All the myrth that es made es markide in me." Looking at himself, Lucifer sees his brightness as the "marke" of an independently constituted being. Does his line mean "All created joy is signified in me"? "is noted/perceived in me"? "finds its boundary in me"? The issue is one of signs and interpreters, and therefore of distance and difference.[20] Marking only the marks and not the mark-maker, Lucifer is released from the signing authorial presence into a burst of intense and gleeful self-improvisation. Unlike the Angels, Lucifer sees himself as an object of action and contemplation, a source rather than a medium: "The bemes of my brighthode ar byrnande so bryghte, / And I so semely in syghte my selfe now I se."

From this liberation into self, Lucifer's language acquires at once greater energy and greater metaphoric plasticity, and his emulous urge grows more agonistic as he asserts an absolute primacy: "More fayrear by far than my feres / In me is no poynte that may payre, / I fele me fetys and fayre, / My powar es passande my peres." Words bend to his will in the creation of startling puns here: Lucifer's "peres" will "payre" before him, they are his "feres," but he is "fayrear." The image in the "merour" intuits self-reliance and asserts its primacy by imagining the conquest of rivals. Lucifer turns to hyperbole as the chief gesture of the agonistic and sublime mode he is inventing. His alliterative rhythms take on a racy sweep: "O! What I am fetys and fayre and fygyred full fytt! / The forme of all fayrehede apon me es feste / All welth in my weelde es" (lines 65–7). He does not pause to consider from what he is "fygyred." Worshiping his own will, he is the first solipsist of the imagination.

Hyperbole is an unstable and self-subverting engine. With his hot language, Lucifer is committed to a restlessness that constantly changes as it feeds on self-observation. But God has made the continued enjoyment of beatitude conditional on "stability": "To-whils ȝhe are stabill in thoghte" (line 30, dutifully repeated by an Angel at line 62). The rhetorical counterpart of this "stability" and its connection with vocation are emphasized:

Ang. seraphyn.
With all the wytt at we welde we wyrschip thi wyll,
Thu gloryus god that es grunde of all grace,
Ay with stedefaste steuen lat vs stande styll,
Lorde! to be fede with the fode of thi fayre face.
In lyfe that es lely ay lastande,
Thi dale, lorde, es ay daynetethly delande,
And who so that fode may be felande
To se thi fayre face es noght fastande.   (lines 73–80)

Alliterative rhythm here has nothing to do with energetic self-revision, but locally reinforces a serenity and commonality of tone corresponding to a "stedefast steuen" in which one may "stande styll." To understand the will is fully to hear the voice, see the face and receive the food (a sacramental ambience appears here), all of which ground and nourish being and insulate it from Luciferian becoming. By contrast, not to hear the voice is to be insecure and hungry, afloat on a wild and violent sea. Lucifer feeds on himself, his voice not "stabyll" but dynamic, hyperbolic, and infinitely aspiring. He can only exclaim the primacy of his own brightness in ever-more-grandiose gestures:

Owe! certes! what I am worthely wroghte with wyrschip, i-wys!
For in a glorius gle my gleteryng it glemes,
I am so mightyly made my mirth may noghte mys,
Ay sall I byde in this blys thorowe brightnes of bemes.   (lines 81–4)

And as Lucifer uses up the fuel on which he feeds, his light begins to flicker and dance. From "bemes of brighthode" (line 50) to "schemer-ande and schynande" (line 69), to "gleteryng ... glemes" (line 82), the images move from general radiance towards fiery pulsation. In a final burst of imaginative vigor, tracing the arc of the sublime visionary even as it also moralizes his fate, Lucifer appropriates the power of creation, leaps breathtakingly across the stanza gap to set up his Heaven of "selfe" – and falls on the other:

All welth in my welde haue I weledande,
Abowne ʒhit sall I be beeldand,
On heghte in the hyeste of hewen

Ther sall I set my selfe, full semely to seyghte,
To ressayve my reuerence thorowe righte o renowne,
I sall be lyke unto hym that es hyeste on heghte;
Owe! what I am derworth and defte. Owe! dewes! all goes downe!
(lines 88–92)

At the acme of his exultation, where a Longinian "height" is itself his theme, the watchers in history see their ironic knowledge spring upon Lucifer at last: his vaunted originality is the older, colder voice of a familiar quotation from Isaiah.[21] His very originality at once turns into the belatedness of echo through the paradox of our foreknowledge. This remarkable and instant metamorphosis of *hypsos* into *bathos*, here literally a plunging into the depths, coincides precisely with the discovery of citation. Though they are temporally Lucifer's successors, the audience therefore precede him in the order of knowledge, and the play confronts its own narrative order with an apocalyptic one that transumes and "speaks through" it. Citation supervenes over self-improvisation to show the containment of Luciferian language within the seamless network of the Word. Helpless, out of control, Lucifer tries a nascent colloquialism, and we hear it cut with a sharply literal edge: "Helpe! felawes, in faythe I am fallande" (line 94). He who has ears to hear, let him hear.

The relevance of this catastrophe for the creative project of the cycle-plays is clear. Even as it initiates the York cycle, the play warns against the danger of an imagination producing self-confirming but unstable and ungrounded versions of its own desires in place of the "food" of God's voice. God himself names this kind of imagination with the Greek-derived term later so dear to the Renaissance: it is all "fantasyes" (line 129). So that orthodoxy can exercise a policing function in the shaping of the action, the opening play calls attention to the necessity of keeping an ear cocked for what speaks through the multiplicity of materials, incidents, and emotions in the immediate dramatic moment. The York play uses the very transgressive and boundary-breaking energies of wonder against themselves by containing their insistent "newness" within a recognized order of familiar oldness. If we have reveled in Lucifer's rhythms of self-making, we can hear and learn our error and stand aside just when he can no longer do so.

What awaits Lucifer and his cohorts in Hell, the black hole of his supernova imagination, is an exact reversal of his previous state, and antithesis dominates there:

> *13. Lucifer deiabolus [sic] in inferno.*
> Owte owte! harrowe! helples, slyke hote at es here,
> This es a dongon of dole that I am to-dyghte,
> Whare es my kynde be-come, so cumly and clere,
> Nowe am I laytheste, allas! that are was lighte.
> My bryghtnes es blakkeste and blo nowe;
> My bale es ay betande and brynande,
> That gares ane go growlande and gyrnande.
> Owe! ay walaway! I well enew in wo nowe!
>
> *14. Secundus diabolus.*
> Owte! owte! I go wode for wo, my wytte es all wente nowe,
> All oure fode es but filth, we fynde us beforn,

We that ware beelded in blys in bale are we brent nowe,
Owte! on the Lucifer, lurdan! oure lyghte has thu lorne.

(lines 97–108)

The diabolic is not after all a restless overthrowing, but a reflective "mirroring" of God in the negative mode of reversal. It is characteristic of the playwright that the Second Devil describes his trajectory at line 107 with a chiasmus, a scheme of reversal that here momentarily becomes a bitter trope for God's active enclosure of diabolic aspiration. What was "beelded" is now "brent," and it is not in the devils' power to rebuild it. All the key terms of the first half of the play reappear in dark and antithetical versions: light, height, beauty, bliss, eloquence, food, creation ("beeldande") are matched with "blakkeste," "dongon," "laytheste," "bale," "gyrnande," "filth," and "brynande." The plasticity of language with which Lucifer hailed his primacy reappears as mere lying:

> Luc. in inf.
> Vnthryuandly threpe ȝhe, I sayde but a thoghte.
>
> Secund. diab.
> We! lurdan, thu lost vs.
>
> Luc. in inf.
> ȝhe ly, owte! allas!
> I wyste noghte this wo schulde be wroghte.
> Owte on ȝhow! lurdans, ȝhe smore me in smoke.   (lines 114–16)

Hanning remarks on the dramatic consequences of this newly divided and divisive epistemology that "only here, in the new, fallen space of the dramatic world, does dialogue become possible, but it is the dialogue of quarrel, of attack and defense, issuing in a physical melee which is the only kind of interaction possible among creatures, each of whom has set out to pretend to be his own God."[22]

With the cosmos now polarized into rival versions of reflection, God stabilizes the division. The "twinning" (line 153, cf. Chester line 10) of light and dark is codified as a structure of oppositions, with the earth a middle ground between Heaven and Hell. God also bids his angels join in the management of the cosmos as his agents. His instruction of them to act as mediators of his light renews the image of them as "merours" and offers an alternative to the Luciferian imagination meditating on itself. As long as the plays can claim the same status, all is well. But to do this, they must maintain "stedefast steuen" and be constantly alert. The sublimity of conception in Lucifer's image of himself as self-imagined is not offered by the York play as an emotional key to the cycle. Instead it is presented as a claim to be resisted if we are to preserve the integrity of the godly community. In giving this metadramatic inflection to his opening play, the York playwright outlines an entire poetics for the cycle.

II

Medieval epistemology recognized two ways to acquire knowledge: one via the representation of images ("phantasmata") to the senses, the other via direct inspiration.[23] The connection of the Transfiguration with the issues of knowing and witnessing is strongly attested in Catholic theology.[24] Aquinas comments that "Christ through his Transfiguration revealed to the disciples the body's glory, which pertains to humans alone" (*Summa* 3a.45.3, ad 1). According to Aquinas, this glorification was attested by representatives: Moses (for the dead and the Law), Elijah (the blessed and the Prophets), and the living Apostles.[25] To this select company the York play admits the modern witnesses in its audience. The focus of this witnessing is explicitly the incarnate body of Christ, so that the play addresses the issues of sacramental embodiment subtending the whole structure. That the play anticipates this revelation will be an extraordinary sight is clear from the outset:

> *Jesus.* Petir, myne awne discipill dere,
> And James and John, my cosyns two,
> Takis hartely hede, for ȝe schall here
> that I wille telle vnto nomoo.
> And als ȝe schall see sightis seere,
> Whilke none schall see bot ȝe alsoo,
> Therfore comes forth, with me in fere,
> For to ȝone mountayne will I goo.
> Ther schall ȝe see a sight
>   Whilk ȝe haue ȝerned lange.   (lines 1–10)

Jesus carefully distinguishes earlier discussions of his true nature (John 14.8 and Luke 9.18–22) from the experience at hand by categorizing the former as inspired, while the latter are to be experienced directly:

> I askid ȝiff ȝe ought wiste
> Who I was, by youre witte.
> You aunswered, Petir, for thy prowe,
> And said that I was Crist, God sonne;
> Bot of thy selfe that had noght thowe,
> My Fadir hadde that grace be-gonne.
> Therfore bese bolde and biddis now
> To tyme ȝe haue my Fadir sonne.   (lines 35–42)

We have no record of how it was staged, but when the Transfiguration occurs, the York play stresses the full force of the disciples' amazement. Their dazed senses and disorientation suggest the headlong breakthrough of an overwhelming experience of wonder. They are almost overcome: it is clear for instance that they cannot or do not hear the first speeches of Moses and Elijah and thus remain uncertain who they are or what is happening. Their bodies can hardly support the strain:

> *Petrus.*
> Brethir, what euere ꝫone brightnes be?
> Swilk burdis be-forne was neuere sene,
> It marres my myght, I may not see,
> So selcouth thyng was neuere sene.
> *Jacob.*
> What it will worthe, that wote noꝫt wee,
> How wayke I waxe, ꝫe will not wene,
> Are was ther one, now is ther thre,
> We thynke oure maistir is be-twene. . . .
> *Petrus.* [To Elias and Moses]
> My bredir, if that ꝫe be come
>   To make clere Cristis name,
> Telles here till vs thre,
>   For we seke to the same.   (lines 85–92; 105–8)

As the play proves, "to make clere Cristis name" demands a clarification above all of his voice, and it is with clarity of speech that Jesus concerns himself:

> And for youre sake thus are thei sought
> To saie ꝫou, his sone am I.
> So schall bothe heucn and helle
>   Be demers of this dede,
> And ꝫe in erth schall tell
>   My name wher itt is nede.   (lines 139–44)

To understand the name imposes a duty to "tell" that name, a duty which extends analogously to the audience also. But bodily sight remains important. Peter makes a point of thanking Jesus specifically for it:

> *Petrus.*
> A! loued be thou euere, my lord Jesus,
> That all this solempne sight has sent,
> That ffouchest saffe to shew the thus,
> So that thi myghtis may be kende.   (lines 145–8)

This ratification of revealed truth in the bodily senses is important to the audience just as it was to Peter and the other disciples.

Yet the play is not naive about the status of its dramatic images as substitutes for what the disciples in fact perceived, and it remains wary of claiming direct sensual access to divine knowledge. The link between knowing and experiencing, pushed to a limit in the transfigured form of Jesus (lines 97–100), breaks down in what follows. Without warning the Father appears in a brilliant cloud and declares his identity with the Son and its meaning:

> Where he is, thare am I,
> He is myne and I am his,
> Who trowis this stedfastly
> Shall byde in endles blisse.

(lines 177–80)

This instruction is clearly heard by the audience, who are presumably among those addressed as "ȝe ffebil of faithe!" But it transpires when Jesus asks them that the disciples have neither seen the vision nor heard the message.[26] They recall "this glorious gleme" and affirm they "saugh pleynly" the "persones thre," but they give no indication of having perceived the Father in the cloud or his words, which they heard only as "noys":

> *Petrus.*
> There come a clowde of the skye,
> Lyght als the lemys on thame lent,
> And nowe fares all as fantasye,
> For wote noȝt [we] how thai are wente.
> *Jacob.*
> That clowde cloumsed vs clene,
>   That come schynand so clere,
> Such syght was never sene,
>   To seke all sydis seere.
>
> *Joh.*
> Nay, nay, that noys noyed vs more,
> That here was herde so hydously.
> *Jesus.*
> Frendis, be noght afferde afore,
> I schall ȝou saye encheson why.

(lines 197–208)

For the audience to hear more of the truth of this scene than the apostles do is a slightly odd predicament.[27] The experience of the spectators is both less immediate than Peter's – they were not present at the historical epiphany – and more complete in that they perceive in the event what he does not. Playing has allowed a saving accommodation of the overwhelming truth to us through a veil of secondary figuration. This veil is the staging and performance, whose very self-consciousness about its creaky theatricality concedes its status as a pretext: the real work is done instead in following the Father's command to listen. The Transfiguration play offers dramatic representation paradoxically as a kind of "via negativa" pointing beyond its own materiality to the imperative of voice beyond.

Jesus' explanation to Peter of why the disciples might not "see / Thy ffadirs face in his fayrenes" articulates this gesture of withholding:

> *Jesus*. Petir, thou askis over grete degree,
> That grace may noȝt be graunted the, I gesse.
> In his godhed so high is he
> As all ȝoure prophetis names expresse,
> That langar of lyffe schall he noght be
> That seys his godhede as it is.
> Here haue ȝe sene in sight
>   Poyntes of his privite,
> Als mekill as erthely wighte
>   May suffre in erthe to see.   (lines 219–28)

The last four lines especially help us to formulate the relation between the dangerous visual presentation of God's "privite" and the vocal message carried through it, apparently comprehensible only to the audience. Peter and the other disciples come close to direct visual contact with God, where the senses and the image-forming faculty which mediates knowledge fail to function. Peter characterizes this experience as "fantasye" (line 199): the product of an overtaxed imagination and, as with Lucifer, the aberrant double of true "visionary" knowledge. The cloud which conceals God is obscure through an excess of radiance, and the disciples cannot straighten out into perception what they experience only too fully as plenitude. This disjunction exposes a difference between direct perception and intellectual or spiritual understanding (here couched in the voice) directly applicable to the occasion of performance. By having the disciples experience the force of the event, but actors and audience witness its significance, the play glosses the limitations and advantages of reconstituting history as drama. The wonder in the original epiphany, expressed in the disciples' confusion, is transferred from the visual spectacle to the greater but less "striking" miracle of the intellectual order that underlies it, leading away from the visual towards the larger verbal order of revelation where the disciples' failure to see is recuperated by the audience's success in hearing. But by miming the overwhelming power of the divine spectacle to stun, block, and confound at the same time as its meaning in an overall pattern is clearly presented "over the heads" of the disciples, the play strikes a bargain between force and signification. The disciples represent mortals as incapable of divine contact; the audience acknowledge this limit but also pass beyond it through self-conscious accommodation. The experience comes to rest in a hermeneutic moment, the object of which is the incarnate Word transfigured at once under its aspect of the knowable and the unknowable, the representable and the unrepresentable.

III

It is above all in the Resurrection plays that the lynch-pin of the sacramental order, the incarnate body of Christ, has to be faced and recognized. It is not enough that the historical fact of Resurrection and return be mimed by actors: somehow these plays must dramatize not merely ancient story, but the inner order to the story that shapes the audience's common present. The Resurrection plays stand synecdochically for the whole relation of representation and authority, vision and vocation in the cycle-plays.

Peter Travis comments that the "recurring dramatic imperative" of the cycle-plays, to "Behold and believe,"

> is most emphatically employed in the sequence of episodes that opens with Christ's Resurrection and climaxes at Thomas's conversion. The paradigm of this sequence ... is an intense and prolonged trial of faith, wherein skepticism and middling conviction time and time again confront accumulating evidence of the reality of Christ's Resurrection and of his physical return to the world of men.[28]

Yet as we have seen, "Behold and believe" is a condition to which these plays aspire, but also one shot through with anxieties about this seeing as a route to the divine. Frequently the preference is for the more penetrative and mysterious medium of the Word. In the light of the "Transfiguration" play, with its preference for what we hear over what we see, naive reliance on what the Lollard author calls "sight without" is difficult to sustain.[29] Christ's meeting with Mary Magdalene from the N-Town cycle will serve as a final example of these tensions at work. Even in John's Gospel, the encounter is a curious one, and in all the cycle-plays it occurs in an environment of great uncertainty and emotional stress.[30]

Mary Magdalene makes an ideal point of contact between audience and action. As the recipient of Christ's particular forgiveness, she had come by the late Middle Ages to be the principal human image of penitential and emotive devotion.[31] In the N-Town play, her meeting with Christ is more recognizably like the audience's own predicament as uncertain seekers after grace and assurance than is that of the Virgin which precedes it. She has the angel's word, she sees the empty tomb, yet she is unsure.

Unlike Mary, the audience are privy to the actual moment of Resurrection, where Christ speaks directly to them of the sacramental significance of his flesh. "Anima Christi" returns to revive the mortal body it has left behind. The body wakes a bit stiff, but Christ's tone at rising is remarkable for its matter-of-fact blend of weariness and triumph, a blend that emphasizes for the audience at once his likeness and unlikeness:

> *Anima Christi*
> Now is 3our ffoo boundyn in helle
> that evyr was besy 3ow for to qwelle
> now wele I rysyn flesch and felle
>   that rent was for 3our sake
> myn owyn body that hynge on rode
> And be the jewys nevyr so wode
> It xal a-ryse both flesch and blode
>   my body now wyl I take.

> *Tunc transiet anima christi ad resuscitandum corpus quo resuscitato*
>   *dicat Jhesus*

> harde gatys haue I gon
> And peynes sofryd many on
> Stomblyd at stake and at ston
> ny3 thre and thretty 3ere
> I light out of my faderys trone
> ffor to Amende mannys mone
> my flesch was betyn to the bon
> my blood I bledde clere.

> Ffor mannys loue I tholyd dede
> and for mannys loue I am rysyn up rede
> ffor man I haue mad my body in brede
> his sowle for to fede
> Man and thou lete me thus gone
> and wylt not folwyn me a-none
> such a frende fyndyst thou nevyr none
> to help the at thi nede.   (lines 1416–1439)

The vitality of the actor's body as it pretends to be dead flesh is used here as the nub of a theological point, even when he "wakes" to speak of pain and exhaustion. The task of accepting seems simple, the presence of Christ as incarnate body almost immediate, despite the odd stage trick whereby a body plays a soul. But when he withdraws, this presence cedes to conflicting and dubious testimony. A procession of witnesses follows: the guards at the tomb, the three Marys on Easter morning, Peter and John at the sepulcher, all variously receive news or encounter evidence. Pilate conspires to hush the matter up. Peter is uncertain what to believe about the bits and pieces in the tomb, but seems to change his mind under skeptical pressure from Thomas:

> The trewth to tellyn it passyth oure witt

> Whethyr he be resyn thorwe his owyn myght
> Or ellys stolyn out of his pitt
> be sum man prevely be nyght
> That he is gon we saw with syght
> Ffor in his graue he is nowth
> we can not tellyn in what plyght
> Out of his graue that he is browth.   (lines 159–66)

It is almost as though Peter has been reading Aristotle's discussion of the varieties of recognition in *Poetics* 16. How much would even seeing convince the determined skeptic? What proof is enough?[32] In this climate of conflicting surmise, where the Angel's "opyn voys" (line 109) is still precarious through censorship or doubt, Mary Magdalene's recognition scene begins.

We might have expected that the "opyn syght" vouchsafed Mary would be sufficient to confirm the "opyn voys." But the staging teases the process of recognition out. As she "goth to the graue and wepyth," Mary herself seems to believe mere seeing would be enough:

> Myn owyn dere lorde and kyng of gras
> that vii develys ffro me dyd take
> I kan nat se hym Alas Alas
> he is stolyn awey owt of this lake.   (lines 5–8)

"He is stolyn" does not resolve the question of agency raised by Peter and Pilate, but in answer to an apocryphal Angel, she seems to settle on disbelief: "my lord is take out of his graue / Stolyn awey and fro me lore" (lines 14–15). At this point an unusual and specific stage-direction intervenes. I transcribe the entire exchange in the layout of the MS:[33]

> *hic parum deambulet A sepulchro dicens*
> Alas Alas what xal I do
> my lord awey is fro me take
> A woful wrecche whedyr xal I go
> My joye is gon owth of this lake.
>
> — Jhesus
> Woman suche mornynge why dost thou make
> Why is thi chere so hevy and badde
> Why dost thou sythe so sore and qwake
> Why dost thou wepe so sore and sadde.
>
> — Maria Magdalene
> A gretter cawse had nevyr woman
> Ffor to wepe both nyth and day
> than I myself haue in sertyn
> for to sorwyn evyr and Ay
> Alas ffor sorwe myn hert doth blede

my lord is take fro me A-way
I must nedys sore wepe and grede
where he is put I kan not say.

but jentyl gardener I pray to thee
If thou hym took out of his graue
telle me quere I may hym se
that I may go my lorde to haue.

— Jhesus

M. A. R. I. A. spectans

— Maria Magdalene

A[h] mayster and lorde to the I crave
As thou art lord and kynge of blys
Graunt me lord and thou vowchesave
thyn holy ffete that I may kys.   (lines 17–41)

Mary moves down ("deambulet") from one of the *loca* (the tomb) into the open space of the *platea* and towards the audience. As she does so, her account of what has happened becomes both more definite and more personal: Jesus has been taken away from her. Her move down onto the open *platea* is a dramaturgical sign of her increasing estrangement from the firmer belief represented by the tokens in the tomb. Her approach to the audience raises the stakes by confronting them with her pain at close quarters, challenging them to measure their own skepticism. They can even perhaps see Christ entering behind, producing a tension between involvement with her predicament and knowledge of its solution.[34]

As Mary's lament reaches its most personal ("My joye is gon owth of this lake" line 20), Jesus speaks to her – and she fails to recognize him. Revelation is deferred yet once more; it seems the proofs will never be enough. The scene plays out the same dialectic of narrative advance and self-conscious deferral we observed in the *Oedipus* example. Mary's movement down the stage is arrested when she meets Christ, but instead of immediate recognition, a short exchange ensues which is virtually a repetition of the one with the Angel ten lines earlier. The dialogue itself is a mere tissue of repetitions and Mary's failure to recognize Jesus even in person is made quite clear. "Behold and believe" is inadequate to explain this moment, for it is clearly not enough for Mary simply to *see*: to be recognized, Jesus must be seen in a certain way, a way somehow withheld until he produces her name: "M.A.R.I.A."

N-Town is the only one of the cycles to content itself with the simple name, as did John. It is placed self-consciously outside the normal pattern of the verse, as an extrametric line in the very center of an abab/ bcbc stanza, just where the rhymes reverse. To rend the stanza in halves like this and yet not disrupt its symmetrical flow suggests that the act of recognition is both part of the ongoing process of the narrative, and yet is effected by a power strictly outside its scope, through a sudden break into temporal patterning. That this break, with something of the simple condensed energy Longinus remarked in the Hebrew Genesis, should be a naming is all the more important, and the manuscript of the plays registers its importance by magnifying it and, as it were, slowing it down, spelling it out in capitals with a period between each.[35] Mary cannot recognize Christ until he calls upon her, gives her leave, admits her to him by giving her her name. The simplicity of the moment is crucial to its power. One feels there ought to be more, and the other cycles oblige by expanding the remark.[36] Yet the impressiveness of the N-Town staging is precisely in its reticence, so that its full wonder rests upon the simplicity of the naming which is allowed to fill with a deliberately unmeasured – we are to infer, an unmeasurable – plenitude. It is especially notable that Christ uses the Latin name, rather than the English one employed elsewhere in the play (lines 25, 42), as though this is the name she must here answer to. As the precise word used in the Vulgate it carries the full authority of Scripture and its formality marks the shift of perspective or of "tonality" which comes at the moment of recognition. In an instant the voice remakes the weeping Mary into "M.A.R.I.A." – a woman blessed with the sight of God, permitted to "behold and believe" where before she could not.

The N-Town recognition scene presents the pattern of alienation and recall as a narrative broken open and suddenly transformed by the power of the divine voice calling. In responding to the scene of recognition, the medieval audience give themselves over to that power in wonder in much the same way that Longinus describes responding to the sublime: they undergo the authority of a greater power that breaks suddenly into the ordinary world and reshapes it in its own image, bending to its will understanding, faculties, and even the right of naming.

These brief examples demonstrate how the crises of vocation in the cycle-plays, those cardinal points at which the medieval audience is invited to recognize its collective character and destiny as a Christian community, are dramatized through the dialectic of identification and detachment which is characteristic of the theatre of wonder. Though that theatre takes specific, historical forms of articulation in relation to the intellectual and institutional framework of the medieval stage, and in particular to the sacramental theology of Corpus Christi, some typical markers of the dramaturgy of wonder recur that are recognizable as in important ways transhistorical.

3   Compounding "*Errors*"

The sea, in fact, is that state of barbaric vagueness and disorder out
of which civilisation has emerged, and into which, unless saved by
the effort of gods and men, it is always liable to relapse.

W. H. Auden

Let it suffice that we have not arrived at a wall, but at interminable
oceans.

Emerson

The aim of this chapter is to argue that Shakespeare's *Comedy of Errors*
provides us with an explicitly germinal model of his dramatic practice at
once in its narrative, poetic and social dimensions, and that the conclusion
of the work turns to the dramatic dynamic of wonder in order to enact
Shakespeare's own recognition of his practice. In order to approach this
intricate nexus, we must first consider the larger question of the institution
for and out of which Shakespeare wrote, to suggest how he responded to
changes in English society and culture by reframing the question of the
work that narrative does, in effect retroping old plots in the new context of
the professional theatre. Shakespeare's work is in this way informed by a
revisionary conservatism by which he self-consciously subjects the stories
he inherits to analysis and critique in order to regenerate them for present
uses. Apparently exiled from the plays, wonder returns in the end to
recoup and transfigure the scattered fragments in a reunion that speaks
also to the function of dramatic narrative in Shakespeare's hands. The
hyperbolic and overdetermined spectacle of wonder thus invoked becomes
a site of plenitude informed in its forcefulness by the resistance of the
very skepticism it has had to overcome.

I

Complex factors determine the transition from late medieval to
Elizabethan drama.[1] We need to note first some significant shifts in the
character of performance as a social occasion. The medieval plays of the
last chapter emerge from a community-based, large-scale organization of

a recurrent and participatory nature. They are part of a perennial festival where plans are laid and expenses defrayed collectively through guilds and other associations. A substantial part of the purpose and pleasure of this theatre is likewise communal: there is a common involvement in a common project that aims to expound a common knowledge.[2] Though economic motives could nerve the festivals as potential sources of trade and prestige, they were not principally commercial ventures. Indeed, the large cost of mounting them at a time of economic difficulty for many late sixteenth-century towns may have contributed to their disappearance.[3]

While the influence of the medieval festival plays on aspects of Elizabethan drama has been disputed, it is clear that the overall shapes of the two institutions and of their characteristic products are very different. The medieval plays are carefully attuned to their particular institutional context, and hence too specialized to provide a model of dramatic form flexible enough for a secular, professional theatre. Although Emrys Jones, for instance, has argued cogently for some similarities in structure, such as between the Passion of Christ and the baiting of Gloucester in Shakespeare's *Henry VI Part Two*, even such striking parallels are largely a question of local patterns of action rather than of a general indebtedness in conception.[4]

The institution of the professional acting company, its attachment to specific patrons, and the eventual settlement of at least some companies in permanent, continuously running theatre venues in the later sixteenth century determined a new shape for the social occasion of performance. At these explicitly commercial concerns, audiences pay the performers not the project. Performances, even before the monarch, are in an important way services for customers, and the nature and quality of the performance impinges not on the honor of a community, but on the commercial viability of the company and the livelihoods of its members. The audience need have no quotidian, community-based relation to the actors on which to draw. Relations "across the footlights" are much more a nonce affair, to a great extent limited to the professional occasion itself, and the openness of these relations to improvisation may well form part of the matter of the play. "Novelty" of both story and occasion becomes an important element in commercial success, and accordingly the public theatres of the late sixteenth century produce and experiment with new plays at a prodigious rate: as high as twenty new plays a year in an uninterrupted season, or about one every two weeks.[5]

The theatre thus occupied a very different place within the civic life of Elizabethan London from the great five- and seven-day celebrations recorded intermittently but consistently there from the late twelfth century.[6] The Elizabethan public theatre was a focus for *ad hoc* outings and celebration by individuals or small groups (apprentices, law students, families) seeking temporary relief from everyday duties. It could be enjoyed at any time it was open, and was set up to answer, within certain limits, a steady demand. While much of the theatrical calendar was still hitched to traditional timetables (such as the Lenten inhibitions or the Christmas festivals), there was no longer any discernible shaping connection between the ritual life of the community and its theatrical entertainments.[7] What was offered was a much more local transaction, which might make use of older forms of festivity and communality, but confined their invocation to the space of the "wooden O" and the duration of the performance. Barring disruptions by plague, riot, or political upheaval (though these were common enough), the public theatres could expect to be open for business continuously for long periods, necessitating a constant and renewable appeal to a public who came by choice and on no common timetable. The collective exploration of traditional forms of common life could have only a very limited role in this theatre. *Twelfth Night*, for instance, might be played on its name date or else when you would, since nothing in the play ties it to a particular day. What features survive in it from the calendar association are better understood as tropes for psychological and social processes in general than as specific to a particular ceremonial order. For a certain fee, the ludic privileges of a mobilized Epiphany can be enjoyed at any time of year. This is a key liberation for the full-time professional theatre, but the emancipation also makes the company dependent on securing the audience's assent to the performance and its occasion in ways that become increasingly self-conscious. Medieval plays might roar and browbeat their audiences into silence. The gambits of Elizabethan Prologue and Epilogue, with their often nervous rhetoric of placation and apology and their language of bonds, amends, and amity, suggest a very different relation.

But it is not only the changed lineaments of the social occasion that alter the kinds of plays the Elizabethan theatre nurtures. In the cycleplays, the performed action and its recognitions are framed by the semiotic complex of the Incarnation and the Eucharist within the institution of the Church. A gesture thither always closes down the potential for either play or skepticism, as none of these authorities can be effectively challenged. Hence in the most experimental or testing plays of this tradition, a gap or rift may open up between the central theological enactment and the elaboration or parody attached to it. In the Wakefield *Secunda Pastorum*, famous for its social protest and gameful pre-plot of the stolen sheep, this disarticulation is particularly plain. As long as the authority of the structuring institutions remains unimpeachable, such rifting cannot itself be addressed in the play. It remains a symptom rather than a topic.

The sixteenth century, however, saw the appearance and development of an increasingly powerful and institutionalized current of what we might now call "cultural criticism." The reformist polemicists against the theatre have often been noted, yet the wider ramifications of the succession of spokesmen, from Gosson and Stubbes to Prynne, have been less considered. Their importance lies as much in how they indicate the progressive factionalizing of English culture at large as in their specific raillery against the playhouses. Such iconoclasm was not confined to anti-theatrical polemic; its wide range suggests the extent to which skepticism was becoming a posture generally available, as much to playwrights as to their opponents, as Christopher Marlowe's turbulent example shows. What we see emerging for the first time is an extensive cultural dialectic of critique and affirmation, much more fraught and much more concerned to entrench itself in particular institutions than heretofore.[8]

This does not mean that older, communal functions entirely disappeared. Though it is obvious that the cycle-plays are not an appropriate formal vehicle for the new theatre, which must find pleasures more "packageable" for an increasingly various economic, social, and intellectual order, it does not follow that their function of exploring the nature and modes of collective self-understanding disappeared. A conservative and tradition-minded society, such as Renaissance England largely was, does not lightly discard social forms and ceremonial structures that have served it well, even in the face of critique. With a playwright of socially conservative preferences, as Shakespeare by and large was, the older uses of performance might re-emerge grafted onto or articulated through another dramatic structure – as happens with holiday customs in *Twelfth Night*. C. L. Barber, for one, argued that the rhythms and forms of traditional popular festivity underlie a great deal of Shakespeare's work in comedy, and that these plays made use of the elements and energies of old holiday, both in the construction of the narrative on stage and in evoking a para-ritual ambience for the contemporary audience. Barber's work showed remarkably clearly the process of co-optation that adapted old communal traditions to new dramatic occasions, and this transition reflects with unusual clarity and detail aspects of the more general movement away from a medieval towards a modern order in sixteenth-century England.[9]

That Barber's central subject was inevitably Shakespeare tells us something in particular about the latter's attitude to older forms of social celebration and regulation. Unlike the more radical voices either of Stephen Gosson or Ben Jonson – both playwrights and later polemicists against the public theatre from political persuasions we might describe as Reformist and Royalist respectively – Shakespeare's brand of conservatism did not seek to root out the cultural forms of the past in order to assert its own claims. It preferred to absorb them, imagining its relation to the past not as polemic opposition but as metaphor and metamorphosis. Such a position is in general nativist rather than international, evolutionary rather than revolutionary. In some ways it is like Sir Edward Coke's insistence that the common law was a peculiar institution and handed down "immemorial customs" *toto divisos orbe Brittannos.* A theatre emerging from such a pragmatically conservative stance does not confront its audience, or even seek to settle with it as an independent contracting party, as Jonson does in inducting *Bartholomew Fair.* Wherever such a theatre goes, like the Chorus in *Henry V*, it wishes to secure the community's collective assent and imaginative implication first. It seeks to make the story and the theatrical occasion theirs for the telling.

We should consider closely what it means to assert that Shakespeare was conservative in this way, and examine the roots and lineaments of this conservatism and its implications for dramatic structures answering his commercial and professional needs. Some possible misunderstandings can be headed off at once by asserting that to be conservative in this sense is to be like neither Spenser nor Jonson. Along with Shakespeare, both of these figures were staunch supporters of the English monarchy, and in that sense "conservative" as we might see the term. But that is hardly an Elizabethan political position: it is more like the point at which Elizabethan (and Jacobean) politics begins. It should be emphasized that there were no significant opponents of monarchy in England in this period, and that such opponents of the current monarch as there were – basically radical Catholics – were staunchly in favor of monarchy as such and themselves divided as to how far they should go in opposing Elizabeth and James. Even the organizers of rebellions and risings were hardly calling for the destruction of monarchy as a basis for civil order: the traditional order was most often what they saw as under threat when they rose. Though what might be called the "preconditions" for the much more radical political ferment of forty years later were perhaps present, it would be mistaken to read those developments back too far as "oppositional" alternatives.

On the other hand, both Spenser and Jonson *were* strongly in favor of various kinds of "reform" in the relations between government and people. Spenser's association with the more ardent Protestant reformers not infrequently brought him into conflict with Elizabethan arrangements, and the kind of apocalypticism displayed in Book One of *The Faerie Queene*, even if oriented towards restoration of the "true Church," required a radical break with much of the recent past which Elizabeth for one was reluctant to make. Jonson, though decidedly of the other religious party and uncomfortable with Spenserian fervencies, also supported a more or less radical revision of the political terms of government towards an imperial profile and away from the more delicate politics of equilibrium and consensus which Elizabeth, along with her ministers, had managed for so long. Though the imperial impulse had been gathering for some time in English politics and law and was by no means a Jacobean invention, it emerged into full articulation with James, and Jonson strongly endorsed it. Recent political criticism of Shakespeare has sometimes overlooked the fact that to be politically "avant-garde" in both Church and State matters in the period meant embracing either Puritanism or Absolutism. The latter stances could also themselves agree in welcoming the image of a strong central figure, as was the case with Prince Henry. At least in the period from 1590 to 1610, "radical" English aesthetics and politics were as often moving towards the imperial monarchy as away from it.

If modern political categories will not help to define Shakespeare as an Elizabethan "conservative," one way of broaching the question is to reflect on the fact – to some extent unusual among his peers – of Shakespeare's lifelong maintenance of relations with the community of his birth. Unsatisfactory though his biographical records are, they are insistently traversed by the thread of Stratford-on-Avon and Shakespeare's concern with the position of his family there. Emphasis on his links with the milieu and politics of the court has tended to obscure this, yet it gives us significant information about Shakespeare's underlying sense of his filiations and community.[10] Also of some significance here may be that Shakespeare was never initiated into the "second home" at the universities, which so often eclipsed the natal community with a prestige language and a sense of the common fellowship of learning. Again, the contrast with Jonson is instructive. There is no sign that Shakespeare, unlike Jonson, sought to overcome his scholarly "deficit" or surmount his humble origins either by prodigious application to learning or by small revisions of name and family history, and this despite the ridicule his lack of "nurture" seems to have cost him at various hands, most notoriously Robert Greene's.[11] But though important aspects of Shakespeare's work remain close to the pattern of rural and small-town life, this does not mean he was not acutely aware of the challenge presented, for instance, by Stubbes's critique of rural summer celebrations. The task was to discern whether and how older functions could be retained, even if performed by new instruments. Coke's attitude is again instructive: he claimed that English judges found within the customary structures of the common law what was necessary to the present case. They did not alter the law in so doing: they revealed more of it, still and always at work.[12]

The idea or pattern of cultural activity embraced by such a view of the world is one that does not insist on radical separation from its community or its own history. Where patterns of communal recognition and reflection such as the cycle-plays disappeared, the emerging professional troupes might be inserted on occasion into their room. A discontinuity of formal and logistic organization need not necessitate one at the level of communal function, and while Chester and York clung stoutly to their traditional plays, and Coventry kept up its cycle into Shakespeare's lifetime and subsequently attempted to replace it with a comparable civic drama, other communities might have seen the business more as a matter of "farming out" a community function previously, as it were, performed "in-house."[13] Such a tactic preserves what can be preserved and adapts to a new form or occasion those elements that cannot in a process of improvisatory adjustment.

There survives one remarkable account tending to confirm that this is more or less what at least some communities did. In 1639 at the age of 75 – which makes him Shakespeare's exact contemporary – Ralph Willis included a childhood reminiscence of the stage in his penitential treatise, *Mount Tabor*. Willis's story is well-known but deserves quotation in full:

In the city of Gloucester the manner is (as I think it is in other like corporations) that when the players of enterludes come to towne, they first attend the Mayor to enforme him what noble-mans servants they are, and so to get a licence for their publike playing; and if the Mayor like the actors, or would shew respect to their lord and master, he appoints them to play their first play before himselfe and the Aldermen and Common Counsel of the city; and that is called the Mayor's play, where every one that will comes in without money, the Mayor giving the players a reward as he thinks fit to shew respect unto them. At such a play, my father took me with him and made me stand betweene his leggs, as he sate upon one of the benches where wee saw and heard very well. The play was called, *The Cradle of Security*, wherin was personated a king or some great prince with his courtiers of severall kinds, amongst which three ladies were in speciall grace with him; and they keeping him in delights and pleasures, drew him from his graver counsellors, hearing of sermons, and listening to good counsell, and admonitions, that in the end they got him to lie down in a cradle upon the stage, where these three ladies joyning in a sweet song rocked him asleep, that he snorted againe, and in the mean time closely conveyed under the cloaths where withall he was covered, a vizard like a swine's snout upon his face, with three wire chains fastened thereunto, the other three end wherof being holden severally by those ladies, who fall to singing againe, and then discovered his face, that the spectators might see how they had transformed him, going on with their singing.

Whilst all this was acting, there came forth of another doore at the farthest end of the stage two old men, the one in blew with a serjeant-at-armes mace on his shoulder, the other in red with a drawn sword in his hand and leaning with the other hand upon the others shoulder; and so they two went along in a soft pace round about by the skirt of the stage, till at last they came to the cradle, when all the court was in greatest jollity; and then the foremost old man with his mace stroke a fearful blow upon the cradle, whereat all the courtiers, with the three ladies and the vizard, all vanished; and the desolate prince starting up bare-faced and finding himself thus sent for to judgment, made a lamentable complaint of his miserable case, and so was carried away by wicked spirits. . . .

This sight tooke such impression in me that, when I came towards mans estate, it was as fresh in my memory as if I had seen it newly acted.[14]

Willis's recollection shows quite clearly the relation between the professional players and the community they play for, aside from its demonstration of the lasting impact dramatic images could have on the Elizabethan spectator, even from what seems to us so bare-bones a piece as *The Cradle of Security*. The performance is from the first implicated in the hierarchical network of social life, with its mutual privileges and duties. The troupe of actors is both a professional organization and a roving limb of the nobleman who sponsors them: the Mayor has his choice which of these aspects he will regard. For him to sponsor "the Mayor's play" is to assert his pre-eminence, but also to fulfill his duty to promote the honor and well-being of the commonality, presumably at his own expense. To attend the play is to acknowledge in return both of these gestures. The play in turn moralizes on the duties and dangers of high place and its failure in vivid, eschatological images, and thus also participates in glossing its occasion. Its appropriateness is complete even down to its suspicious treatment of the female figures elsewhere excluded from Willis's recollection of his civic and personal fathers.

Though Gloucester was larger than Stratford-on-Avon, it seems fair to assume this is the kind of thing which the documented visits to that town of the professional troupes of actors in 1583–4 and 1586–7 involved, and such a context is most likely to have been that in which Shakespeare first encountered the Elizabethan theatre.[15] It is in accord with such a view that he depicts players when he comes to write: his troupes, professional or scratch, are very much aware of the social dimension of their work. Though they tend to be overeager, naive or insufficiently *au fait* with the complexity of their moment (whether the poisoned milieu of *Hamlet* or the aristocratic churlishness of *Love's Labours Lost*), they are always conceived as absorbing into themselves the ambient energies of the occasion they play to. What distinguishes their shortcomings from the work of the Lord Chamberlain's Men is not only a difference in technical skill, but the latter's added resources of deliberate critique to add to those of fellowship and service in its repertoire of stances.

II

One recent critic who has sought to address the Elizabethan theatre in this way as an active site of cultural reflection in the moment of performance is Louis A. Montrose. Seeking what he calls "a Shakespearean anthropology," Montrose surveys sixteenth-century English history, emphasizing a galloping disequilibrium and a burgeoning anxiety among a bourgeoisie increasingly unsure of its bearings. From this, Montrose proposes that the Elizabethan theatre became a self-conscious site of surrogate ritual in a world whose reassuring solidity of symbolic practice was being eroded: "I am suggesting ... that the public theatre absorbs some vital functions of ritual within Shakespeare's society. These functions are not adequately performed by more central and officially sanctioned institutions, and are in some ways inimical to them."[16] This is an exhilarating vista, yet so much remains unspoken as to give one pause. The assertion that Shakespeare's theatre was a species of collective ritual is by no means a new one, going back as it does at least to Francis Fergusson's attempt to assimilate *Hamlet* to a model of Sophoclean drama derived from the Cambridge anthropologists, a claim later refashioned by O. B. Hardison with Christian ritual as the model.[17] The difficulty here is to specify in what the ritual aspect inheres and how it is addressed and understood by the playwright and taken up by the audience. In both Ferguson and Hardison, "ritual" remains in some sense archeological, an inherited rather than a meditated condition. In Montrose's view, its invocation seems a kind of secret or unconscious gesture in response to an equally unformulable discomfort with established religion. At the same time, the underlying assumption about the expressive or cathartic inadequacies of Elizabethan religion is highly speculative: inadequate for whom? one is entitled to ask, and how do we know? Those who objected most vociferously to the established religious order tended to be those who also strongly denounced the theatre. Though it is certainly true that Shakespeare's plays "present exemplary fictions in which human characters are confronted by change within the self, the family, the body politic, the cosmos," it is hard to see this as a historically specific assertion about Elizabethan drama: it does just as well for Euripides, Goethe, Chekhov, or even Brecht.[18]

Montrose's remarks are the more frustrating because he is surely right about Shakespeare's attentiveness to the ritual aspects of the dramatic language and action he inherits, though whether the same description will do for Greene or Jonson (i.e. whether it is really a general condition of Elizabethan drama) is another question. A powerful impulse to draw on the magical and world-shaping energies of ritual does inhabit Shakespeare's plays. But if ritual informs Shakespeare's theatre, it is less because of some non-specific malaise in the churchgoing public that the theatre struggles to identify and physic, and more through a quite specific response to the forms of story and dramatic occasion it inherits. The principal place we should look to establish the historicity of a work such as a play is less to a rather nebulous history of the culture at large, and rather to the textures of the work itself understood as the mediated and meditated product of histories at once formal, institutional, social, and vocational. To reduce any one of these to an epiphenomenon of another is to move away from a full appreciation of the work's history and "historicity" rather than towards it.[19] In the current instance, neither the assertion of O. B. Hardison that "continuity" characterizes the relation between medieval ecclesiastical ritual and Shakespearean drama nor Montrose's stress on "the essential feature of discontinuity" will really do. It is the intertwining of retention and transformation that is the fullest measure of Shakespeare's historical consciousness. Analysis needs to unfold where this process of adaptation is chiefly accomplished: where continuity and discontinuity confront each other in the metamorphic absorption and troping of older modes of dramatic story into newer ones.

The Eucharistic fusion of word and matter that underlies the dramaturgy of the cycles is a crucial instance of how Shakespeare folds received cultural schemas into his theatre's transformed task. There can be no doubt that the power of this ritual event remained active in Elizabethan society. The very persistence of intense controversy around it testifies to that. As they are absorbed into Shakespearean drama, these struggles over the central symbol of the Christian order re-emerge, linked to questions at once of the continuity of English historical experience and of the performance of that experience on stage. This is particularly explicit in *Richard II*, where the central action articulates a struggle between the desire to affirm the miraculous corporeality of sacramental kingship (tied directly to the actor's performance of Richard in and on his body) and a counter-desire to drain the action of that very mystique in favor of a roughcut and contingent pragmatism of office and role. The identification of workable schemas to interpret the body's action becomes a primary goal, but the play entertains the option of a sacramental solution only as a dream whose fullness, like Gaunt's health, is ebbing almost from before the outset. That Gaunt refers to the Incarnation while himself dying, even as the actor playing him is faced with the daunting technical task of performing the famous long aria to "this sceptered isle," indicates the extent to which the political and the dramaturgical are intertwined through the question of "embodiment." Old symbol and new context, nostalgia and critique, icon and actor self-consciously confront one another. All through Shakespeare's career, questions of "embodiment" framed in relation to the sacramental model are central to his thinking-through of the meaning of theatrical performance. But while a deep desire for the tangibility of the body is pervasive, so also is a sense of the difficulty of grasping such a moment. What was merely dichotomy in the *Secunda Pastorum* has become a restive dialectic.[20]

In putting the issue this way, I have in mind a discussion of the self-consciousness of fictive form as representation, in which John Hollander cites the remark of Friedrich Schlegel that "In all its descriptions, this poetry should describe itself, and always be simultaneously poetry and the poetry of poetry." Hollander comments that "a closely guarded poetic secret peers out of the last clause. ... [which] hides a more powerful assertion – not 'and' but '*because*.' "[21] We could restate and extend this point here by proposing that poetry expresses its historical conditions most fully, since it also there expresses how it does and does not understand them, where it renders those conditions available to itself in deliberate inflection. To read a poem as an act of historical awareness is to attempt to chart its successes and failures in the struggle for consciousness of its own ways of knowing the world in and through itself.[22]

In this dialectic of affirmation and critique in Shakespeare's theatre, the dynamic of wonder becomes crucial. Wonder as a conscious crisis of the integrity of knowledge unfolds at just the point where, according to Schlegel and Hollander, the characteristically poetic is to be sought, so that the self-consciousness characteristic of this emotion generates precisely a double orientation on "poetry and the poetry of poetry." In Shakespeare's work, the outbreak of wonder registers interplay and negotiation between simultaneous desires for continuity and discontinuity, between the impulse to successful solution and the forcefulness of a critique that resists easy satisfaction. In tragedy, wonder's turbulent power stems directly from the force that has destroyed the protagonists and their world, even as it also guarantees the audience's relative protection from that force by the saving grace of figuration. In comedy, even more crucially, wonder absorbs into itself the resistance of skepticism, and its force measures that resistance even as the latter is overcome and sublated. Resistance braces the desire to affirm surviving powers of recognition and articulation, and in particular, the reconstruction and survival of the institutions of continuity, chief among them marriage. A variable tempering of wonder and skepticism against one another across different plays marks out a continuum in Shakespeare's comic practice, along which critical argument has in turn arrayed itself.

The language of doubling and twinning which haunts the instabilities of wonder, as we saw in Chapter One, appears specifically in Shakespeare's plays at the level of plotting in his recurrent preoccupation with stories of twins – including the pretend twins of *Much Ado about Nothing*, the anti-twins Edgar and Edmund, and those twin-like abstractions Art and Nature in *The Winter's Tale*. What is at stake here is the poetic recognition of the interest the plays and their audiences have in the dialectical mirroring of continuity and discontinuity in one another as motives for theatrical representation. In most cases, the end of the play stages a critical confrontation between these character pairs that is framed by and produces wonder.

In what follows, I will argue that scenes of wondrous speculation, present from the first, articulate in this way much of Shakespeare's concern with the theatre as poetic and social event, and that these scenes focus a particularly Shakespearean self-consciousness in language and action. Careful reading can demonstrate in what way they meditate on continuity as their chief aspiration, one whose difficulty in turn gauges their historical consciousness. In particular these plays use the dynamic of wonder to think through their impulse to absorb and adapt their own cultural history, to be "at once theatre and the theatre of theatre."

III

When Shakespeare chose to frame Plautus' play of the twins of Epidamnum with the venerable romance of the shipwrecked family, he did more than merely complicate the plot: he immeasurably enlarged the scope of the whole dramatic structure. Modern critics have been quick to see the paired stories of the father and his sons as segregated by style or genre or some other consideration, but fixing overrigid boundaries between "frame story" and the central action tends to obscure the links between them in a way the play explicitly refuses.[23] The central action and concern of the opening scene is the power of Egeon's narrative to create a community of mutual interest, even in the face of political and social antagonism. The question of what narrative is *for* is before us from the outset, and the opening tableau sets forth large images of the play's stakes which are then worked out in more elaborate detail through the Plautine material. By fusing Plautus' rambunctious plot with the life-and-death romance of Egeon's quest, and both with allusions to St. Paul (as though Plautus and Paulus were anagrammatic twins), Shakespeare's hybrid tests their respective modes of narration, as though asking "Which kind of story, if any, can help us stave off death?"[24]

This is a weighty question, perhaps too much so for such a slight piece. Yet it is the play's own initial question. Consider the opening tableau. A bound prisoner stands before his judge and asks – for mercy? On the contrary – he asks only for a speedy death:

> Proceed, Solinus, to procure my fall
> And by the doom of death, end woes and all.   (I.i.1–2)

The action, it seems, will be over before it has even begun; the play threatens to contract itself into the few moments needed to utter the sentence and chop off the head. Such an end seems altogether too forbidding and abrupt. Its absoluteness, the anonymity of the speaker, his "fall" with its "doom of death," hint at the image of a more general or final "proceeding" and judgment. His judge continues these intimations in speaking of his Syracusan counterpart whose victims:

> Wanting guilders to redeem their lives
> Have sealed his rigorous statutes with their blood. . . .   (I.i.8–9)

These are hints only, but they evoke a complex of images and notions about time, death, and judgment familiar enough to an Elizabethan audience and suggest, without being too explicit about it, that the overall resolution will address some sort of "redemption." We seem to be engaging in a kind of theological oneupmanship on Plautus here. Roman comedy being the work of pagans, it is hardly surprising that such a vocabulary was unavailable to it. But such a play in a Christian society claims it sees further into the life – and death – of things.

These images are unusually stark for opening a comedy, and before their fatality Egeon seems already to have quailed. Duke Solinus for one seems to want the prisoner to begin the play differently. He responds not to Egeon's call for death, but to some imagined plea for mercy: "Merchant of Syracusa, plead no more. / I am not partial to infringe our laws" (I.i.3–4). And though playing stern, he deliberately invites Egeon to re-forge just the ties of sympathy to the community at large that the old man seems most eager to break off. All through the scene, Solinus forces Egeon to return to his story, where Egeon is eager to abridge it, to take it as read. "Gather the sequel by what went before," he insists, as though it were all a self-evident matter of mere logic. Egeon wants to tell us that the world is always fatal, nature and time the twin wheels of a slow, small grinding. There is no point in recounting it all over again: the sentence reaches its period, the great axe falls. That's all there is to it.

Solinus shares this much with Egeon: for him too syntax is an absolute ruler: "passed sentence may not be recalled / But to our honour's great disparagement." Yet Egeon's despair goes deeper and links itself to the general process of time and the bell. Life cures us of itself:

> Yet this my comfort, when your words are done,
> My woes end likewise with the evening sun.   (I.i.26–7)

By making him tell the whole tale over, Solinus not only puts off the end Egeon seeks, he works to repair the very social connections Egeon wishes to sunder. Inspired to pity, if not fear, Solinus throws Egeon back on the community for rescue. His task, an almost parabolic one, is to find a redeemer among "all the friends thou hast in Ephesus." This is not to Egeon's liking and he views it as merely one more futile episode in a narrative whose end he has long since longed for: "Hopeless and helpless doth Egeon wend / But to procrastinate his lifeless end." He is a figure of Despair: for him all time is drained of vitality, all story points only deathwards. "Lifeless" is as much an epithet of the speaker as of his expected end.

Does all story, all time uncover only an image of death? Must the rigorous logic of cause and effect lead us to submit to an Iron Law, not "partial to infringement," that stands grimly behind narrative? When is an end not an End? Solinus' "limit" puts these questions before us, so that whenever in the subsequent action we are told what time it is – and we are so insistently – we may recall Egeon's quest. Yet a curious jingle of phonemes all through the course of Egeon's lamentable narrative tells a more lively, lucky "undertale" than their speaker knows. A quartet of terms chimes an arbitrary, serendipitous consonance in the world which brings "hope" and "help" to make "hap" at last "happy."[25] This is not logic. On the contrary, these doublings and echoes are silly happenstance, a gratuitous accident of language. Yet their tale outweighs Egeon's in the end, and from their very plasticity Shakespeare will generate a marvelous world of plenitude, of strange and happy miracle.

Meanwhile, the vision of time as an inhuman controlling law ticking away on its ineluctable path is not confined to the first scene. Such a strict sense of time is taken into the play as an integral part of the basic narrative apparatus of classical comedy. T. W. Baldwin argues that this feature is derived specifically less from *Menaechmi* than from Shakespeare's whole understanding of classical comedy: "Shakespeare already knew these unities; he did not learn them from *Menaechmi*; at

least, not at this time."[26] Indeed, the "limit of this day" is so integral
to the design of the Antipholus section of the play that its deep
connection to the opening scene is often overlooked. Narratively, and to
some extent thematically, Egeon's story and that of his sons are
segregated, but both put in play a conception of time as one-dimensional,
an inflexible linear process in which Death follows Judgment as verb
follows subject as two o'clock follows one.

Time as an irreversible sequence of effects organizes both events and
conversation for much of the play. As the breakneck, mechanical rhythm
of farce comes to orchestrate the action, the intentions of the characters
seem more and more to lag behind the onward sweep of the minute hand.
From Antipholus of Syracuse's first conversation with a Merchant who
rushes off to a business lunch, it is clear that Ephesus keeps as strict a
clock as it does a law-court. As with Egeon, though in a less desperate
key, time is money, and money is life. The secular, commercial community is bound to time as its vital, regulatory engine. But with Ephesian
Dromio's first entrance the mortal clock starts to accelerate and takes on
a striking inhumanity:

> Returned so soon! Rather approached too late.
> The capon burns, the pig falls from the spit;
> The clock hath strucken twelve upon the bell;
> My mistress made it one upon my cheek.
> She is so hot because the meat is cold;
> The meat is cold because you come not home;
> You come not home because you have no stomach;
> You have no stomach having broke your fast.
> But we, that know what 'tis to fast and pray,
> Are penitent for your default today.   (I.ii.43–52)

Dromio's lines hunt temporal process back along a line of causally
related points which has as its latest term the infliction of violence upon
him. The traditional vulnerability of the clown's body to attack is here
the result of living at the mercy of a rigorous time which servant
Dromio's logic maps out rhetorically line by line. Dromio's very name
has both the aspect of breakneck speed and linear movement: it means
"one who runs," "one who races."[27]

Clowns are always in danger of becoming sorry cogs in a mechanistic
universe under whose laws they suffered long before Newton. In *Errors*,
the life of the body generally is governed by a remorseless temporal
violence. The body, thinks Dromio, itself ties one to time: "Methinks
your maw, like mine, should be your clock" (I.ii.66), and later, in a
pathetic outburst, this same Dromio sums up his whole life as a series of
moments struck into his body one by one:

I have served him from the hour of my nativity to this instant, and have nothing for my service but blows. When I am cold, he heats me with beating; when I am warm, he cools me with beating. I am waked with it when I sleep, raised with it when I sit, driven out of doors with it when I go from home, welcomed home with it when I return; nay, I bear it on my shoulders, as a beggar wont her brat; and, I think, when he hath lamed me, I shall beg with it from door to door. (IV.iv.29–40)

The body of a Dromio is an object at the mercy of physical laws, like the football one compares himself to (II.i.83). Narration for him is always only one step away from a beating if he is "out of season": "Ay, ay, he told his mind upon mine ear" (II.ii.48). In this farcical view of things, time, money and violence link up in every "striking" of the bell. Each new event "tells," as a bell, a coin, a blow, consequent on its forebear with clarity and remorseless precision.

Several passages of the play that otherwise seem digressive or excrescent are related to this thematic and metadramatic preoccupation with "telling" time. During one of their periodic interludes, the Syracusan pair conduct a peculiar conversation about the baldness of Father Time. Antipholus observes that "there's a time for all things." Dromio denies this by what might be called his First Law of Time: "There's no time for a man to recover his hair that grows bald by nature" (II.ii.71). The somewhat strained banter that follows includes references to legal remedies for time's trespass and to "the world's end," which Antipholus calls "a bald conclusion." The comic routine, itself only "marking time" in the action, puts before us again a temporal order which goes in one direction only: Egeon's deadly time progressively stripping its hapless, hairless victims.

The play's principal dramatic image for narrative as an expression of the First Law of Time, an image that comes to dominate both action and language, is the line. We could plot the whole play as a set of vectors on a street map of Ephesus, where each intersection would mark a staged incident. This linearity reflects and reflects on the nature of narrative generally. Critical discussions of narrative have always used linear imagery – it seems to be a primary human way of conceiving time – but the real witchcraft of Ephesus seems to lie in the way this narrative design keeps incarnating itself everywhere, coming alive from page to prop-box in the lines, ropes, chains, whips, and snares that gradually entangle and constrict the characters. The opening image of the play is of a man bound for death, and rope-bonds thence proliferate. Dromio's tale of being struck because of a spitted pig is told insistently in serried lines. The verse-writing throughout includes many different kinds of "lines" and line patterns, more than is usual in Shakespeare. Alexandrines, fourteeners, quatrains, couplets, stichomythia ("line-story"), all make their appearance. This may have to do with the "earliness" of the play, but it also fits its preoccupation with its own method of story-telling. "What kind of story gets told in lines?" seems the implied question.

Egeon's opening narrative has begun the process of imagining lines. Maplike, it encourages us to chart the movements of the family across the sea: he ships from Syracuse to Epidamnum, she follows, they return. It is these same lines that he and his son are now attempting to trace or decipher, a linear trajectory forcibly "splitted" when the wooden line to which the family was literally bound – the "small, spare mast" – hit the rock.[28] Shipwrecks are everywhere in romances, but the detail of that splitting mast, original with Shakespeare's version, turns out to be much more than variation on a cliché. It is an image integrally bound up with the poetics of narrative in the play. And it may have an even deeper metadramatic dimension. Lars Engle points out that the mast to which the family are bound is also a secret emblem for the linear design of the action: from end to end the family are strung along their mast in the very order in which they speak: Egeon–Syr. Antipholus–Syr. Dromio–Eph. Dromio–Eph. Antipholus–Emilia.[29]

It is not linear conceptions of time only on which Ephesian social life runs. The whole community is undergirded and held together by a poetics of the line, the bond, the limit, and the boundary. Ephesians are always "drawing the line" at something, as Solinus does when he refuses to "infringe our laws." Each thing, each sign in the city has its appointed place and bonded meaning: the social order, the commercial network, the very town geography are mapped with clarity and semiotic rigor. We dine at the Tiger and host at the Centaur, Adriana stays at the Phoenix, the Courtesan at the Porpentine and so forth. Unfortunately for social and semiotic order alike, walking homophonic puns (or are they metaphors?) are now usurping the names Antipholus and Dromio.

Both the appeal and the danger of a life kept in line are made dramatically concrete in the goldsmith's chain that comes to play such an important part in the action. This prop is first mentioned pat as Adriana is lamenting the fraying of her own bond:

> I know his eye doth homage otherwhere,
> Or else what lets it but it would be here?
> Sister, you know he promised me a chain.   (II.i.104–6)

It is for a moment as though Adriana is speaking of her marriage vow. And when Angelo the goldsmith brings in the prop in question in a later scene, his entrance is likewise carefully timed to crystallize the Syracusan brother's nervous fantasy of a Luciana who,

Possessed with such a gentle sovereign grace,
Of such enchanting presence and discourse,
Hath almost made me traitor to myself.
But, lest myself be guilty to self-wrong,
I'll stop mine ears against the mermaid's song.
Enter Angelo with the chain   (III.ii.160–4)[30]

In the succeeding seventeen lines, the word "chain" appears five times, concluding with:

But this I think, there's no man is so vain
That would refuse so fair an offered chain.   (III.ii.185–6)

The metaphoric connection between the two offers is sustained by that chain of "chains," just as it comes to represent commercial obligation (and especially the bondage of debt) by a similar verbal obsessiveness in the following scene. There the chain appears no fewer than thirteen times in forty-five lines (IV.i.20–65), interwoven with terms like "bound," "bond," "attach," and with references to the pressing march of time.

The increasing confusion of the plot at this point suggests that the importance of this strand of gold is not only in the various "social bonds" that Adriana, both Antipholuses, and the Goldsmith take it for. The chain also becomes an image of the linkages of assumption and inference which give the play its hilarious, increasingly desperate drive. In short, it is a neatly-imaged "chain of events," comically literal, materializing the audience's own attachment to an increasingly knotty plot. We may even see it as an emblem of metaphor itself, appearing as it does so charged with figurative linkages. As these emblematic and metadramatic functions multiply, this polysemous chain of chains comes to head a class of linear counters in an exploration of acts of linkage for good and ill in the play.

For instance, we might also consider the fortunes of the chain's poor cousin: the "rope's end" for which Ephesian Antipholus sends his Dromio in the middle of the "chain" discussion, and with which he intends to beat his wife. The other Dromio shortly appears sans rope and, when duly berated, offers a bewildered pun on death by the hangman's rope, presumably another "end of the line" joke (IV.i.99). As Antipholus is haled off to prison, this same Dromio is sent to Adriana for bail. When the first Dromio later returns, with his rope, the sequence resumes:

ANTIPHOLUS   To what end did I bid thee hie thee home?
DROMIO   To a rope's end, sir, and to that end am I returned.
ANTIPHOLUS   And to that end, sir, I will welcome you. *Beats Dromio*
                                                       (IV.iv.15–17)

This rather suggests that Antipholus here whips Dromio with that same rope. But there is yet more. The women appear with the Doctor, and Dromio warns: "Mistress, *respice finem*, respect your end; or rather, the prophecy like the parrot, 'beware the rope's end'" (IV.iv.42–4).[31] The hanging joke is common, but here it seems to have come to life. When he later asserts that "God and the rope-maker bear me witness / That I was sent for nothing but a rope" (IV.iv.91), it looks for a moment as if God has himself turned rope-maker. Pinch decides that "They must be bound, and laid in some dark room" (IV.iv.95).

The notion of "bonds" has thus gradually been extended by the play to cover more and more territory. Ordinary dead metaphors of being "bound" to do this or go there begin to chafe uncomfortably (e.g. IV.i.3). The play fills with instances of lines, boundaries, and acts of crossing over. The comic scene at the locked gate, for example, turns on a structural boundary that cannot be crossed, across which names themselves start to break their bonds with referents:

> E. DROMIO   Maud, Bridget, Marian, Cicely, Gillian, Ginn!
> S. DROMIO   Mome, malt-horse, capon, coxcomb, idiot, patch!
>
> (III.i.31–2)

One Dromio here calls names, the other replies in playful parallel with abuse (*abusio*) and name-calling. And what is an insult but a name emphatically *not* ours? Antipholus is dissuaded from breaking down the wall in rage only because it would invite a circulation of bad names for himself and his wife over which he would have no binding or regulatory power:

> If by strong hand you offer to break in,
> Now in the stirring passage of the day,
> A vulgar comment will be made of it;
> And that supposed by the common rout
> Against your yet ungalled estimation,
> That may with foul intrusion enter in,
> And dwell upon your grave when you are dead.... (III.i.98–104)

Names are becoming alarmingly deathless succubi that usurp the lives of people. Ephesian "credit" as a whole depends on a one-to-one correspondence between a name and its *nominatum*, but the ever-intersecting paths of the twins function like crossed wires, disrupting the flow of information, mismatching the links that bind all things in their "proper" places. It is here that Antipholus decides to divert the chain from his wife to the Courtesan.

The Plautine poetics of line and limit in Ephesus thus governs at once linguistics, narratology, and anthropology. The alarming implications of this poetics do not go unnoticed or uncriticized by the play. The end-driven regulatory scheme of cause and effect, name and referent, is glossed by a set of references scattered through the play to Biblical, and especially soteriological, history. We have already noted the hints of a "fall and judgment" pattern in the opening scene. These resonances return sharpened when Egeon reappears unsuccessful at the end of his "grace period":

> By this, I think, the dial points at five;
> Anon, I'm sure, the Duke himself in person
> Comes this way to the melancholy vale,
> The place of death and sorry execution,
> Behind the ditches of the abbey here.   (V.i.118–22)

The "melancholy vale" and "place of death" echo the Biblical "valley of the shadow" and "place of the skull" and take their place in a string of allusions through the play to the Fall and consequent sentence of Death. For instance, when Dromio runs to beg Adriana for money to set Antipholus free, he says his master is "in Tartar limbo, worse than hell," the captive of "A devil in an everlasting garment" and "One that, before the judgment, carries poor souls to hell" (IV.ii.32–3, 40). Luciana in her turn has become "Mistress Redemption." When he returns with the bail to find the other Antipholus unarrested, he enquires: "What, have you got the picture of old Adam new-appareled?"

Not that Adam that kept the Paradise, but that Adam that keeps the prison; he that goes in the calf's skin that was killed for the Prodigal; he that came behind you, sir, like an evil angel, and bid you forsake your liberty. (IV.iii.16–21)

It is St. Paul's "Adam in whom all die" that is in the picture here, the first patriarch in Hell. All the play's talk of fiends and devils in Ephesus suggests a community still under the dominion of "the penalty of Adam," inhabited by fiends of whom "It is written, they appear to men like angels of light" (IV.iii.56).[32] Images of divine judgment haunt the play. Even the glorious figure of Nell (Knell?) the kitchen wench, whose name is not rope enough to measure her body, is an apocalyptic giant: her grime is "in grain. Noah's flood could not do it" and "If she lives til Doomsday, she'll burn a week longer than the whole world" (III.ii.106, 100). The hapless characters enmeshed by the linear poetics of classical comedy are assimilated to St. Paul's Ephesians that were "dead in trespasses and sinnes, Wherein, in time past ye walked, according to the course of this world" (Ephes. 2.1–2).[33] When Dromio fears the devil-Courtesan will "shake her chain, and fright us with it," it is the Devil of Revelation who is behind her, and binding in a pit that is indeed at hand.[34]

That the regulation of the communal order of Plautine Ephesus is in the end a deathward process is made clear by its final champion: the would-be exorcist Dr. Pinch, whose talk is all the fiend and whose very name is constraint. He gets hold of those who have reached the end of their tether, and the "dark and dankish vault" to which he carts them is like enough to hell. But it is his appearance which clinches the matter:

> ... a hungry lean-faced villain;
> A mere anatomy, a mountebank,
> A threadbare juggler and a fortune teller,
> A needy-hollow-eyed-sharp-looking wretch;
> A living dead man.   (V.i.238–42)

Within necessity's sharp Pinch lurks a figure familiar from countless homilies. St. Paul would have seen through Pinch at once: under his disguise of family therapist, he is Death's point-man in Ephesus.[35]

At the end of the line, the wear and tear of Time on hapless mortality crystallizes in Egeon's final appearance, having failed to secure a community of friends to change his iron bonds for human ones and save his life. In the play's most moving passage, Egeon longs for something more than the body of this death, and the death of this body:

> O time's extremity,
> Hast thou so cracked and splitted my poor tongue
> In seven short years, that here my only son
> Knows not my feeble key of untuned cares?
> Though now this grainèd face of mine be hid
> In sap-consuming winter's drizzled snow,
> And all the conduits of my blood froze up,
> Yet hath my night of life some memory;
> My wasting lamps some fading glimmer left;
> My dull deaf ears a little use to hear.   (V.i.308–17)

This is where the rhetoric of the opening scene pointed, the victimization of "one thing after another" and the partition of community – the tongue like the mast – in cracking and splitting. The play has staged the temporal drive of classical comedy itself as a drive towards death.

Confronting this deadly world of bond and line, its story-books ruled by antique precept, are two alternative sites of imagery: one an equally inhuman contrary, the other a sublation the play hopes will transfigure both contraries alike. The first alternative Egeon's family faced on their "helpful bark" in the dissolute violence of the storm and the all-melting ocean of natural chaos.[36] In this environment we can no more survive than under the iron government of Time's Law. Law in Ephesus opposes and seeks to shape the always incipiently chaotic flux of natural process. To this extent it is presented as fitfully appealing. Errant Antipholus of

Syracuse longs for the stable order of bounded social life when he lands on the firm ground of the mart, bringing the very marine dissolution of which Egeon has just spoken with him into Ephesus. A famous speech expresses the pathos of oceanic boundlessness:

> I to the world am like a drop of water
> That in the ocean seeks another drop,
> Who, falling there to find his fellow forth,
> Unseen, inquisitive, confounds himself.   (I.ii.35–8)

Boundary in these lines has become fluid, evanescent, and meta-morphic.[37] The pathos of its imminent loss is curiously cosmic, perhaps through the submerged connection between world and drop, as though a person were not less a node than a globe of manifold possibilities, a little Nell made cunningly. Indeed, the threat to Dromio of Nell's magnitude belongs with this sense of the uncontrollable flux of the world as a potential solvent of personal identity, as too does the element of fear mixed with desire in his master's response to Luciana. For these men, women have too much fluidity about them.

If the contraries of rope and ocean, law and nature, were the only alternatives, it would be a grim lookout. Some mediating term or passage is needed between them. For this transfiguration the play turns to two sources: intellectually to the language of the sacramental, emotionally and dramaturgically to the theatre of wonder with its dialectic of surrender and self-consciousness. Death and earth, the penalty of Adam, is only half the story. Out of Paul's redemptive contrary ("Even so in Christ shall all be made alive") Shakespeare produces a third possibility, a deeper tide towards a breakdown of order not into death but life. Between the two opponents of Time-as-Law there is some commerce: both stress the availability of sudden, improvisatory breakthroughs. Hence the language of wandering and ocean occasionally coalesces with the language of the sacramental under the banner of fluidity. But their two tendencies are fundamentally distinct: one divides and fragments only, where the other does so in order to generate a more vital compounding. Unlike so many of his Protestant contemporaries, but very like those who wrote and performed the medieval cycle-plays, Shakespeare's principal point of connection to theology is not through sin but through the notions of incarnation and the sacramental, where word and matter, spirit and flesh are explicitly confounded in the creation of communal forms of life.

Apart from the hint of "redemption" in the opening scene, various reminiscences of the Incarnation pepper the middle of the play: Dromio refers to his "nativity," there is a character called Balthasar and a merchant who has been waiting since "Pentecost." And when Ephesian Antipholus chooses not to break down the door of his house for fear his credit will suffer, we might see a worldling's distant anti-echo of the liberation and epiphany played out before the infernal gate and its rapscallion Porter.[38] The "undoing" of time's tyranny also appears when Dromio comes to "Mistress Redemption" for bail. First there is a telling reminder of three familiar images for the bondage of time and story:

> ADRIANA   Tell me, was he arrested on a band?
> DROMIO   Not on a band, but on a stronger thing:
>   A chain, a chain! Do you not hear it ring?
> ADRIANA   What the chain?
> DROMIO   No, no, the bell; 'tis time that I were gone.   (IV.ii.49–53)

Bond, chain, and bell are cardinal images of the world's rigor. But the hint of new, more liberal possibilities follows:

> DROMIO   It was two ere I left him, and now the clock strikes one.
> ADRIANA   The hours come back! That did I never hear.
> DROMIO   O yes, if any hour meet a sergeant, 'a turns back for very
>   fear.
> ADRIANA   As if time were in debt! How fondly dost thou reason!
> DROMIO   Time is a very bankrupt, and owes more than he's worth
>   to season.
>   Nay he's a thief too: have you not heard men say,
>   That time comes stealing on by night and day?
>   If 'a be in debt and theft, and a sergeant in the way,
>   Hath he not reason to turn back an hour in a day?
>   (IV.ii.54–62)

This corresponds to the earlier jokes about Time's baldness, but now Time is fugitive rather than bailiff. If Time still steals from us, runs away too fast, he now begins to show a capacity for the unexpected and transgressive. If Time can run backwards, there is no telling what may happen. If Time is a thief, we glimpse a world less dominated by logic, more open to improvisation and even miracle, in which "the day of the Lord wil come as a thief in the night" (2 Pet. 3.10). This new vision of time is associated directly with the redemption of Antipholus from his bonds, and when Dromio hands over the money, he does so with a reference to St. Peter's release from prison, itself instance and echo of Christ's power to liberate: "Here are the angels that you sent for to deliver you" (IV.iii.41).[39]

The linear imagery of Ephesus also appears again strangely shifted and fused with the fluidity of ocean in Antipholus' evocation of Luciana's hair as a bed afloat on the surface of the ocean:

> Spread o'er the silver waves thy golden hairs,
> And as a bed I'll take them, and there lie,
> And in that glorious supposition think
> He gains by death that hath such means to die:
> Let Love, being light, be drowned if she sink.   (III.i.48–52)

The thin meniscus that screens life from death is sustained and made viable by the magically erotic, a power that will allow Antipholus to float luxuriantly on a raft of hair, close to but not concerned at the danger of drowning in nature's deep.[40] Metamorphic Eros occupies the middle ground between rope and water, "error" as fatal mistake and "error" as endless deviation.[41] This fusion of the erotic with the sacramental is a combination that comes to be characteristic of Shakespeare's work. It is by no means always a stable combination, and can turn bitter in the extreme as it does for Othello. But in *The Comedy of Errors*, as for Adriana, the language of ocean is eroticized and attracted towards the sacramental:

> For know, my love, as easy mayst thou fall
> A drop of water in the breaking gulf,
> And take unmingled thence that drop again
> Without addition or diminishing
> As take from me thyself, and not me too.   (II.ii.126–30)

The breaking gulf as the sacrament of marriage described in Ephesians is Shakespeare's most important image of lived *contaminatio*.[42] If the gulf breaks, it is a dynamic and creative fracture, as the bonds of most Ephesian institutions are not. Its surging energies at once sustain and mobilize the central social institution. The crucial importance of Paul's letter to the play thus comes into clearer focus. Paul's vision of erotic desire in marriage as a social counterpart to the Word-as-Flesh undergirds Shakespeare's contamination of boundary with flux, a move that at once dissolves law and circumscribes ocean.

The Shakespearean drama of *contaminatio* that unfolds in *The Comedy of Errors* has, like its classical counterparts in the play, its metanarrative emblems. Consider again the "chain" as an image of narrative. As a figure of bondage, it points us to the world of rigor and Old Law. But as a figure of metaphor, it points on the contrary to a power in language that desires and makes new pertinencies, new constituencies, new connections with the world. That the chain's first associations should be to erotic emotion is therefore deeply appropriate, since in Shakespeare Love is the sign *par excellence* of the promise of new community, as well as that under which all of Paul's unifications occur. The chain thus both looks to the marriages of the conclusion and recalls the ropes and mast

that bound the shipwrecked family together as the play's first images of
bonds that protect from the blind chaos of mere nature.

The resuscitation of community through clarification of the vital
significance of narrative turns out to be the play's deepest impulse, and
explains the pervasive use of the Ephesians' epistle. Paul's theology there
is oriented especially to the maintenance of community: the letter is
written to bolster and encourage the cohesion of a Church threatened
with fragmentation. Against Egeon's vision of the tongue "cracked and
splitted," we can set Paul's image of a body that has overcome such
attrition:

For he is our peace, whiche hath made both one: and hath broken downe the wal
that was a stoppe betweene us,/ Taking away in his fleshe the hatred, (even) the
law of commaundementes (contayned) in ordinaunces, for to make of twayne one
newe man in hym selfe, so makyng peace:/ And that he might reconcile both unto
God in one body through (his) crosse, and slue hatred thereby. (Ephes. 2.14–16,
Bishops' Bible)

What Shakespeare takes from Paul's writings is less a particular doctrine
than a kind of figurative substrate of images and associations in which
incarnation is the principal trope for all kinds of unification, including
that which creates new community between the play and its audience.
This commitment to incarnation as the goal of poetry has a kind of
secular "real presence" as its dramatic ideal, and imagines language itself
as a ubiquitous informing power. Verbal utterance at this level deeply
creates and roots itself in a form of life and experience, where the world
fits itself to one's desire and a language can be found that mediates each
to the other. Such an ideal language does not constrain, constrict, bully,
or scar: language that does that is what Ephesus deals in when it writes
its governing signs, as Dromio laments, directly into the flesh in bruising
and chaining. The language of Shakespearean incarnation, on the other
hand, seeks a sacrament-like function which can express the life of the
flesh, and inform that life with its own vitality. Language is in this way
itself a creative activity, not a merely secondary one, welling up from
some deep source which is also the source of experience. The plasticity of
language and the mutability of experience are twin – or one – in their
interinanimation. They are a vital unity of a kind usefully imaginable
through the older theological conception of the sign that acts.

Shakespeare's poetry does what medieval drama always threatened to
do, what Aquinas indicated was always implied by the logic of a
sacramental semiosis: it unbinds itself and its shaping power from the
Church. At the heart of Shakespeare's drama is a power confident that
words can incarnate lives before the eyes of an audience without the

institutional apparatus of the Church to guarantee their orthodoxy, and without a structure of dogma external to the dramatic occasion. Though such a stance suggests that the playwright is in direct competition with God, no sense of struggle ever emerges, either in abjection or self-aggrandisement (Marlowe is an instructive comparison here). The universe of verbal creation is capacious enough to allow for both. It follows that one can only with some restriction speak of the Shakespearean project as a "secularization." One could just as easily call it a radical resacralization of the world. For Shakespeare words are all, but a great all inseparable from the continuing life of the world itself, and whose deepest energy springs from the ever-metamorphic reproduction of the world. It is as though Shakespeare read the Bible as an epic poem written by Ovid.

The problem finally to be faced is by what counter-magic the trixiness of metaphor can be reconciled with the hunger for persistence, how the pun can be made flesh. It is here that we encounter the play's own rabbit-out-of-the-hat in the person of Emilia. Nothing in the classical logic of the narrative requires her presence: all that is required is that the two Antipholuses (or even the two Dromios) finally run into one another in the street. In Shakespeare's play, this encounter is shepherded by Emilia, who seems to grasp at once the precise shape of the resolution called for. She becomes its focal point, stands in in her own person for the redemptive figure that the Pauline allusions have led us to expect. Why should the body of the mother, whose labor as mother is explicitly announced as finally accomplished at the point of reunion, replace the body of Christ?[43]

The play is almost explicit about this compounding of Emilia's gestation with the Incarnation. Emilia declares "Thirty-three years have I but gone in travail / Of you, my sons, and till this present hour / My heavy burthen ne'er delivered" (V.i.401-3). That odd time interval corresponds to no chronology mapped out anywhere else in the play, indeed it contradicts Egeon's tale.[44] Shakespeare is notoriously careless about such details, but that will not explain this particular choice of number. The answer is, of course, that thirty-three years was the period of the Incarnation, at the end of which the clock was turned back, the chain broken, and the fatal debt paid.[45] Emilia's "thirty-three years" of "travail" end likewise in liberation from bonds, forgiveness of debt, and redemption of time – all accomplished in the moment of recognition. This image of a labor to deliver the world anew redefines the nature of narrative as a temporal process and supervenes over the old images and mechanisms of plot closure. Its gargantuan – and rather disturbing – pain was after all not towards death, but towards new life, and the

Plautine logic which drew us to expect, as early as I.ii, that Antipholus'
"thousand marks" would in the end redeem Egeon, is pointedly set aside
by Solinus: "it shall not need, thy father hath his life." The late and
peculiar completion of the twins' "suspended" nativity translates the
characters back in time to a "gossips' feast" to be held in the sacral space
of the Abbey, in which all will join to break down "the wal that was a
stoppe betweene us." Nativity (rhyming with itself in Emilia's closing
speech), incarnation, baptism, marriage: the sacramental counters pile up
upon one another, but are also absorbed into the natural image of
childbirth, here understood as the redelivery of its own vitality to the
community.

The "poetics of incarnation" plays a still deeper role in the scene. It
has to do with Shakespeare's feel for our knowledge of the world in our
language: how language can deliver the world as a gestated presence to
us for naming and recognition. We can glimpse this if we consider again
Shakespeare's attraction to fictions of identical twins. Linguistic witchcraft such as metaphor, pun and double reference have materialized
throughout the play as twinning. The scene of recognition where the
twins finally meet puts flesh on these verbal two-in-one paradoxes, and
the dissolution of identity and boundary which Paul's sacramental
language imagines is also crystallized for them and us when they stand
before one another. Instead of the romance cliché of recognition tokens –
what Stephen Gosson sneered at as the "broken ring, . . . handkercher, or
piece of a cockle shell"[46] – we have a matching pair of living bodies, a
pair that yet comprise or share, so the language seems inclined to claim,
one spirit:

> One of these men is genius to the other;
> And so of these, which is the natural man,
> And which the spirit? Who deciphers them?   (V.i.333–5)

Flesh and spirit are each in each here, and cannot be extricated.
Romance *anagnorisis* provides the dramatic and emotional occasion to
focus a profound feeling both for language as a discoverer of the world
and for theatre as a site of knowledge ("theory"). It almost seems that
the scene, with its language of mirroring and of confrontation with a
miraculous other self, is a response to Paul's famous formulation of how
our limited knowledge is to be completed: "for now we see through a
glass, darkly, but then face to face." Each twin is both self and other, as
the lovers were without knowing it in Plato's *Phaedrus*.

We may seem to have erred far in our turn from the matter of
"wonder," but the strange and satisfying paradox of the identical twins
who face one another at the play's end returns us to it. It is the first of

Shakespeare's many scenes that exploit this feeling of the world made over in wonder, and it shows us just how involved his dramaturgy is with the issues of knowledge and its ground that wonder engenders. In sharing in a mutual wonder "across the footlights," the characters are for the first time equal with the audience, as the secret we have held for so long is now made common knowledge.[47] Each Antipholus (= "reciprocal love") facing himself tastes the audience's delight in the realization of knowledge released, transferred, freely given, incarnate for all to see.[48] The boundaries between stage and audience are deliberately made porous. No one is quite sure of what his or her bearings ought to be: all the characters will assert is that the world has become somehow both theirs to live in and at the same time beyond them, that they can embrace it only between affirmation and denial. Gingerly they explore the world's new shape, linking it together piece by piece, feeling at its edges with the mind's fingertips as skepticism and elation hold one another in tension:

> ANGELO   That is the chain, sir, which you had of me.
> ANTIPHOLUS   I think it be, sir, I deny it not.
> ANGELO   And you, sir, for this chain arrested me.
> ANTIPHOLUS   I think I did, sir, I deny it not.   (V.i.378–81)

We can hear language's adequacy to the world being felt out. The double drift of separation and identification that marks theatrical wonder's relation to the world it meets reappears here through the reunited twins. One Dromio at least has a strong sense that he may be seeing himself – one rather gets the impression that it is for the first time: "Methinks you are my glass, and not my brother; / I see by you I am a sweet-faced youth" (V.i.418–19). The discovery of his beauty is a joke, of course, but it also focuses the general sense that the world is a newly beautiful place where the self is potentially at home with itself, where narcissistic delight can be true without being invidious or damaging.

Gestation is the play's final image of itself, replacing the rope of classical poetics and the sea of romance flux with umbilical cords and amniotic fluid. It may also give something of Shakespeare's sense of himself as a nascent playwright. The end of the process that Egeon figured as deathward turns out to be an image of the society and family gradually re-membered into a living body. Re-membering is also the image of the work of the play itself, and of its working *on* itself over the course of the narrative to articulate characteristic procedures and conceptions of Shakespearean drama. If we have always felt that Nell was the play's most striking figure, the end proves this intuition right by revealing her as the play's great comic image of the body that can contain us all, that will by its very material cohesion resist the Flood and postpone death "a week longer than the rest of the world." Nell is the play's early, popular foreshadowing of the figure of the mother produced as the final site of unification. The incarnative imagination casts itself revealingly as a female principle of vivification which stands in for the body of Christ. Feared in Nell as too overwhelmingly material, this principle is embraced in Emilia as the site where the social body can be revealed in its most concrete, but also most wonderful, work of reproduction.[49]

At the end of the play, romance recognition, heterosexual marriage, sacramental semiotics are assimilated to one another as common images of a credible faith in the world.[50] The body of Christ resurrected becomes the body of Emilia delivered. The final attachment of this comic vision to the world rather than to a supernatural aspiration is summed up in the *topos* of reproduction within the verbal order of matrimony. By linking the conservative notion of "legitimacy" with the transformational power of incarnative trope, Shakespeare registers at once inheritance and renewal. The impetus to matrimony that will drive the whole of Shakespeare's writing in comedy is a response therefore not only to social and political conditions, as many have argued, but to questions of cultural and poetic self-consciousness at the widest level.

IV

This sense of comedic resolution as a "fitting together" of contraries – and the discovery of how deeply they may answer each other – can be said to describe not only Shakespeare's attraction to a particular kind of story, but a preoccupation and a sensibility that manifests itself at all levels of his writing. From his consistent attention to erotic experience (both hetero- and homo-), to his predilection for exploiting the unclassical indecorums of the Elizabethan stage, to his notably dense and paradoxical metaphoric language, his impulse is to discover a figurative complement, to push apparent difference towards some deeper reciprocal unity, sometimes imagined beyond language itself, as in "The Phoenix and the Turtle." Consider, for instance, the large number of phrases that condense crucial moments of entire plays in a stark and baffling paradox that demands to be understood, and, even more surprisingly, that we think we can and do understand: "Mine own and not mine own"; "Nothing is but what is not"; "I am not what I am"; "This is, and is not, Cressid"; "A natural perspective that is and is not"; "I confess nothing, nor I deny nothing"; "I did love you once. ... I loved you not."[51] These are not merely clever paradoxes, inward-looking mirrors, for they are deployed to register their plays' sense of sources of language, feeling or knowledge ever beyond the horizon of the expressible, which only such teasing, even maddening, formulae can index. Rhetorician Puttenham called such figures "The Wondrer" and certainly in their dramatic context they often have the qualities at once of profound representational power and of equally profound self-consciousness that we have associated with the dynamic of that emotion.[52]

To take just one more instance, consider how the paradoxes of doubling and doubt shape this radiant moment of discovery in *A Midsummer Night's Dream*:

> DEMETRIUS These things seem small and undistinguishable,
> Like far-off mountains turned into clouds.
> HERMIA Methinks I see these things with parted eye,
> When everything seems double.
> HELENA   So methinks;
> And I have found Demetrius like a jewel,
> Mine own and not mine own.   (IV.i.187–92)

It is not only the heady evaporation of dream mixed with the open-mouthed discovery that "all is true" that makes this so exciting and joyous. It is the gradual discovery, through successive, gingerly approximations, of *just* the language for this very state. Helena's grasp of the right way to word the world in her feeling catches its own quality of stumbling on truth right there for us: her metaphor crystallizes as the wonderful jewel of itself. We hold it breathless, sparkling in the hand. The possibility of metaphor as the granting of the world we want, our own and not our own, catches up the vibration of erotic desire in its strong toil of grace. In Shakespeare's comedy, language's love for the world can be requited.

4   *Pericles*; or, the past as fate and miracle

Perhaps there are moments of awakening,
Extreme, fortuitous, personal, in which

We more than awaken, sit on the edge of sleep,
As on an elevation, and behold
The academies like structures in a mist.

Wallace Stevens

Blessing and curse, euphemism and slander, praise and blame under-
mine statement. However neutral or objective words seem to be,
there is always a tilt of this kind, produced by the very effort to
speak. There are those who must curse in order to speak, and those
who must bless in order to speak: some interlard their words with
obscenities, some kill them with kindness expressions. These are the
extreme cases that suggest how close we are to muteness: to not
speaking at all unless we untangle these contrary modes.

Geoffrey Hartman

In *Pericles, Prince of Tyre* Shakespeare deliberately set out to resuscitate
a dramatic style some twenty years out of date, and thereby made
transmission and revival the central concerns of the play. This return to
stylistic "first principles" in simplicity of design and directness of address
joins the play's concern with the fortunes of family to link questions of
biological and cultural reproduction. The overall action first presents the
loss of family and language and ends by staging their recovery in a
sequence of wondrous reparations. The curtailment of complex narrative
interplay focuses attention on the role of story-telling in these moments:
what it is and what it does, its pleasures and its dangers. Such is the
intensity of the play's investment in narration that it is difficult to resist
repeating the story in discussion, as though one could not properly value
it without having traversed it. Accordingly, I shall concentrate on
moments of narration, recovery, and recognition – together with their
counterparts, dumbness and blankness – and on the relation to those
moments of the bodies that perform them, in the fiction and in the
theatre.

I

Story-telling is everywhere in *Pericles*. The play begins with the ancient rites (and rights) of the poet-singer, and throughout people engage one another with the stories of their lives. For Gower, story is the vehicle and purpose of life, and for its pleasure and illumination he offers to use up his own "like taper-light." A god in the end commands the tale to be retold in her own precincts. The impulse to story-telling is not a personal property, but a transpersonal and communal one, even a transhistorical one. The play's wager seems to be that we will come away in turn restored and restoried. Yet the achievement of the "right" story is revealed by the play to be fragile and elusive, its attainment itself an occasion for wonder. In the final reunions of *Pericles*, the tangibility of recovery stands in delicate balance with the bare sufficiency of time and flesh to hold the visible shape of a narrative embodied.

We are placed from the outset into a network of story as a reciprocal and dynamic exchange between past and present. Gower is merely a medium; the tale did not originate with him, nor is he its proprietor. His entrance emphasizes – visually as well as aurally, if the title page of Wilkins' *Painfull Adventures* is a guide[1] – traditional aspects of his role as "old master."[2] His "song" in the Globe revives high and low narrative traditions at once, fusing epic poet and folk-balladist. This traditional, almost cosy, context for story offers us pleasures that, if in the end non-physical, speak first to the simple senses:

> To sing a song that old was sung,
> From ashes ancient Gower is come,
> Assuming man's infirmities,
> To glad your ear, and please your eyes.   (I.Pr.1–4)[3]

The emphasis on the matching of body and story here is important to the play's overall conception of narrative as a fundamental activity of human life. In order to tell the story, Gower must asssume a body, which has, along with its vulnerabilities, certain sensuous pleasures. Story-telling is deeply linked to the bodily life: the senses have aesthetic appetites and words satisfy those that take pleasure in them. The Globe troupe offer their incarnational abilities as actors for the recovery of old pleasures that effect somatic processes of ceremonial purgation and festive renewal:

> It hath been sung at festivals,
> On ember-eves and holy-ales;
> And lords and ladies in their lives
> Have read it for restoratives:

> The purchase is to make men glorious,
> *Et bonum quo antiquius eo melius.*   (I.Pr.5–10)

The theatre is not simply a purveyor of consumable "productions." It has a re-creative, even therapeutic agency. The restorative reading formerly reserved to "lords and ladies" fuses with popular Church festival, and Gower's incarnation now proffers both to his new, modern audience:

> If you, born in these latter times,
> When wit's more ripe, accept my rimes,
> And that to hear an old man sing
> May to your wishes pleasure bring,
> I life would wish, and that I might
> Waste it for you like taper-light.   (I.Pr.11–16)

Steven Mullaney has recently argued that this Gower anticipates "an emerging figure of the author that would eventually eclipse the popular stage and Shakespearean dramaturgy."[4] But the kind of "authorship" of which Mullaney speaks is more like the failure of what Gower claims, and will fill the shell of his role like a hermit crab. Gower is at pains to insist that his authority is not personal, that it is his only through modes and functions of story-telling such as those of the bard and holiday spieler. If anything, modernity is represented as Gower's antithesis, a time "when wit's more ripe." Nor is Gower at all "an embodiment of the play's effort to divorce itself from the cultural grounds of theatrical activity in Jacobean London."[5] Gower comes before us to explain just how this play understands those grounds. The play is very clear about its relation to its history and occasion.[6] And while it is true that the play strives for a transhistorical potency, its success is in doubt from the start: the assertion that "*bonum quo antiquius eo melius*" is immediately tested.

If Gower worries that the "more ripe" present will refuse what the past has to offer, the opening of his tale presents a complementary failure of continuity: the past refusing to hand over to the present what it needs. Cultural transmission is always fragile, since the parties to it must concede their mutual insufficiency. This avowal of essential impotence is difficult, and not only in the erosions of time and nature can tradition fail, but in a fierce recalcitrance that conceals the hoarding of self behind a mask of benevolence, and baits its very hostility with pleasure. Antiochus the Great embodies this will-to-self in the play, and the scene in which he "presents" his daughter casts the problem of narrative and cultural inheritance in terms of family romance. Its complicities, silences, and coded disclosures are metanarrative as well as personal.

Pericles presents Antiochus and his daughter as an emblem of sexual and familial involution and opacity controlled by the father's rapacious will:

> Bad child, worse father to entice his own
> To evil should be done by none.
> But custom what they did begin
> Was with long use account'd no sin.
> The beauty of this sinful dame
> Made many princes thither frame,
> To seek her as a bed-fellow,
> In marriage pleasure's play-fellow;
> Which to prevent he made a law,
> To keep her still, and men in awe[.][7]   (I.Pr.27–36)

The arrested quality of this family knot is nicely given by the ghost of immobility in "to keep her still" and reinforced by the daughter's silence. The scene Antiochus stages is a coercive theatrical mechanism from which there is no escape; the suitor's eye once caught "in awe" can only wilt before the father's authority, which holds all speech fast in its grip. The heads that stud the background of the set mark how the suitors are never allowed to look away: the spectacle compels even in dismemberment and death. Wonder is here a theatre of deadly paralysis. The verbal model for this stasis is the riddle, impenetrable itself and picturing a family without beginning or end, "like a viper" which has swallowed its own tail. Like the riddle, Antiochus' show oscillates between offering and withholding, enticing and forbidding. Its signs point inextricably several ways at once, as with his description of the daughter "clothed like a bride / For the embracements even of Jove himself," with its coded hint of just the kind of violent and incestuous rape that has occurred. Nothing is named with its name, and yet everything is patent. The theatrical pageant casts a retrospective pall over the humbler pretensions of Gower only moments before, and the parallel is reinforced by the repetition of Gower's odd verb "to glad." What if Gower's offer of pleasure were merely another version of the same desire to arrest the eye and subject it to the will of the past?

As contestant, Pericles enters fully into the father's mode of both acknowledgment and denial. The two join in an appreciative chorus for the daughter's absolute exposure to their gaze:

> "Bring in our daughter, clothed like a bride ..."
> "See, where she comes apparell'd like the spring ..."

In sharing Antiochus' posture, Pericles enters a dangerous rhetorical environment where he stands to inherit more than he suspects – not just the daughter herself, but a way of regarding her. Such an insight, or failure of it, is couched in his next image:

> Her face the book of praises, where is read
> Nothing but curious pleasures, as from thence
> Sorrow were ever raz'd, and testy wrath
> Could never be her mild companion. (I.i.16–19)

Playing the father's theatre game allows the secret to appear, but nothing can be done about it. Though Pericles can still read or intuit what sort of thing has been erased from the text of the expurgated face, he is somehow blind to it. His blazon reproduces the tension of exhibition and concealment that marks Antiochus' power-play as a whole.

The situation is further glossed as Pericles turns away into an apostrophe to the "gods" on the origins of sexual desire, which Antiochus completes. The exchange frames Pericles' first assertion of his dynastic and sexual ambition and suggests he sees Antiochus as one of the gods to be appeased:

PERICLES	You gods, that made me man, and sway in love,
	That have inflam'd desire in my breast
	To taste the fruit of yon celestial tree
	Or die in the adventure, be my helps,
	As I am son and servant to your will,
	To compass such a boundless happiness.
ANTIOCHUS	Prince Pericles –
PERICLES	That would be son to great Antiochus.
ANTIOCHUS	Before thee stands this fair Hesperides,
	With golden fruit, but dangerous to be touch'd;
	For death-like dragons here affright thee hard.

(I.i.20–30)

The parable of the tree is curiously double. Hercules' labor in the garden of Hesperus is Antiochus' gloss. But Pericles' version involves not simply Hercules' task of picking the fruit but also tasting it, and this suggests as well an eroticized version of Genesis. The Edenic and Herculean analogues contaminate each other, producing a third myth of a sexual knowledge which divinity, as God and Dragon/Serpent, at once promotes and prohibits. Pericles must both transgress and obey powers which both encourage and forbid – just as the godlike Antiochus has both revealed and concealed the truth, offered and withheld the daughter. Antiochus' gloss completes the double-bind, so that Pericles' "Or" (line 23) must really be "And" – death will come tasting or not tasting, speaking or not speaking. The lesson is that the gods kill man for the very aspiration to see the world through their eyes that they have implanted within him. The strange blending of Hesperidean and Biblical stories identifies god as a jealous father who holds all the cards. Turning back to his daughter's "enticing" face, Antiochus imagines it as "like heaven," a distant realm which men, unlike himself, may "view" but not reach for:

> Her face, like heaven, enticeth thee to view
> Her countless glory, which desert must gain;
> And which, without desert because thine eye
> Presumes to reach, all the whole heap must die.   (I.i.31–4)

The face is strangely both tangible and diffuse here, Heaven both close and remote; one can be punished for reaching for it, yet one could not have touched it in any case. The "reaching eye" is Antiochus' catachresis for wonder's double sense of intimacy and distance, and the violence of wonder is here the sky-god's jealousy. Antiochus points to the heads of the failed suitors, like Pericles "Drawn by report, advent'rous by desire," now a blank and silent spectacle. Their threat is a stymied astonishment: dumbness and dismemberment.

This exchange preceding the presentation of the riddle intimates less some sin or fault in Pericles, as some critics have held, than a series of subtle inveiglings between Pericles and Antiochus which ends with the former recognizing the secret commonality of their desire.[8] To solve the riddle, one must share the desire, see the kinship between God and serpent. But the answer is that the fate of desire is deadly either way – buying in or opting out. The obscurant language of the riddle migrates by contagion into Pericles' reply. Challenger and possessor co-operate in keeping the secret hidden, and the daughter remains the baffled victim of an abuse so deep she is unable to speak it. She is hardly more than a cipher, yet the morsel she can say may reach out pathetically for a salvation through speech which Pericles is unable to accomplish:

> Of all sayd yet may'st thou prove prosperous.
> Of all sayd yet, I wish thee happiness.   (I.i.60–1)[9]

What *Pericles* seeks, from the moment of Gower's appearance, is some other way to cheat time of its prey, so that desire need not be merely an endless repetition that abjects the self before a larger, darker authority whose instrument it becomes. But the opening scene shows the ethos of male challenge and desire as ruled by a logic of repetitive violence from which there is no escape.

The effect on Pericles of solving the riddle is a radical doubt about the reliability of perception, a doubt which echoes throughout the story.[10] In reaction, Pericles calls for a general curse on seeing. The "countless glory" of the daughter is now a sight to be avoided by the "countless eyes" of heaven. The gods must cloud all eyes so that no-one may know, and the ambiguous "their" suggests the blinding is pervasive:

> ... but O you powers
> That gives heaven countless eyes to view men's acts:
> Why cloud they not their sights perpetually,
> If this be true, which makes me pale to read it? (I.i.73–6)

For Pericles it is too late. The innocent eye that relied on the truth of surface yields to a paranoid one that suspects a hidden knowledge everywhere. Disillusion crystallizes as a repugnance for the female body, whose interiority masks the dirty secret of death:

> Fair glass of light, I lov'd you, and could still,
> Were not this glorious casket stor'd with ill.
> But I must tell you, now my thoughts revolt;
> For he's no man on whom perfections wait
> That, knowing sin within, will touch the gate. (I.i.77–81)

Hearing likewise is infected in the image of the "fair viol," within which we cannot not hear "vile" and perhaps also subliminally a casket-like "vial."[11] If neither eye nor ear can mediate and interpret the world cleanly and clearly, how can an audience be comfortable in the "pleasures" of Gower's play tale? Such pleasures in language and desire alike here curdle.

In answer to Antiochus' demand, Pericles reveals how he has taken the infection, revoicing the double-bind by a piece of indirection which also reveals and conceals:

> Great king,
> Few love to hear the sins they love to act;
> 'Twould braid yourself too near for me to tell it.
> Who has a book of all that monarchs do,
> He's more secure to keep it shut than shown. (I.i.92–6)

One may have knowledge but yet no way to use or live with it. Even the attempt at concealment is doomed to failure. Pericles reveals what he knows to Antiochus and no-one else – the secret understanding between them remains intact:

> For vice repeated is like the wand'ring wind,
> Blows dust in others' eyes to spread itself;
> And yet the end of all is bought thus dear,
> The breath is gone, and the sore eyes see clear
> To stop the air would hurt them. (I.i.97–101)

The language is opaque, parabolic, has its own secret interior. Yet Antiochus sees into it, knows that Pericles knows because he cannot not reveal himself. Given the privy strangling in the last line, it might be better to be blind. Yet blindness is just as deadly, as it is with the "blind mole" which dares tell tales on its oppressor. Neither blindness nor insight will serve and Pericles bows to the bare ubiquity of power ("and if Jove stray, who dares say Jove doth ill"), and imposes a "speechless tongue" upon himself.

Act I, scene ii clearly shows Pericles' condition of infected knowledge in his melancholy withdrawal and desultory loss of pleasure:

> Here pleasures court mine eyes, and mine eyes shun them,
> And danger, which I fear'd, is at Antioch,
> Whose arm seems far too short to hit me here;
> Yet neither pleasure's art can joy my spirits,
> Nor yet the other's distance comfort me.
> Then it is thus: the passions of the mind
> That have their first conception by mis-dread
> Have after-nourishment and life by care.   (I.ii.7–14)

Pericles has returned from Antioch with a breeding "fear" which he nurses pathologically. Wilson Knight's comment is apposite: "He seems to feel guilt, yet is uncertain how far the 'offence' is his own."[12] This uncertainty over collusion is just the point. Pericles himself glosses this "mis-dread" (an odd coinage – as though he understands he has feared the wrong object) as an obsession with Antiochus' military power, but it is clear that it is as much the thought of his "greatness" that disables a Pericles who is "too little to contend." The obsessive, nightmarish quality of the meditation points to an overshadowing by the "bed of blackness," in which he admits (lines 19–20) he is implicated willy-nilly. Hallucinations of national abjection mime his own stance before the internal image of this bloated potentate, with whom, having colluded, it is impossible to compete:

> With hostile forces he'll o'erspread the land,
> And with th'ostent of war will look so huge,
> Amazement shall drive courage from the state,
> Our men be vanquished e'er they do resist,
> And subjects punish'd that ne'er thought offence.   (I.ii.25–9)

As Pericles sees it, he is doing Antiochus' job for him in a defensive gesture of atonement and self-emasculation before the hideously sublime spectacle of his opponent. Crouched before the jealous god in whom Aristotle did not believe, Pericles endures a twofold nightmare in which the world of natural plenty becomes a universe of death and the world of signs a play of deathly surfaces. The middle movements of the play will oscillate between and combine these two visions under the rubrics of the sea and the kingdom, tyrannies of nature and of artifice. How can plenitude and clarity be reconciled, sign and world reunited? The urgency of this question is generated not only from the antinomies of the tale, but from the general cultural situation of Shakespeare's drama in its restless concern with the promise of dramatic incarnation as a mode of inter-weaving natural and verbal/intellectual orders. The very emblematic simplicity of the scene with Helicanus bears within it the recognition of a melancholy it cannot correct:

> ... I went to Antioch,
> Whereas thou know'st, against the face of death
> I sought the purchase of a glorious beauty,
> From whence an issue I might propagate,
> Are arms to princes and bring joys to subjects.
> Her face was to mine eye beyond all wonder;
> The rest, hark in thine ear, as black as incest. (I.ii.70–6)

Death and wonder occupy the face together here, and again we hear the language of Gower's promise to us ("the purchase is to make men glorious"). Again the aesthetic and semiotic problem of the false surface turns into the intimation of mortality. The face of beauty screens that of death, like the "glorious casket stored with ill."

II

The opening section of *Pericles* presents us with a tale in which the common pleasures that keep the human attached to a habitable world become heavily shadowed by intimations of concealment and force. Language becomes opaquely figurative, desire a tangled knot, beauty fatal delusion. The play's own increasing fragmentation in space and time, its reversion to simplicities (if not banalities) of action and staging, may be a response to this strain. There are signs that it wishes to imagine a repair. Pericles' intervention at famine-struck Tharsus is one attempt to reverse some of the damage, to correct both the universe of death where mothers eat their babies (I.iv.42–4), and the deceit of signs through Pericles' white sails that mean, despite Cleon's misgivings, just what they seem to (lines 74–5). But though Pericles is monumentalized at Tharsus, where they "Build his statue to make him glorious" (II.Pr.14) the play is not satisfied with the material persistence of objects like statues as an image of survival: statues tell no tales. Mere good deeds will not suffice.

The diffuseness of the middle Acts, especially Act II, may be thus less a structural weakness than a kind of symptom. Part chivalric fantasy and part populist romp, Act II seems to respond at some level to the twofold generic roots referred to in Gower's opening, but the mix is uneasy, and the play's reliance on a simple emblematic style makes it endearing but vulnerable to the suspicion that one's sympathies are being programmed. The play seems not to have understood the implications of the opening scene about the coercive potential of theatrical spectacle. Through the Act, the destructive rapacity of the "merely" natural is counterposed against a fantasy of social goodwill and community. Aristocratic merit, peasant ebullience, and unjealous paternity are all bathed in the warmth of common generosity like a nostalgic cartoon. Instead of paranoia, we get Pollyannaism. One can almost hear Ben Jonson shudder.

The opening of Act II also presents the first of the play's "dumb-shows," those archaic-seeming mimes. Though Gower introduces these vignettes for "your eyes" with the contentious question "what need speak I?" they remain stiff devices: simple in design, but remarkably difficult to interpret. Emblematic truths of the eye are not alone sufficient. It is important to the play's concern with transmission that all three dumb-shows (II.i, III.i, and IV.iv) concern the delivery of messages, and that we keep being assured that apparent meanings are true. They both fore-shorten the narrative, drawing attention to the technical aspects of getting a story told, and recall the potential of shows to become screens: the pageant of Marina's false monument (IV.iv) is only the most obvious example.

Beneath the rubrics alike of sentimental pictorialism and manipulative power-politics, the play keeps returning to scarcity and chaos as limit conditions of human life. At the outset of Act II, this is bodied forth as the sea from which a "wet" Pericles emerges:

> Yet cease your ire, you angry stars of heaven!
> Wind, rain, and thunder, remember, earthly man
> Is but a substance that must yield to you;
> And I, as fits my nature, do obey you.
> Alas, the seas hath cast me on the rocks,
> Washed me from shore to shore, and left me breath
> Nothing to think on but ensuing death.
> Let it suffice the greatness of your powers
> To have bereft a prince of all his fortunes;
> And having thrown him from your wat'ry grave,
> Here to have death in peace is all he'll crave.   (II.i.1–11)

The similarity to *Lear* is striking, but the note is resignation rather than outrage. Yet from this watery ascesis, the play at once pulls back into a kind of littoral pastoral in the fishermen, who combine the language of festive renewal with Christian populism. The scene is full of references to English customs and conditions which mark it as self-consciously popular, if not populist; it is the generic counterpart to Gower's archaic dumb-shows with their *Gorboduc* pedigree.

The chivalric society of Simonides' court at Pentapolis also matches the style of the fisher commune: a cartoonish feudalism where all is ceremonial order.[13] Amid its pageantry and picture-book *imprese*, King

Simonides is just the figure the play needs to weigh against Antiochus.[14] When the lords mock Pericles at the pre-tournament ride-by, Simonides complains: "Opinion's but a fool that makes us scan / The outward habit for the inward man," forecasting Pericles' upset victory.[15] As at Tharsus, Pericles reverses the expectations of a world-weary cynicism, and as if in answer, the gods choose this precise moment to strike down Antiochus "even in the height and pride of all his glory," a vengeance that lifts the gaudy surface and seems to restore faith in the clarity of signs.[16] This reversal of Antiochan paranoia is even clearer in what follows. Understandably wary of royal fathers where marriage is concerned, Pericles assumes that the letter from Thaisa which Simonides angrily proffers is "the king's subtlety to have my life" (II.v.44). The sequel is a burlesque of the tensions which made the first scene so unfunny. Simonides is quite happy to play jealous father for a nuptial purpose. His threatening "I'll tame you" is promptly disarmed by a joke which undoes the old double-bind of Antioch. This time around, Pericles cannot not be married:

> Therefore hear your mistress: either frame
> Your will to mine; and you, sir, hear you:
> Either be rul'd by me, or I'll make you –
> Man and wife.   (II.v.80–3)

This strangely simple wish-father then boots the bewildered couple into bed and slams the door on the second Act.

The throwback dramaturgy of Presenter and dumb-show, the sententious sentimentality of fishermen and ogre-Fathers, even the romantic evocation of a wide and wild world invite attention to both the pleasures and pitfalls of cultural nostalgia. By the end of the second Act, Pericles has traversed the narrative design of a marriage comedy, with its shaping of a general arena of consent between generations and sexes that allows characters and audience to turn to a future outside the play. But if these Acts at first present and then defuse the threat of a rapaciously selfish and tyrannical past that will let nothing escape into the future, the underlying condition of that threat – the vulnerability of human life to change and decay – appears at the outset of the third Act, and demands in answer greater poetic and dramaturgical resources than a smiling Simonides.

III

The diction and rhythms that open Act III (generally felt by readers to mark a new level of skill in the play) recall particularly the closing tetrameters of *A Midsummer Night's Dream*, with the snores, the household mice, and the sexual activity of the wedding-night.[17] In *Pericles*, the end of the "marriage comedy" is only another threshold: "Hymen hath brought the bride to bed, / Where by the loss of maidenhead / A babe is moulded" (III.Pr.9–11). The rest of the play will explore this economy of loss and recompense, locating the work of tales and imagination in relation to procreation and sexuality.

As if at once to highlight and overcome the risk of total loss suggested in Thaisa's disastrous labor, just here Gower's commentary strikes a newly urgent note: "Be attent, / And time that is so briefly spent / With your fine fancies quaintly eche; / What's dumb in show I'll plain with speech" (III.Pr.11–14). "Eching" is the play's term for the collective creativity of tale-making or re-making, one shared among actors and audience. There may even be a homophonic ghost suggesting that "each" listener will remake the tale according to particular need of "fancy." Gower's offer to "waste" his life finds its answer in the audience's willingness to augment or supplement his labor:

> I nill relate, action may
> Conveniently the rest convey;
> Which might not what by me is told.
> In your imagination hold
> This stage the ship, upon whose deck
> The sea-tost Pericles appears to speak.   (III.Pr.55–60)

The site of the narrative is doubled here over the enjambment "hold / This stage," where "hold" means at once "consider" and "contain," just as the antecedent of "whose deck" is both "imagination" and "ship," so that the place of the story is both the material stage and "your imagination." Narration is not an event about the world only, but also an event in and about the mind and its faculties as they apprehend and construe the world. The imagination is a kind of creative "hold" like that of a ship, or perhaps, given the narrative context, like a kind of womb.

But the storm at sea suggests the world may be simply too strong and painful to be borne by a merely human mind at its mercy. In the world-as-storm drastic measures are necessary which fragment all our continuities, leaving them abrupt and diminished. Storm shadows the turbulent strait that runs between generations, the risk inherent in reproduction, the dependence of mind on body. With the death of Thaisa, his baby daughter is presented to Pericles as a consolatory fragment or synecdoche:

LYCHORIDA   ... Take in your arms this piece
                  Of your dead queen.
PERICLES   How? How, Lychorida?
LYCHORIDA   Patience, good sir; do not assist the storm.
                  Here's all that is left living of your queen,
                  A little daughter: for the sake of it,
                  Be manly and take comfort.
PERICLES   O you gods!
                  Why do you make us love your goodly gifts,
                  And snatch them straight away?   (III.i.17–24)

Time's economy is loss and restitution. The world is ruffled by a blustering rapacity made bearable only by the ambivalent gift of forgetting: "We here below / Recall not what we give and therein may / Use honour with you" (24–6). Though Lychorida urges "Patience," Pericles refuses recompense and denies synecdoche its consolatory or representational magic: "Even at the first thy [the child's] loss is more than can / Thy portage quit, with all thou canst find here" (III.i.35–6). Eventually the play will suggest a more recuperative economy: that the fragment or trope not only compensates for the whole, but is the only human means of recovering that whole through a dialectic of wounding and mending, fate and miracle, which parallels biological processes.

Already in this scene there are hints of a counter-movement. The unnamed baby is "this fresh new seafarer" – an epithet which suggests a congregation of literal and figurative meaning. This child's position as sponsor or locus of magically true names is heightened by Shakespeare's decision to have her called "Marina."[18] What offsets the losses of nature and time, it appears, is the richness of meaning that language has the power to sediment, which includes a power not only to name the world, but to translate into it by that naming the pressure of human need and desire.

So far however, the dialectical counter-movement of language remains no more than a bare hint, and in the meantime the sailors insist that Thaisa's corpse be jettisoned so that the storm can abate, a superstition that follows the storm's own logic of loss. Over Thaisa's body, as the storm rages, Pericles speaks his famous elegy:

A terrible childbed hast thou had, my dear;
No light, no fire: th'unfriendly elements
Forgot thee utterly; nor have I time
To give thee hallow'd to thy grave, but straight
Must cast thee, scarcely coffin'd, in the ooze;
Where, for a monument upon thy bones,
And e'er-remaining lamps, the belching whale
And humming water must o'erwhelm thy corpse,

Lying with simple shells. O Lychorida,
Bid Nestor bring me spices, ink and paper,
My casket and my jewels; and bid Nicander
Bring me the satin coffer; lay the babe
Upon the pillow; hie thee. . . .   (III.i.56–68)

Again there are counter-hints in the very description of Thaisa's resting-place. In place of formal memorial, there is the strange music of "belching whale and humming water." The whale's belch in an earlier scene (II.i) had brought the fisherman's swallowed parish back up again, and though Thaisa's stasis seems of an almost unearthly quiet, "lying with simple shells," the whale and the general air of large turbulent process above the sea-floor seem already to expect her restoration from some deep but not lasting relegation.[19] This hint is carried through when Thaisa's casket is recovered by Cerimon's men, one of whom comments that "If the sea's stomach be o'ercharged with gold, / 'Tis a good constraint of fortune / It belches upon us" (III.ii.54–6).

When Cerimon restores Thaisa to the world from her rich and strange chrysalis, he works through all the natural senses – sight, smell, touch, hearing, and taste – if Wilkins's account is an index to stage action:[20]

I GENT   The heavens, through you, increase our wonder,
            And set up your fame forever.
CERIMON   She is alive!
            Behold, her eyelids, cases to those
            Heavenly jewels which Pericles hath lost,
            Begin to part their fringes of bright gold.
            The diamonds of a most praised water
            Doth appear to make the world twice rich. Live,
            And make us weep to hear your fate, fair creature,
            Rare as you seem to be. (*She moves.*)
THAISA   O dear Diana,
            Where am I? Where's my lord? What world is this?
                                                    (III.ii.99–108)

As in *A Midsummer Night's Dream*, it is as though humans had briefly acquired the clarity and permanence, but also the strangeness, of jewels. The wonder of the scene is focused in eyes and the act of looking, in the very slowness with which Cerimon unfurls the revival, as though something were slowly crystallizing in the "water" (is it tears?) of those eye-diamonds.[21] The emotional tone of the moment depends on a sense of the newness of the objects presented to the viewers' eyes, but also on their willingness to welcome these objects into their world. And this willingness is immediately linked to a lively sense of the theatre's powers of vivification. Cerimon's pronouncement "She is alive" has about it the delightful air of stating the obvious: of course she is, we might say, anyone can see that. But only in the self-conscious ambience of that moment can we re-examine in such exquisite detail what it means to see another's liveliness. Notably too, the astonished inspection of the living body leads directly to a demand for narration, which will fulfill the desire for significant contact that visual inspection has begun.

The "delivery" of Thaisa out of her watery box, so that she keeps something of the watery about her – in her eyes and her listeners' tears – suggests a connection with the (absent) scene of her death in childbirth. There is something of the "midwife" about Cerimon here, as though he and Lychorida were counterparts in delivering life from the maelstrom, as though the undersea world of "belching whale and humming porpoise" were a kind of *in vivo* amniotic tumult. Thaisa's first exclamation also bespeaks her sense of delivery into a strange new world. This would make Cerimon's medicinal expertise the third of a set of renovators of the human in the play (along with Pericles at Tharsus and Gower in his tale). All three modes are eventually subsumed in Marina. It would also explain the felt link between Cerimon and Prospero and connect intellectual and scientific knowledge to the play's larger questions about the re-creative function of human pleasure:

> I hold it ever,
> Virtue and cunning were endowments greater
> Than nobleness and riches; careless heirs
> May the two latter darken and expend,
> But immortality attends the former,
> Making a man a god. 'Tis known I ever
> Have studied physic ... which doth give me
> A more content in course of true delight
> Than to be thirsty after tottering honour,
> Or tie my pleasure up in silken bags,
> To please the fool and death. (III.ii.26–32, 38–42)

Science is a form of "pleasure," as much a part of human destiny as sexual pleasure.[22]

The question of gender in Shakespearean romance bears further examination, however. The cardinal importance of daughters in Shakespeare's plays of marriage, heightened in these late plays, has been frequently remarked. Recent feminist criticism has stressed the interest of early-modern society, if not all human society, in monitoring and delimiting reproduction. But Shakespeare's interest in sexual difference is not only societal. It is also connected to his recurrent concern to define the relation between the broad world of natural process within which human life unfolds and the narrative and metaphoric processes by which human agency and consciousness are asserted within that horizon. Any observer of human life cannot help noting that the burden of reproduction falls unequally on the sexes. Childbirth imposes a high risk of death on women, a risk much graver before the advent of modern medicine. A decision to engage in sexual activity in such a situation must involve some notion of wager, perhaps even a consciousness of gift. It is the shadow of this gift, and the love which it moralizes, that imparts the very real pathos as well as energy to many of Shakespeare's comic heroines. It lies in part behind Beatrice's melancholy before the image of her cousin Hero about to be married, in her sense that her birth, far from being "a merry hour," was a time when "my mother cried" (and perhaps died). Along with the social costs and benefits of the marriage market, Shakespeare never forgets the darker core of biological need and threat.

Childbirth is thus linked in a basic way in these plays to story-telling: both are forms of creative maintenance. It may be that Shakespeare did not regard sex as a specialized "reproductive practice" set off from others, but as part of a continuum of semantic activities broadly nameable as "bringing the human into the world." Story-telling is another aspect of this continuum, and especially theatre insofar as it produces actual bodies that incarnate their stories in space and time. Shakespeare's attraction to the erotic as a primary topic of dramatic representation is involved here, as is also his sense of the generative, even erotic, charge that words bear, a charge that seeks the world as its counterpart.[23] Terry Eagleton's suggestive assertion that Shakespeare's central dream is of language united to the body goes only part of the way.[24] It is not "unity" that language and body seek, it is something more like "correspondence" – a dialectical interanimation by which each realizes the other's needs and desires in the world. Nor is that world a Newtonian flatness of dead matter: its objects are themselves charged with the desires that other, earlier language has shaped in them. Language seeks incorporation as part of its ultimate task of delivering the world to mental touch, as a body driven by erotic desire seeks another body. Sex is therefore the moment at which Shakespeare's characters seek in the profoundest sense to know the world. And there is always risk in that encounter.

To be a woman in such a universe involves a heavier share of both risk and gain. This conjunction helps explain why the economic and the erotic so frequently trope each other in the plays. As potential child-bearers, women also figure, or rather "participate," the conjunction of word and world in the strange magic of linguistic incarnation.[25] Thus women are most often the guardians of language in Shakespeare's plays of sexual success, and the less that stewardship is active or effective, the more brittle tend to be the energies of the play – as in *Measure for Measure*, for instance, or *The Tempest*.

There is likewise in these plays a link between sexual reproduction and the dramaturgy of wonder which explains their consistent turn to the recovery of female, and especially maternal, figures in their climactic scenes. The reproduction of the past, its availability to the present, even, perhaps especially, in a shape modified by the pressure of time – as a child is both like and unlike its parents – is a cardinal object of wonder in Shakespeare. *Pericles* has named the cognate task in the theatre the "eching" – the enlargement or augmentation – of the story. It is as though for Shakespeare there were a deep truth to the etymological connection between the *res gestae* or "chanson de geste," the "gester" as public entertainer, and "gestation."

IV

It is not surprising then that Gower links Marina's artistic ability intimately to her sexuality:

> Now to Marina bend your mind,
> Whom our fast-growing scene must find
> At Tharsus, and by Cleon train'd
> In music's letters; who hath gain'd
> Of education all the grace,
> Which makes her both the heart and place
> Of general wonder. . . .
> Be't when she weav'd the sleided silk
> With fingers long, small, white as milk;
> Or when she would with sharp neele wound
> The cambric, which she made more sound
> By hurting it; or when to th'lute
> She sung, and made the night-bird mute
> That still records with moan; or when
> She would with rich and constant pen
> Vail to her mistress Dian.   (IV.Pr.5–11, 21–9)

In embroidery, Marina's skill balances trauma with recompense, breach with strengthening, just as did the account of her conception. Sexual wounding also surfaces in Marina's singing, which silences the ancient rape that the nightingale "still records with moan." A small fiction of therapy flits in this image of the singing voice, as though Marina had for a moment assuaged Philomela's pain. Her poetry locates the origin of these powers in Marina's virginity – "rich and constant" like her pen – but in this it always points to, has to do with, sexual experience. It is minutely close to the actively sexual, yet skirts it. The skill with which Marina treads this boundary, alluding to sexual contact without under-going it, is part of the play's strategic fascination with her, and glosses the centrality of women making sexual choices throughout the romances. Marina is a liminal figure, even a fantasy one, combining virginity and sexuality in a highly charged compound. Her activities with "neele" and "pcn" displace and convert the violence and risk of sex in the service of a creativity glossed as a female control. To see these implements (and perhaps the nightingale's thorn also) as incipiently or "properly" male would be to close a metaphoric gap from which the play derives great power – though Shakespeare himself, for whom biological and cultural reproduction are always interinvolved, will eventually do just this.

When she appears, the scene fills with echoes of Proserpina – another flower-culling virgin confronting sexual violence – and with the claims of memory, as she strews her flowers on Lychorida's grave. She is quite aware of the implications of her name and peculiar history as a strange site of union between literal and metaphoric:

> Ay me! poor maid,
> Born in a tempest, when my mother died,
> This world to me is as a lasting storm,
> Whirring me from my friends.   (IV.i.17–20)

This concern unfolds too in her sojourn in the Mitylene brothel, where she resists a series of attempts to represent her in any way that refuses to acknowledge the literal state of her predicament.[26] Verbal evasions of its human meaning are the very stuff of the brothel business. Routinely, the bawds speak of their girls as commodities: "creatures," "stuff," and "baggage." Marina is a "sapling," a "joint," a horse for the "manage." Twice she is a "piece," perhaps recalling her birth as a "piece of your dead queen" though this time the synecdoche is a commercial parcelling. Every attribute has its particular market value:

BAWD Boult, take you the marks of her, the colour of her hair, complexion, height, her age, with warrant of her virginity, and cry "He that will give most shall have her first." Such a maidenhead were no cheap thing, if men were as they have been. (IV.ii.53–5)

This crying abroad repeats the theatrical show of Antiochus' daughter. Boult "draw[s] her picture with [his] voice" (IV.ii.92), and the hearers listen "as they would have hearken'd to their father's testament." Piecemeal, she becomes the price of her hymen.

The Bawds urge Marina to suppress before the customers the true names for where she is. The goal of this dissimulation is greater profit by exciting in equal parts pity and desire in the customers and flattering their self-esteem:

BAWD Mark me: you must seem to do that fearfully which you commit willingly; despise profit where you have most gain. To weep that you live as ye do ... begets you a good opinion, and that opinion a mere profit.
MARINA I understand you not. (IV.ii.115–21)

Marina in fact carries out these instructions quite literally. When we see her before Lysimachus she staunchly refuses to behave, or to allow her situation to be named, any way but directly. She relentlessly insists that Lysimachus put names to his desires precisely where he wishes to mask in expedient pseudonyms:

LYSIMACHUS   Now, pretty one, how long have you been at this trade?
MARINA   What trade, sir?
LYSIMACHUS   Why, I cannot name't but I shall offend.
MARINA   I cannot be offended with my trade. Please you to name it.
LYSIMACHUS   How long have you been of this profession?
MARINA   E'er since I can remember.
LYSIMACHUS   Did you go to't so young? Were you a gamester at five or at seven?
MARINA   Earlier too, sir, if now I be one. (IV.vi.65–75)

This insistence on having the literal names of the intended acts spoken keeps Marina safe, as a storm of euphemisms, slang, and abuse rages in comic fury around her. Lysimachus, like all the brothel's clients, cannot bring himself to name what he wants and therefore cannot perform it. Behind this verbal niceness we note the obscuring riddle which opened the play and the crippled silence of Antiochus' daughter, who could find no clear route into speech for what was done to her.[27]

Against Marina's singular insistence on a clarity both representational and moral, a violence that might fragment her consistency is the only recourse. The Bawd's exasperated instruction to Boult to "Crack the glass of her virginity, and make the rest malleable" (IV.vi.142) again suggests the "fair glass of light" which was Antiochus' daughter. But the notion of virginity as a "glass" also points to Marina's saving knack of reflecting back images of her clients as they most deeply do not wish to see themselves. Maidenhead has here a power like Hamlet's magic mirror, and finding the right language clarifies the stakes of a moment. In this respect, Marina can be taken as an emblem of Shakespearean representation itself, at least in one of its aspects.

Stephen Mullaney's very suggestive discussion of these scenes finds in them a deliberate avoidance of any analogy between the commercial theatre and the brothel as a site for selling tales.[28] Yet though the scenes do omit the telling of her story that Marina's counterpart in Twine performs, the sense of Marina as a scrupulous shaper of words maintains the play's concern with verbal transmission.[29] What Marina points to is a consciousness of when and how a tale may be told that subsists, even with the emergence of a market-place for narrative. Marina challenges what a suspicious hermeneutic would deny: that commerce must necessarily debase the exchange of narratives as cultural work. This might be called a sentimental fantasy, but the issue is surely neither as simple nor as closed as that – as the outcome of *Pericles* will attempt to show by justifying the audience's expense by its recompense.

V

Marina's recovery of Pericles from the dumb, frozen, and barely human figure he has become is the play's final example of the power of story-telling to give human consciousness a bearable habitation in the world. The scene is set up so that the progressive "opening" of experience and world to each other is inflected through the turbulent passage of wonder from violence to knowledge and recognition.

Gower's prologue to Act V again proclaims Marina's accomplishments, and connects her sexually liminal status and her miraculous ability to "deliver" (the word is increasingly important) human artifice into the world as its counterpart:

> Deep clerks she dumbs, and with her neele composes
> Nature's own shape, of bud, bird, branch, or berry,
> That even her art sisters the natural roses;
> Her inkle, silk twin with the rubied cherry.   (V.i.5–8)

Marina has apparently the same effect on "deep clerks" that Antiochus' daughter had on suitors – though there is no suggestion that a secret power is being deployed to malicious advantage. She resembles the daughter also in that, though she is not as absolutely foreclosed, she has her own dumbness. Not every story can be told all the time, it appears, and the end of the play will be much occupied with what the conditions of possibility of a telling are. It is not "learning" that makes for creative skill in narration.

The citation of Marina's needlework returns us to the links between creativity and sexuality. Here the play seems deliberately to recall the Helena of *A Midsummer Night's Dream* who lamented how she and Hermia had embroidered together like "two artificial gods" or "a double cherry seeming parted." With Marina the anticipation of loss, focused for us in the economy of needlework's wounding, twins not with a second self (Dionysa's daughter, for instance) but with the "natural roses." The verse insists on a sisterhood of word and thing: the world is made up and offered to human ears out of phonemes that voice out its fruitful unfolding on the lips and tongue as "bud, bird, branch, or berry." The subtle declension of sound, here almost Keatsian, suggests there is a developmental power in language akin to the process that animates the world. Artifice reveals and illuminates that power, as the multiple echoing in "inkle, silk twin" embroiders the lines and underscores the sistering and the twinning.

Against this image of a dialectic between word and world, the play sets Pericles, for whom both have assumed the unyielding quality of a stone. He is discovered immobile, fixed and speechless, a male Niobe fulfilling the curse laid on him by Antiochus so long ago, of "speechless tongue and semblance pale." Marina's approach to him is both a seduction and an assault: "with her sweet harmony / And other chosen attractions" to "allure, / And make a batt'ry through his deafen'd ports, / Which now are midway stopp'd" (V.i.44–7). A simultaneous drawing out and bursting in will overcome what is conceived as a blockage to intercourse with the world. The language of difficulty and force mixed with pleasure here should alert us at once to the presence of the dynamic of wonder, imagined as a psychotherapy blasting its way back to erotic springs of vitality. There is a sense of Pericles as sunk, somewhat like Thaisa, into an almost unreachable depth. When Marina pledges to "use / My utmost skill in his recovery" (V.i.75–6) the phrasing gives a particularly active, verb-like force to the final noun.[30]

Marina's first attempt, an unrecorded song, elicits nothing from Pericles.[31] Her request that he "lend ear" at least gets a response – a grunt and a shove.[32] Perhaps surprised at the depth and violence of Pericles' resistance, Marina breaks into a rather exasperated speech in which she offers herself first as an object appealing to the eye, second as a fellow sufferer comparing griefs, third as a member of a noble family with a disastrous history:

> I am a maid,
> My lord, that ne'er before invited eyes,
> But have been gaz'd on like a comet; she speaks,
> My lord, that, may be, hath endur'd a grief
> Might equal yours, if both were justly weigh'd.
> Though wayward fortune did malign my state,
> My derivation was from ancestors
> Who stood equivalent with mighty kings;
> But time hath rooted out my parentage,
> And to the world and awkward casualties
> Bound me in servitude.   (V.i.84–94)

There is at first surprise and even disappointment at Pericles' unresponsiveness. Evoking wonder in onlookers has been her means of survival, but also, it appears, a burden that has distanced her from them and disabled intimacy. It has concealed behind the dazzle "a grief" at bondage to "the world and awkward casualties." Though she moves to go, she is prompted back by a mysterious blushing voice: "I will desist; / But there is something glows upon my cheek, / And whispers in mine ear 'Go not till he speak'" (V.i.94–6). This has a distinctly erotic sound, coinciding with the unexpected rise of Pericles to the word "parentage," which he anticipates as "good parentage – / To equal mine." With hesitant, dim reminiscence he breaks off: "You're something like that –" but the glimpse is enough. What startles Pericles out of himself and towards speech and the world is an unexpected moment of doubling: before his eyes suddenly floats and speaks an embodied image he had thought his silent and particular property. It is a measure of Shakespeare's confidence in the mind's fittedness for the world that recognition is so swift. Pericles cannot help seeing in Marina what there is to see. We take in the world before we speak it. The moment is a kind of reverse "uncanny" where the doubt that flickers about the strange incarnation from within is not of fear, but hope.

Marina offers in response to his urgency what sounds like a riddle on her paradoxically literal history:

> PERICLES   ... [Are you] of these shores?
> MARINA   No, nor of any shores;
>   Yet was I mortally brought forth, and am
>   No other than I appear.
> PERICLES   I am great with woe
>   And shall deliver weeping.   (V.i.103–6)

This suggests resolution through a "riddle-and-answer" encounter echoing the opening scene. Shakespeare had used this tactic in both *Measure for Measure* and *All's Well that Ends Well* and it is that of his sources, where the daughter's identity is discovered through riddles she puts to her father.[33] But Pericles ignores the riddle and focuses instead on the seeing and telling that unfolds from the figure before him. His image for this picks up the earlier suggestion of blockage and tropes it into an image of childbirth that responds precisely to the nest of associations Marina's figure has galvanized into motion: "I am great with woe / And shall deliver weeping." Weeping here is both action and result, noun and adjective. He weeps and cries, and the life he delivers is that weeping and that woe, a birthing that gives him back to the world through emotional attachment to what he sees before him. Lychorida's consolatory synecdoche has retained its power, and paid recompense in its own coin. The fact of family resemblance, a natural sign, allows the traumatic cargo of experience to be brought into the world. Marina opens a figurative link between inner and outer registers of experience:

> I am great with woe
> And shall deliver weeping. My dearest wife
> Was like this maid, and such a one
> My daughter might have been: my queen's square brows;
> Her stature to an inch; as wand-like straight;
> As silver-voic'd; her eyes as jewel-like
> And cas'd as richly; in pace another Juno;
> Who starves the ears she feeds, and makes them hungry
> The more she gives them speech.   (V.i.105–13)

By the end of this speech it is not entirely clear whether Pericles is speaking of Thaisa or Marina, and as the two merge he evokes a dynamic kind of erotic and emotional economy, of filling and emptying at once.[34] The lines are worth dwelling on. Their ultimate ancestor seems to be the Ovidian paradox "inopem me copia fecit" of Narcissus (*Metamorphoses* III): an economic image for the relation of a bounteous self to an erotic desire that meets no answering object and, prevented from circulating into the world and returning enriched by exchange, stifles in surfeit. Pericles' desire is directed not to a self-image, but to an image of the self's own erotic success, even if that success is marked by loss. For him the doubling of Marina's image with Thaisa's invests both with a plenitude of desire which gives him a hold on a world of real objects and persons. Unlike Ovid's Narcissus, it is not a phantasm of desire written on the reflective surface of a "thin film of water" ("exigua prohibemur aqua"), the "almost nothing" ("minimum est") of a difference between literal and figure.[35] The therapeutic efficacy of Marina's image stems from a biographical fact which underpins the figure and gives it the heightened ambience of miracle. This fragile consonance tropes the Antiochan sexual hunger so close to the scene into one for recognition, speech, and story-telling. Language is the register where the world is remade in order to manage the dangers of the literal, but Marina guarantees that the figurative recompense can have its own truth. Ovid's frustration and skepticism are replaced by a strange confidence in an ability to see, know, and tell. This confidence works its way forward through the energies of wonder towards a mutual fluidity and responsiveness of self, language, and world.

One way to see the importance of this move for Shakespeare's poetics as a whole is to see in it just how Shakespeare identifies the work of his dramatic poetry as the assertion of what we might call a belief in the "proper metaphor." Theories of metaphor from Aristotle onwards often speak in terms of a disruptive difference from a "proper" language for naming the world. In Shakespeare, a surplus of signification in language is set over against a surging at once of desires in the self and of ever-shifting forms in the world. At the same time, there subsists a profound belief in the possibility of correspondence between self, world, and language through their very fluidity. That this is difficult to achieve gives bite to his tragedies; that it is possible gives them their profound sense of something narrowly if irrevocably missed. We have seen how one formulation for its achievement is put in the marriage comedies as Helena's sense of the beloved as "my own and not my own." In later plays, as here in *Pericles*, the miracle is that metaphor is true. Metaphor is revealed as precisely that which is adequate to the world, which by its very fluidity is proper to both world and self. Recall for instance Marina's singing and needlework which so successfully matched ima-ginary and real objects and scenes of desire, and thereby managed her knowledge of the world, including its threats. By metaphor, the world is redelivered to the self, which discovers in that delivery its own deep desire for the world. The extension of the notion of the "proper metaphor" towards the dimension of the world's temporal unfolding brings us directly to the need to "tell" – to spin world and self alike into narration in order to match their shiftings to each other. Narration is an attempt to find a livable truth for the world that self confronts; it keeps up the links to living. Hence, narration is a fundamental and natural human desire – part of a continuum of drives towards commerce with the world that includes those for food and sex. As Pericles begins to recover, he emerges into love and narration at once as a starving man might. His ears demand their food.

Marina, however, is suspicious of Pericles' eagerness, as well she might be given her sense of her own tale as similarly obstructed: we are told that "being demanded that, / She would sit still and weep" (V.i.188–9). Even she, it seems, can hardly believe in her story's credibility as narrative: "If I should tell my history, 'twould seem / Like lies, disdain'd in the reporting" (V.i.118–19). Pericles, however, bases his confidence on the conviction of his remembered desire:

> Falseness cannot come from thee, for thou look'st
> Modest as Justice, and thou seem'st a palace
> For the crown'd Truth to dwell in. I will believe thee,
> And make my senses credit thy relation
> To points that seem impossible; for thou look'st
> Like one I loved indeed.   (V.i.120–5)

A peculiar jerky momentum or oscillation develops between narration and stasis. Marina appears as an abstract and atemporal personification, at the same time as she looks "like one I loved indeed." The scene wishes to emblematize Marina into an allegorical image, thus giving her an unchanging value, and yet not to freeze her in this way – it fluctuates and heaves with an emotion it calls "opening" (line 132) that at once suggests a therapeutic procedure performed on some improperly healed wound and recollects the various revelatory openings through the play – of eyes, of chests, of caskets, and even of the fearful "bed of blackness" (I.ii.89). Categories and hierarchies threaten to dissolve under the pressure of such "opening": Pericles envisions a radical reversal of sexual and psychological roles and of normal temporal logic in the exchange of griefs. Again there is the rhythm of hesitation, backtracking, and the recourse – part celebration, part defense – to allegorical abstraction:

> Tell thy story;
> If thine consider'd prove the thousandth part
> Of my endurance, thou art a man, and I
> Have suffer'd like a girl; yet thou dost look
> Like Patience gazing on kings' graves, and smiling
> Extremity out of act. (V.i.134–9)

Where Marina hesitates, Pericles demands, and he hangs back where she speaks. He cries "O stop there a little" as if to stretch out his emotions and explore their unfolding moment. He insists "I'll hear you more" when she in turn attempts to break off. She must demand over and over his attentive faith in literal narrative truths that intimately resemble impossible metaphors. Narrative itself comes to feel like metaphor: the work of story-telling puts the past back together into intelligible sequence (here Aristotle nods agreement), but its ability to do so is itself hardly short of the miraculous. The success of the play, of the mind, in doing this for itself is a source of great power – and hence of a potential, if unexpected, threat to the very self that recognizes and uses that success. The curious oscillation of the scene between blockage and progress, pain and delight, resistance and recovery maps very closely the unstable dynamic of wonder as it disrupts commonplaces of self and world in just this way.

Pericles promises at last that "I will believe you by the syllable / Of what you shall deliver" (V.i.167–8). This delivery is once again both message and child, and that child Pericles himself:

> O Helicanus, strike me, honour'd sir!
> Give me a gash, put me to present pain,
> Lest this great sea of joys rushing upon me
> O'erbear the shores of my mortality,
> And drown me with their sweetness. O, come hither,
> Thou that beget'st him that did thee beget;

Thou that wast born at sea, buried at Tharsus,
And found at sea again.   (V.i.190–7)

The first image here manages emotional stress through an imagined preventive bodily pain – a determinate and controlled wound to still a violence of recovered desire which threatens to overwhelm. This apocalyptic flood invokes all the elements of boundary-transgression and supervening force which we have isolated as characteristic of wonder. The anti-narrative elements in the scene are here at their most forceful: language goes backwards and forwards, reverses itself even as it is strung out into sentences. Under such conditions, normal progressions and hierarchies – semantic, familial, erotic, temporal – double and disrupt themselves. But a balance is maintained: past and present transform each other; memory and desire fructify without concealment; sublimation and incarnation hold each other in equilibrium. And as daughter and father "beget" each other in mutual figuration ("Oh I am mock'd," cries Pericles), so the scene illuminates the model of resurrective participation through mutual "pleasure" that Gower has offered us: the tale is enlarged ("eched") by its listener as a figure for his or her own experience. The authority of the tale is not imposed from without, but elected by those who choose or find it for their own need and moment, to free them from whatever muteness they may have sunk into. Its metaphors offer themselves for attachment to some literal need for restoration in a listener's present. Those with different needs find different tales.

The uprush of bottled energy in Pericles, directly correspondent to the intransigence of his withdrawal, brings back the eye and ear with an overplus of forcefulness. He declares himself "wild in my beholding," speaks with an intensity of blessing, and hears a sudden supernal music. Much has been said about the role of music in mediating shifts in levels of experience in these plays and in providing an image for an orderly arrangement of natural phenomena into patterns. Pericles certainly calls what he hears "the music of the spheres," but it feels here less like an insight into celestial mechanics than an overflowing response to the possibility of coherent and satisfying pattern in what had seemed "awkward casualties," that is, to the truth of narrative itself as a kind of miracle of design.[36] The vision of Ephesian Diana is unlike a medieval theophany in that it produces no supernatural transformation of the action. It is an epiphany in which merely human knowledge is transfigured into pattern but not superseded or revoked.[37] Diana's charge to Pericles is simply to tell the story again in a sanctified space, to give it "repetition to the life" (line 244).

In the Temple at Ephesus, Thaisa's first reaction to Pericles' tale, to "voice and favour," is a rehearsal of her own death and revival. Her recognition of his ring is a formality showing the extent to which the previous scene had worked in a deeper mode. A kind of joke on narrative structure, it carries also a sense of a superfluity of astonished knowledge that can only overflow into more and more confirmatory signs, as though the signifying power of signs were part of the joy.[38] Yet Thaisa's reappearance has also a peculiarly sobering effect. As with the "great sea of joys o'erbearing mortality" in the earlier scene, recompense is accompanied by a movement of melting or annihilation:

> PERICLES   This, this: no more. You gods, your present kindness
>   Makes my past miseries sports. You shall do well,
>   That on the touching of her lips I may
>   Melt and no more be seen. O come, be buried
>   A second time within these arms.
> MARINA   My heart
>   Leaps to be gone into my mother's bosom.   (V.iii.40–5)

Renewed contact with the mother smacks very peculiarly of a death-directed joy, as though the perfection of ending had its price. For one thing, if the story is over, Gower's "life" is now used up. If the moment is transitory, it is still seems a necessary component of "this great miracle." The play diverts this feeling into the news that Simonides is dead, so that Pericles, with Thaisa, can take his place, as Lysimachus and Marina take theirs in Tyre. As with many such endings in Shakespeare, the telling is not halted by the end of the play, but is to be resumed elsewhere, both inside the play world and outside it. The existence of story is a kind of guarantee. So likewise, for all its moralizing curtain-call shorthand, Gower's Epilogue turn the play over to us:

> So on your patience evermore attending,
> New joy wait on you! Here our play has ending.   (Epilogue, 17–18)

The slightly peculiar syntax closes our own participation into a continuous loop of patience and joy. The play may have ending, but our pleasure in the tale does not.

VI

In his brief but moving account of Marina's work of "Telling stories," Terence Cave speaks of the intensity of the final recognition as in part a product of the disarticulation of narrative in the rest of the play – its "windy spaces, fragmentary encounters, peregrinations among cities scattered like islands, tempests and temporary havens."[39] Cave sees Pericles' response to Marina's tale as that of "a perfect listener or reader" guessing, crediting, involving himself, only to discover that the tale is his own. He invites us to imagine two alternative conclusions for the play. One is the ancient analogue, eclipsed but still visible in Shakespeare, in which Pericles discovers his daughter's identity too late after he has met her in the brothel. The other is a more modern scene in which, though "lost youth and happiness are irrecoverable [and] the fragmentation brought about by time and accident cannot be reversed," a "talented and sensitive young woman" nevertheless "finds for her patient a story that reaches far back into the past, ... makes some sense for him and allows him to pick up what threads remain of his life."[40] Cave does not need to explore the positioning of the Shakespearean fiction between the archaic and the modern analogue, but his tactic allows us the opportunity to do so, and to ask in turn some pertinent questions about the particularly Shakespearean tactic of rendering the therapeutic relation that modern readers recognize as essentially psycho-analytic in terms of a biological and familial relation between actual bodies. Insight into this insistence on Shakespeare's part will take us again into the concern of Shakespearean poetics with the relation between language and the world.

The specific quality of the wonder of Marina's recognition in *Pericles* depends on the identity of the story she tells and her physical presence. Cave's second therapeutic scenario lacks the particular force of Shakespeare's scene precisely insofar as it lacks the somatic sense of "contact" with what is "mine own and not mine own." Pericles can at some perceptual level "tell" his daughter as soon as he looks at her, before he orders her to tell her story. The two tellings are taken to complement and even to guarantee each other. One is only possible as linguistic and cultural expression, but the other is in a crucial way not a linguistic event, but a prelinguistic one, enacted between humans as direct perceivers of the world. Such recognitions do not depend on language. Animals and infants perform them as well as philosophers. In *Pericles*, Shakespeare uses the immediacy of this non-linguistic faculty of recognition along with linguistic and narrative ones to generate his climax. To perceive Marina as "something like that– " and for her to tell her story both uncover the past in the present, and realize this both as a matter of natural fact ("my queen's square brows / Her stature to an inch") and of narrative contract ("I will believe thee"). These complementary modes of cognition propose a consub-stantiality of natural and cultural processes which has the air of miraculous surplus. Marina becomes an object of thaumaturgical potency because of the way she offers to bridge and merge cultural and natural orders. And this has been so all through the play, from her nativity as "seafarer" to her arts of embroidery and song, where she managed the darker shapes of sexual life through a representational testing.

This sense of Marina as in part a figure for the power of Shakespearean narrative to manage and order potentially damaging impulses has implications for our sense of Shakespeare's own inheritance as a poet, and of the specific way he transformed that inheritance. It also casts light on the position Shakespeare occupies between medieval and modern conceptions of poetry. The miraculous conjunction of the natural with the Verbal is a image with a long and crucial history in Western culture as the trope of the Incarnation. In *Pericles* this conjunction reappears in Marina as Shakespeare's image for his own creativity, hovering at the border of subjection to natural process, but deliberately using that liminality as a source of intensely figurative energy. Of the many possible stances a work may adopt towards its predecessors, Shakespeare's choice of what we might call "gestation" is especially powerful. His assertion of a miraculous yet non-transcendent quality to his own poetic labor in *Pericles* includes a demonstration of renewed incarnative power through the use of his own theatrical inheritance in the form of the play itself – however much Ben Jonson objected to its "mould" – in its archaisms of presentation and language, its reversion to old-fashioned narrative form, its deliberate reference to a "miracle" scene.[41] As Cave suggests, what we are led to wonder at in the closing scenes is to a significant extent the skill and sophistication with which the new playwright has recuperated the fragments of the tale. Enthralling as the scene is, there remains an aura of the virtuoso about it, which directs our attention to the work of composition. Here we can find also what Mullaney misses in the play – acknowledgment of its "authorial" and commercial aspects, amounting to a covert assertion by the playwright that the shaping power of this narrative miracle is his own intervention in it.

Out of this there recurs necessarily the question of gender difference. Why is the figure of this miracle in Shakespeare's later plays so consistently a young woman? Among other hints, Pericles' preposterous reversal of "begettings" explicitly recognizes that sexual relations are crucial to these scenes of restoration, but also that these relations must be as yet imaginary rather than enacted: three of the four heroines of the final plays are not yet more than betrothed, and the fourth has had her husband banished, it would appear, straight after their wedding. What has this peculiar preoccupation with the imminence of sexual experience to do with the prominent metanarrative current of these plays? And what has *that* to do with the cultivation of wonder as their characteristic emotion?

Posing this question of *Pericles* requires us to ask what relation the play makes between Marina and Gower as story-tellers. As Cave points out, in the climactic scene Marina effectively stands in for Gower, performing for Pericles what Gower does for his audience. Gower's only wish, as he says, to "waste" his life so that the story may be renewed sounds on the one hand not unlike a version of a father's blessing. (One might compare Alonso's wish in *The Tempest* that he were "mudded in that oozy bed / Where now my son lies" if Ferdinand and Miranda could be thereby more felicitously bedded in Naples.) Yet the deathwardness of the story-teller father (we recall, in their different fates, Antiochus and Simonides) is balanced in Marina by the equally insistent lifewardness of imminent sexual activity. Sexual pleasure and narrative pleasure are counterparts, just as Shakespeare also bears in mind that the potential immortality of narratives depends upon the medium of perishable bodies.[42]

The choice of a virgin daughter as responsible for narrative continuance therefore derives from Shakespeare's deep concern with a poetics of incarnation, a concern which informs all levels of his poetic and dramatic practice. Yet what shapes the particular presentation of these female characters as active, articulate, and assertive is his desire to realize a dynamic and dialectical relation between mental and physical, conscious and biological processes. What we see as a result are young women endowed and even empowered with a particular self-consciousness about their sexual status, and insistent on managing it and spelling out its meanings for themselves. Even the passive Miranda becomes assertive where Ferdinand is concerned. The two liminal figures that recur in these late plays – aging fathers and marriageable daughters – represent counterposed ends of a spectrum: the former are comparatively disengaged from sexuality and closer to death, the latter likewise not directly involved in the sexual, but contemplating its imminence through consciously deployed representations. Between them stands a figure that Shakespeare finds extremely difficult to represent as a central figure of his narrative: the mature, sexually active woman. It may be that she is too powerful a competitor for his key metaphors. Where she arrives, trouble follows.

Yet this latter figure emerges most often in the non-tragic plays as origin and end, from whom the narrative departs and toward whose recovery it moves. Shakespeare begins *Pericles* with the death of Antiochus' wife and ends it with Thaisa, devotee of Diana. This latter divinity herself shows some significant complexity. Invoked by both Thaisa and Marina, she seems to combine the aspects of Virgin Protectress and Great Mother, a "double Diana" recalling and even glossing the double image of Marina-as-Thaisa which Pericles encounters in Mytilene harbor.[43] This figure of Virgin-Mother seems too full to be allowed to occupy the central action of any play, as though its production could only arrest action into a posture of stasis and admiration.[44] It seems that she is rather that towards which these later plays move, and in whose absence the final scene is apt to cloud with more melancholy thoughts of sin and death, as is the case with Prospero.[45]

Contemplation of the figure of the Virgin Mother as Shakespeare's deepest presider over the scene of reunion returns us unexpectedly to the theatrical dynamics of wonder with which we began. Both the syncretic and the impossible qualities of the figure bear reflection. She combines in fantasied synthesis equal parts, stasis and movement, since she both participates in the deep processes of mutative generation and stands over against it like "Patience gazing on kings' graves." She can therefore enfold and embody the impulses both towards and against narrative that we detected struggling in the dynamic of wonder. She is a figure at once of convulsion and abstraction, change and persistence, not oscillating as with the turbulent rhythms of Pericles' recognition scene, but held in tension as equal alternatives. Yet because the emblem also must freely confess its impossibility, its purely artificial or fantastic status, its production also introduces a note of self-conscious artifice that both stymies and invites inspection. The play can move toward such a figure, but not beyond it.

The figure of virgin maternity also functions in complex ways to allay the more damaging or traumatic suggestions of confrontation and struggle we noted earlier as characteristic of wonder – its recourse to imagery of wounds, blindings, and curse. As mother, the figure has an implied beneficence, as virgin a certain repose and abstraction from mutability: each of these elements checks any potential threat in the other, so that the figure becomes a site of productivity without itself standing for or entering into an excess of risk. As such it provides a kind of guarantee for the unification of motion and rest, choice and compulsion, consciousness and necessity. In its self-consciousness, it also suggests Shakespeare's image of his own tradition: a dynamic and productive site of elaboration at the same time possessed of a continuity that persists through its transformations. Such an image resumes both Shakespeare's conservatism and his often radical and dynamic sense of the necessity to transform traditional culture dialectically to preserve its communal function. In the elusive but compelling figure of the virgin-mother, we may be encountering Shakespeare's invention of a certain modern conservative notion of tradition as a dialectically evolving onus on its every recipient, not a site for a confirmatory mantra-like repetition, but a task involving the continual expenditure of effort to tell the difficult story of the past under the double aspect of what it was and what it was not.

All the same, we are entitled to ask of such fantasies as this of the virgin-mother whether they have no harmful effects, and whether at some point they must be given up in order to save either ourselves or others from damage. Of this one in particular we might ask: what are the consequences for actual women of the creation of such fantasy structures through images of gender? Shakespeare attempted to stage such a crisis and relinquishment in *The Winter's Tale*. In doing so, he turned at last on his own deepest imaginative strategies the eye of critique he had begun by exercising on his forebears.

5 *The Winter's Tale*; or, filling up the graves

O what venerable creatures did the agèd seem! Immortal Cherubims!
And the young men glittering and sparkling Angels, and maids
strange seraphic pieces of life and beauty! I knew not that they were
born or should die; but all things abided eternally.

Thomas Traherne

Gib Deine Hand, Du schön und zart Gebild!
Bin Freund und komme nicht zu strafen.
Sei guten Muts, ich bin nicht wild.
Sollst sanft in meinen Armen schlafen!

Der Tod und das Mädchen

Dum stupet et medio gaudet fallique veretur,
rursus amans rursusque manu sua vota retractat;
corpus erat: saliunt temptatae pollice venae.

Ovid

Shakespeare seems to have been the first English dramatist to give his
plays "poctic" titles, by which I mean not high-flown ones, but ones that
stand in a complex figurative relation to the plays they name. Earlier
dramatists offered proverbial titles such as *Enough is as Good as a Feast*
or *Like Will to Like*, but this is not quite the same thing. The practice
begins as early as *The Comedy of Errors* and *Love's Labours Lost* and
reaches a kind of climax with *Twelfth Night or What You Will*. Given this
attentiveness to the resonance of title, we ought especially to pay
attention when one of the plays makes a point of citing its title during the
action. It does not happen very often, but when it does it orients us
strongly on where the playwright himself sees the network of complex
interrelations having one of its primary interpretive nodes. This is
especially true of his comedies, for which there is a less neutrally
designating set of title conventions than for, say, *The Life of Henry the
Fift* or *The Tragedy of Julius Caesar* (though that "of" teases). At one
point in the middle of his career, Shakespeare seems deliberately to have
set out to mock or wrong-foot this very kind of attention with apparent
throwaway titles like *As You Like It* and *Much Ado about Nothing*. *All's*

Well that Ends Well looks like the same sort of gesture, except that the phrase then appears twice in increasingly rocky straits on the very lips of the heroine (IV.iv.35, V.i.25) and makes us pay attention.

In both *The Winter's Tale* and *The Tempest*, as if in this they were a pair, this underlining gesture is not merely a secret citation for our ears alone, but a reference to an act or occasion of story-telling itself, with an even higher degree of self-consciousness. Of Prospero we might expect such a metadramatic gambit, since he is at once magician and theatre-manager. He speaks his line to Ariel, almost to himself, looking back on his master-plot as its final suite of gestures is about to unfold:

> PROSPERO   Now does my project gather to a head:
> My charms crack not: my spirits obey, and Time
> Goes upright with his carriage: how's the day?
> ARIEL   On the sixth hour, at which time, my Lord,
> You said our work should cease.
> PROSPERO   I did say so,
> When first I rais'd "The Tempest."   (V.i.3–6)

This punctuation is tendentious, of course, but I think it matches what audiences hear, and the line points them to an enhanced awareness of the closing movement of the whole play.[1]

In *The Winter's Tale*, on the other hand, the title-allusion has little of this deliberate affirmative to it. A small boy makes it, without even quite "getting it right," so that we may even work a bit harder to notice. Why would such a gesture of self-consciousness be given to a minor character in a scene that looks like an introduction or prologue to the main event of the act?[2] Or is Mamillius closer to the center of the play than he appears? What sorts of things do we learn about him in his two short scenes that might justify the dignity of having him allude to the play's title in this canny way? We know, or we may already feel, that he is to be sacrificed. Insofar as his name associates him with his mother, we may wonder whether he can escape his father's blind wrath against her.[3] And though Leontes apparently decides that the child is after all his, solicitude for his son's welfare does not include actually bringing him with him in subsequent scenes: he is as effectively banished from the King's company as his mother is, more so in fact. Whether he cries on being haled from her we do not know, but we are reasonably sure he grieves terribly later on. Even Leontes proclaims this much, though he glosses it as shame at his mother's behavior – or on her behalf.

But what do we see that might help us understand why his small story bears the weight of the whole play? By his own criteria, his is a "winter's tale" – brief and clouded, haunted by haunted figures. His two appearances revolve first around his father, then his mother. "Revolve" as there is a prominent element of oscillation in the boy's movement in each case: he moves away (is pushed away in fact) and returns. This pattern of separation and recovery in relation to both parents is important for defining him as a dramatic figure. The stakes, it will appear, are high both for him and the play in understanding the tentative alternations between identification, detachment, and resistance that these stage movements come to map.[4]

It is in the scene with his mother, more set off from its surroundings than that with his father, that the play marks him for its own. Stanley Cavell has drawn attention to Leontes' discovery of the boy whispering to his mother, and read it as another scene of suspicion to add to his burgeoning fear and rage at the insidious knowledges of him he sees proliferating around him.[5] For Cavell the moment focuses Leontes' secret wish – secret perhaps even from himself – to make away with Mamillius, and through and with him all generation. But the odd thing about Cavell's attention to this scene is that it seems in some ways to repeat Leontes' own gesture by banishing Mamillius himself from real consideration. For we see more of the scene than Leontes, and we know that Mamillius is *not* whispering a secret about him – or at least, not the secret he most fears and desires. What then is he doing with his "sad tale ... of sprites and goblins"? Cavell speaks of the moment between mother and son as "a result of mutually seductive gestures," which is acute, but there are many kinds of seduction. What are the elements of this one that it should issue in this story?

I

The scene begins with Hermione pushing Mamillius – his mother's boy – away, in exasperation at something he has been doing, as if she were afraid he is about to exhaust her patience: "Take the boy to you; he so troubles me, / 'Tis past enduring." She speaks over his head, into an adult world that converts her command into a gamesome and seductive entreaty: "Come, my gracious lord, / Shall I be your playfellow?" But Mamillius knows enough to know what is going on, if not enough to respond with urbanity: "No, I'll none of you. ... You'll kiss me hard and speak to me as if / I were a baby still." If he has been irritating his mother, perhaps the rub has been mutual: he is trying to grow away from a defenseless dependency he considers past. Making his own play for power, he tries to set his antagonist against her companion ("I love you better"), who is indulgent ("And why so, my lord?"). And now Mamillius has a chance to strut his discriminating knowledge of female beauty. Contrary to Polixenes' claims in the previous scene for the lambkin innocence of boyhood, this boy has a keen eye for sexual attractiveness and an interest in seeing how he can exploit what he sees. He even claims to have his lore from his own observation ("I learn'd it out of women's faces"), and he knows and perhaps resents it when his precocity is made fun of ("Nay, that's a mock"). The playfulnesses of this exchange are clear enough, yet they are not the same for boy and women, and the delicate psychological observation of the small scene rests in these differences. Though he relaxes into their indulgent teasing, even uses it to shine in, Mamillius has more to lose, and he finds in the end that their power to hurt is more real than he had hoped when they put before him the image of his strutted independence unpleasantly taken at its word, and begin to speak, again almost over his head, of "women's matters":

> [1.] LADY   Hark ye,
> The Queen your mother rounds apace; we shall
> Present our services to a fine new prince
> One of these days, and then you'ld wanton with us,
> If we would have you.
> 2. LADY   She is spread of late
> Into a goodly bulk. Good time encounter her! (II.i.15–20)

Hermione interrupts the pair at this point with a rebuke, as though she knows the conversation is heading into deeper waters. She readmits the boy to her, offering reassurance of her continued presence and love, as though this were also a pledge for the future: "Come, sir, now / I am for *you* again."[6] The expedient she hits on for letting him show his authority over her is that of story-telling, a move that allows mother and son to collaborate in a mutual dependence where he is active and controlling but still needs her consent and scope for his showcase. The two negotiate and Mamillius plays once more at refusal and aggression, a gambit Hermione is willing, even eager, to accommodate:

> HERMIONE   Pray you sit by us,
> And tell's a tale.
> MAMILLIUS   Merry or sad, shall't be?
> HERMIONE   As merry as you will.
> MAMILLIUS A sad tale's best for winter. I have one
> Of sprites and goblins.
> HERMIONE   Let's have that, good sir.
> Come on, sit down, come on, and do your best
> To fright me with your sprites; you're pow'rful at it.
> MAMILLIUS There was a man –
> HERMIONE   Nay, come sit down; then on.
> MAMILLIUS Dwelt by a churchyard. I will tell it softly,
> Yond crickets shall not hear it.

HERMIONE   Come on then.
       And giv't me in mine ear.
          Enter Leontes, Antigonus, Lords   (II.i.22–32)

This is deft stuff. We watch Mamillius and his mother together shaping the stakes and prospect of his frightening her. No doubt she will exclaim with fear at suitable intervals, giving him the delicious pleasure of mastering at once her and his aggressive impulse against her, since he will know of course that she is not "really" frightened. The "winter's tale" proves a narrative device to stage and explore the psychic strain of their coming separation, alike feared and desired by both. It maps and cycles anxiety into story, just as the spatial movement away from and towards Hermione maps more complex separations ahead of the threat of his displacement – a threat contained in his own maturation, but also threateningly hastened by her insistent "goodly bulk." The story about ghosts itself ghosts much that cannot be directly faced. These are indeed "mutually seductive gestures," but they are carefully hedged by a definite aggression also acknowledged sidelong by both.

What must Mamillius make then of his father's terrible irruption into this scene? It is sometimes asserted that Leontes in some sense "is" the man who "dwelt by a churchyard." For Mamillius, however, the "winter's tale" does not so much continue as spin wildly out of his control and into some weirdly hyper-literal realm, as though he had all along been casting a spell without knowing it. There could hardly be a worse nightmare than the sudden appearance of this dark phantasm of accusation in the person of his father. At some level, this is profoundly *not* what Mamillius had in mind, yet it may seem to him as if his own desires have somehow called forth this vengeful demon in the shape of his father: just how much of Leontes' appalling musings may we think of the boy garnering in the previous scene? As long as there is a medium for managing and so dispelling such forebodings, Mamillius can play secure. But now he must watch his own deeper half-promptings realized in the father who both demands and banishes him, at once fulfillment and retribution for his daring against his mother:

LEONTES   Give me the boy. I am glad you did not nurse him.
           Though he does bear some signs of me, yet you
           Have too much blood in him.
HERMIONE   What is this? Sport?
LEONTES   Bear the boy hence, he shall not come about her.
           Away with him! and let her sport herself
           With that she's big with, for 'tis Polixenes
           Has made thee swell thus.   (II.i.56–62)

To Mamillius, this exchange must be both horrifying and deeply inscrutable. To hear that he "bears some signs of" this Leontes comes too close to what he has been imagining himself: recall his earlier claim to his father "I am like you, they say" – but would he want to be like *this* father? To be forced from his mother's side in this manner, leaving her to "sport" with the new child, is also too much like the way the scene began ("and then you'ld wanton with us, / If we would have you") and carries a darker undercurrent mixing childish and adult sexuality in Leontes' bitter reference to Hermione's "sport." Have his entwined desire for and rejection of independence begotten such a monstrosity as this between them? What relations obtain between the boy's desire against his mother and his desire for her? Is his mother now to suffer for what he has thought and felt, and at the hands of this dark cartoon of himself grown-up?[7]

Such considerations cast a terrible light on what we hear of the boy's decline through the rest of the play. It is important that Leontes' claim on him does not extend to more than enquiring after him, as far as we know. Mamillius is sequestered from both his parents, and Leontes' cry "Away with him" is only the first of many such cries to follow, cries that seek apparently to banish the whole world and leave him in the company only of his own fantasies ("Away with her, to prison"; "Away with that audacious lady"; "My child? Away with't"). Cavell's suggestion that Leontes' rage is against Mamillius as well as Hermione, in spite of his apparent solicitude, seems only too accurate, and although this may be because of the "too much blood in him" of which he speaks, it seems also to speak of a more pervasive aggression, one we find turning even on himself – sleepless, restive, and thought-fretted as he becomes.

Mamillius, then, awakes from a world whose nightmares he controls to one where they are alive, where they strut and glower and spit accusations. His response to what he has done is to sicken, neurotically as we may suppose from Leontes' description, though we need not accept Leontes' specific diagnosis:

LEONTES   How does the boy?
SERVANT   He took good rest tonight;
           'Tis hop'd his sickness is discharg'd.
LEONTES   To see his nobleness,
           Conceiving the dishonour of his mother!
           He straight declin'd, droop'd, took it deeply,
           Fasten'd and fix'd the shame on't in himself,
           Threw off his spirit, his appetite, his sleep,
           And downright languish'd.   (II.iii.10–17)

Cavell on these lines is worth quoting directly: "this sounds more like something Leontes himself has done, and so suggests an identification Leontes has projected between himself and his son. The lines at the same time project an identification with his wife, to the extent to which one permits 'conceiving' in that occurrence to carry on the play's ideas of pregnancy."[8] But may this not also be something Mamillius has done? If Leontes' interpretation of Mamillius' condition is suspect, his description of it need not be. Though "the boy," as he calls his son, has perhaps not "conceived" Hermione's dishonor (and both their notions of "conception" must be important here), he may regard her slander and punishment as in some way his doing, in which case his "fixing" of "the shame on't in himself" would be an attempt to undo what his momentary aggression has so rashly and magically done. This would be acute child psychology certainly, and would explain and complete a strange circle of identifications among the members of this apparently doomed family. Mamillius is trapped between identifications with father and mother. Too like his father in his violence and sleepless languishing, he is now willing himself to take his mother's place in conceiving and drooping. It is indeed a noble gesture, but not quite of the kind Leontes imagines. By it Mamillius attempts to take his mother's part as the object of his father's sexual violence, and to perform this part partly to deny his part in his father (and his father's part in him). Bastardizing himself is, in a sense, the price of redeeming his mother. In effect, he will kill himself for being like his father by becoming like his mother, taking her place to pay for both his own and his father's violence.[9] "With mere conceit and fear / Of the Queen's speed" he races his mother to a death he now identifies as the outcome (and perhaps the engine) of male desire. In this heroic resolution he is all too successful.

There is a sense of Mamillius as having "seen the spider" through these brief glimpses, but the spider in this case is a sexual intimation for which he has inadequate preparation and no expressive recourse save this of his fatal sickening. The question of his mimetic "conception" of his mother's dishonor is shadowed, and perhaps interpreted, by the fact of his own "conception" by her at an earlier time through an act of "sport" not unlike aggression.[10] Paulina's language in describing the etiology of the Prince's decline touches directly on this point, since it sees Leontes' current slanderous rage to "sully the purity and whiteness of my sheets" (his own phrase at I.ii.326–7) as intimately but obscurely connected to the Prince's secret "conception" of the act that created him:

PAULINA   Nor is't directly laid to thee, the death
                   Of the young Prince, whose honourable thoughts,
                   Thoughts high for one so tender, cleft the heart
                   That could conceive a gross and foolish sirc
                   Blemish'd his gracious dam.   (III.ii.194–8)

Paulina here clearly indicates she regards the boy's death as induced by
a "high" revenge enacted on himself for having a "heart" base enough
to "conceive" of his mother's staining by his "gross" father. Some part
of a divided Mamillius has made itself a party to that imagined or real
act of pollution, while another part has determined to wipe it out as far
as he can – by wiping out at once both the cause (his heart) and the
effect (himself). Leontes, more ruthless or more selfish, has meanwhile
chosen to attack what he calls, with his typical obscure clarity, "the
cause ... part o' the cause" (II.iii.3). But children often confuse cause
and effect like this. D. W. Winnicott has spoken of the imaginative
paradox of the "transitional object" in a way that deeply illuminates
Mamillius' predicament:

it can be said that it is a matter of agreement between us and the baby that we
will never ask the question: 'Did you conceive of this or was it presented to you
from without?' The important point is that no decision on this point is expected.
The question is not to be formulated.[11]

For Mamillius the imaginative object has spun horribly out of his
control, and fused itself with dark images of "conception" that point
fearfully to him. The threat to his mother precipitates the need to
formulate and decide the question of "conception" as a matter of
urgency through suggesting that some magical potency in his own
tentative aggressions has re-created the world as a nightmare. Has he
produced his father's accusation or not? If he has, he must punish
himself; if he has not, he must protect his mother. Further underlying
this traumatic complex of ambivalences lies a terrible but obscure
intimation of sexual generation – the very act that produced him, that he
has somehow now repeated – as intimately involved with violence,
staining, and mortality. Rather than consent to his inevitable part in that
nest of spiders, Mamillius revenges himself on mortality by depriving it
of its prize in him.

II

These conjectures on the relation between the Prince and his parents may
seem somewhat overdeveloped, but they follow strictly what we see or
are told, and they have the advantage that they do not rely on Leontes'

surely confused sense of "the cause" to explain what happens to the boy. The obscurity of the connections Mamillius makes is registered by the play both lexically and dramatically, in their withdrawal deep within the texture of his lines, and of his character itself from the action. Where Leontes "stages" his suspicions, for Mamillius the process of violent desire goes on "behind the scenes." The play shows us a complex triangle of identifications in which both males deeply, and perhaps similarly, mistake the nature of their relations with Hermione and with each other. We need therefore now to look at the play's own dreadful "primal scene" of Leontes' suspicions, a scene in which Mamillius is also an intrusive – and, I believe – catalytic, presence.

It has been argued recently that Leontes' resentment and paranoia spring from his suspicion of female generativity in general, and his dependence on Hermione's in particular. His violence has been linked thence to the general history of patriarchy and its simultaneous use and devaluation of childbirth as "the woman's part." There is much truth in this view, yet it also seems to me insufficiently precise to account for just what happens in this case, where, for all the mystery of their genesis, there is a clear and precise notation of "events." One serious problem to be faced by the diagnosis of misogynist suspicion of women as the root cause – though it is certainly the route Leontes' rhetoric takes once mobilized – is that it is touched off not by femaleness in general (as it is in, say, Iago) or even with birth *per se*, but specifically with the birth of a *second* child. If it was merely a matter of suspicion of female sexuality in general, one would have expected it to have broken out with Hermione's first pregnancy, her first evidence of "openness" to male penetration, or even earlier, as it apparently does with Othello, around the initial moment of marital consummation.[12]

But this is not what happens. Instead the crisis precipitates only when mediated through the presence not only of Polixenes but of Mamillius, the latter a genuinely new element in the familial equation. It is worth recalling that the boy is first mentioned in the opening scene, in what seems otherwise a rather awkward transition, immediately after Archidamus has said of the two kings' love: "I think there is not in the world either malice or matter to alter it."[13] And though Leontes comes upon or is seized by his suspicion unprompted by any explicit thought of his boy, its efflorescence is curiously interleaved with another scene in which the child moves towards and away from his parent, alternately embraced and dismissed by him.

Yet if the actual genesis of Leontes' suspicions unfolds independent of Mamillius (though the boy is on stage and presumably doing something, perhaps playing, while his elders talk), the question of the sort of sexual

consciousness boyhood has is very much in the air. It is discussed at
some length between Polixenes and Hermione (does Hermione have her
son in mind? are he and Leontes playing together?), and its nature is
explored in images of a pastoral mutuality elsewhere reserved in Shakespeare for girlhood.[14] What Polixenes recalls, or fantasizes, with especial
plangency is a lack of any sense either of development and change or of
sin, specifically of sexual sinnings associated with the appearance of
women on the scene as occasions or, more strongly, instigators of (male)
desire. The highlighting enjambment at "chang'd" is very relevant here,
as though when we revise its meaning from "altered" to "exchanged" we,
with Polixenes, avoid a thought of mutability:

> HERMIONE   Come, I'll question you
> Of my lord's tricks and yours when you were boys.[15]
> You were pretty lordings then?
> POLIXENES   We were, fair queen,
> Two lads that thought there was no more behind
> But such a day tomorrow as today,
> And to be boy eternal.
> HERMIONE   Was not my lord
> The verier wag o' th' two?
> POLIXENES We were as twinn'd lambs that did frisk i' th' sun,
> And bleat the one at th'other. What we chang'd
> Was innocence for innocence; we knew not
> The doctrine of ill-doing, nor dream'd
> That any did.   (I.ii.60–71)

If we suppose for the sake of argument that Polixenes and Hermione are
here watching Leontes and Mamillius at play, the scene before them
becomes doubled by an imagined scene which peculiarly charges it with a
nostalgic pathos springing from the necessity of whatever was "chang'd"
in adult development. A heretofore perfect economy between equals then
suffered an imbalance, coincident both with the perception of time as
mortality and with "the doctrine of ill-doing." Polixenes seems here
peculiarly to repeat a moment in the past where, like Mamillius in a later
scene, he had to decide whether the "stronger blood" of sexual excitement that bears within it the intuitions of both mortality and punishment
has come to him from within or without. Hermione points out the
implication despite Polixenes' delicate attempt to turn it aside by framing
her as "most sacred":

> Had we pursued that life
> And our weak spirits ne'er been higher rear'd
> With stronger blood, we should have answer'd heaven
> Boldly, "Not guilty"; the imposition clear'd,
> Hereditary ours.

HERMIONE   By this we gather
                You have tripp'd since.
POLIXENES   O my most sacred lady,
                Temptations have since then been born to's: for
                In those unfledg'd days was my wife a girl;
                Your precious self had then not cross'd the eyes
                Of my young playfellow.
HERMIONE   Grace to boot!
                Of this make no conclusion, lest you say
                Your queen and I are devils.   (I.ii.72–83)

Polixenes' way of putting it – of temptation's having been "born to's" – both points to the particular issue at stake and neatly sidesteps the need to decide precisely where the origins were of this "conception" for him and Leontes.[16] His description of Hermione "crossing the eyes" of "my young playfellow" – which sounds rather like Leontes on Mamillius – likewise conceals inside a more neutral phrase a (remembered?) resentment or taunt or sense of damage at her hands. After seeing Hermione, Leontes' vision became faulty, even as his desire fledged.

The later scene between Hermione and Mamillius, from this point of view, explicitly responds to Polixenes' vision of male childhood as insulated innocence, and with it we can be precise about the latter's sentimentality. Sexual knowledge is continually in development, mediated and modulated through play and fantasy and in constant contact with other emotions such as anger and fear. It is not a catastrophic creation from some female "nothing." But the question that needs answering here is: does Leontes too think this is what happened to him? There is some evidence that he does, at some level – though this thought itself may, as we shall see, screen a deeper self-knowledge he wishes *not* to call to account.[17]

If we continue to imagine Leontes as coming into the scene from playing with Mamillius (hence as himself in contact with boyhood, even as Polixenes describes it), we can see at once the relevance of what Polixenes says about "eye-crossing" to what Leontes now finds before him. Indeed Leontes' testing and accusing of the world from here on frequently appeal to the arrant and visible truth of his fantasies to any "head-piece extraordinary." Though the "lower messes" are still "purblind" (as once both he and all were "Blind with the pin and web"), now *he* has "eyes / To see" all that's "beneath the sky" (I.ii.310, 180). His fierce accusation that Camillo is one who "Canst with thine eyes at once see good and evil" (I.ii.303) sounds not unlike resentment at having had his own eyes "cross'd" by his wife. And when he later confronts Hermione, he has the half-indulgent rage of an enlightened demystifier before his former illusion, redeeming himself by helping others on to the cure:

> You, my lords,
> Look on her, mark her well; be but about
> To say she is a goodly lady, and
> The justice of your hearts will thereto add
> 'Tis pity she's not honest – honourable.
> Praise her but for this her without-door form
> (Which on my faith deserves high speech) and straight
> The shrug, the hum or ha (these petty brands
> That calumny doth use – O I am out –
> That mercy does, for calumny will sear
> Virtue itself), these shrugs, these hums and ha's,
> When you have said she's goodly, come between
> Ere you can say she's honest: but be't known
> (From him that has most cause to grieve it should be)
> She's an adultress.
>   (II.i.64–78)

There is a remarkable anticipation here of the eventual image of Hermione's fate at Leontes' hands. With a brutal connoisseurish swagger, Leontes gives his men a tour of his wife as though she were some object of aesthetic pleasure and moral inspection he had unveiled for them, to delight and to instruct. The "aesthetic" distance he thus achieves measures the extent to which he must defend himself from the possibility of responding to her as a human presence. She is as it were an exemplary picture, a monitory emblem labelled "feminine fraud." Only a fool would take her for the real thing. The play here imagines Leontes' aesthetics as a defense against his psychology, against a deeper commitment or a more carnal knowledge. And as usual, wrapped up in his fulminations, Leontes lets a truth slip "out" which he must either ignore or repudiate. Here the neatly chiastic form of the passage – his calumny coming between him and his wife – telegraphs the "insideness" of this truth to Leontes, around which he buttresses the more extravagantly his theatrical, aestheticizing gestures. Now at last, with a colder vision, Leontes thinks he can recognize the truth of Polixenes' charge that Hermione "cross'd his eyes."

Polixenes' low but distinct note of suspicion against Hermione is also picked up and amplified into the theatrical in Leontes' own recollection of his courtship as a time when "Three crabbed months had soured themselves to death, / Ere I could make thee open thy white hand, / And clap thyself my love" (I.ii.102–4). Sexual longing and the intimation of mortality, a sense of being closed out, a sense Leontes has of forcing Hermione, and also a strange and alienating theatrical dependency – as if he were on a stage awaiting Hermione's applause – all intertwine here.

(The last sense prefigures Hermione's scene with Mamillius, where she provides an audience for his performance.) As Leontes watches Hermione now give that same hand to Polixenes, much that was allayed by her speaking then is stirred up again.

If Leontes' experience of childhood and the springing of desire has been as Polixenes describes it, then the relevance of Mamillius to the scene as a potential double of a young Leontes is immediately clear. Leontes himself admits this much, and we need not assume he is fabricating; indeed, *his* sense that he is so hides the deeper truth of a man who keeps his variant self-knowledges precariously concealed from one another:

>   Looking on the lines
> Of my boy's face, methoughts I did recoil
> Twenty-three years, and saw myself unbreech'd
> In my green velvet coat, my dagger muzzled,
> Lest it should bite its master, and so prove
> (As ornament oft does) too dangerous.
> How like (methought) I then was to this kernel,
> This squash, this gentleman. Mine honest friend,
> Will you take eggs for money?
>
> MAMILLIUS No, my lord, I'll fight.
> LEONTES   You will? Why, happy man be's dole!   (I.ii.153–63)

Leontes' identification with his son is quite explicit here, even if the instant of recognition makes him (uncomfortably) "recoil." The figure of "myself unbreech'd" (incidentally revealing Leontes to be younger than we often think: under thirty – Hamlet's age), "unbreech'd" – either "not yet breech'd" or "with breeches removed" – and with his power to hurt in restraint or underdeveloped, is both a regression and an inversion of the adult, revealing by contraries how Leontes now thinks of himself.[18] Particularly worth considering is the dagger: it seems, like a dog, to have a life of its own. In its adult form it is presumably unmuzzled and ready to bite, and its clearly phallic resonance suggests again that sexual maturity and damage go together, though an adult ought to be in control of both. But against whom is it now turned? The fear of the child's dagger biting "its master" might suggest that sexual maturity and desire threaten as much a self-wounding as an aggression directed against others, say against women. Deeper yet, the two potential woundings may be understood as one. Does the perception of desire as a wounding of others or of the self come first? The vision of rape or the vision of castration: can one say which is prior, or do they emerge simultaneously and without hope of disentanglement? Antigonus, a genial chauvinist, later takes his potency and patrimony alike to depend on Hermione's faith. If she is, as Don John would put it, "any man's Hero," then all bloodlines are as good as scrambled, and men might as well castrate themselves ("I had rather glib myself") and find some other means of grasping at the future than generation ("I'll geld 'em all; fourteen they shall not see / To bring false generations"). But Antigonus, with all his huffing and puffing, does not really see what's at stake for Leontes here. What kind of mastery does Leontes imagine himself to have achieved over his own violence, and what relation does that imagined violence have to the reproductive potency that both dagger and son shadow?[19]

Desire and violence are thus very intimately linked. When Hermione "cross'd the eyes" of Leontes, the harmlessness of his muzzled dagger was converted into danger, and it at once bit or breached its master. The "mutually seductive gestures" of the scene between Hermione and Mamillius also gloss the remembered scene of courtship.[20] Leontes' desire to wound Hermione, which she provokes and which is (a response to) his sexual desire, wounds him also by its inhuman aggression, so much against the tenor of a would-be idealization ("O my most sacred lady"). Desire's intimation of mortality and its revelation of himself as an aggressive and stained and staining figure are all alike laid at her door. His resentment and fear of his own violence is (inadequately) cloaked in the intuition of her crime – of her having (yet again) "cross'd his eyes." In response to Winnicott's "question not to be asked" Leontes wishes to reply that his "conception" has come from outside, from her. It was and is all her fault. Hence his central assertion throughout the following scenes, the one intuition that he *must* uphold, is: "It was not *I* who impregnated her." The rest follows from that. ("Yet it was someone *like* me – who better than my brother? Yes, it must have been he: look at him now – disgusting.") It is an implicit rejection of the universe of generation and mortality as one to which Leontes is necessarily bound through his desire.[21] Leontes thinks to stand away from the world of generation and regard it as an object of contemplation, of lessons, even perhaps of beauty, but as fundamentally remote from him. Hence his intense frustration in Act II at his inability to find the "peace" which ought to come with his sequestration.

Such considerations can help us find our way through one of the most deeply obscure passages in Shakespeare, during the course of which Leontes tries to unfold to himself (or fold up in himself) his sense of what is happening to him:

> Can thy dam? – may't be? –
> Affection! Thy intention stabs the centre!
> Thou dost make possible things not so held,
> Communicat'st with dreams (how can this be?),

> With what's unreal thou co-active art,
> And fellow'st nothing. Then 'tis very credent
> Thou may'st conjoin with something, and thou dost
> (And that beyond commission) and I find it
> (And that to the infection of my brains,
> And hardening of my brows).   (I.ii.137–46)

The dark stuttering that gives way to a hectic rhythm here suggests a deep disturbance that moves many ways at once. Leontes seems to be talking at once about perception, imagination, and sexual desire, uncertain where to locate or how to feel any of them: each bleeds over into the next. "Affection!" is a cry that refuses to settle even into clear rhetoric: is it noun? verb? apostrophe? diagnosis? accusation? Is it her emotion or his? Whose center does it stab, even supposing it *is* the referent of the following pronoun? It is at least the cry of itself as it wounds Leontes, as through Leontes it wounds Hermione with its/his unmuzzled dagger. "Thy intention" is equally difficult: as though an emotion could have one – and if it can, there is a sense of Leontes as possessed by some force with its own inscrutable, perhaps malevolent, designs. Is this perhaps a "tenting in" that stabs at some wound in the – heart? genitals? Some such quasi-etymology seems implied. But which way are affection and intention moving: towards or away from Leontes? "Affection" is somehow transformed into "infection," combated as an invader.

Any commentary on these lines threatens to reproduce their own turbulent movement, as the critic's imagination becomes "co-active" and joins in the act of reading Leontes' sense of being pushed around by obscure implicating forces. The same applies to the spectator, for whom the actor's expression and movement may both clarify and complicate.[22] What the lines uncover or create or "fellow" – in a manner at once poetic and sexual – is an indeterminate and alarming hermeneutic plasticity which mimes a vertigo within or surrounding Leontes, where ambivalent cross-currents of attraction and repulsion coincide. All we can really count on is Leontes' sense that he has come across (but does he "find" or create it?) something that causes "infection" and "hardening" – terms that suggest at once groin and head, in a play that inquires how these two sites of knowledge are related. The very non-specificity of Leontes' first suspicious remark becomes important here: "Too hot, too hot! / To mingle friendship far is mingling bloods" (I.ii.108–9). Though the coldness of his irony bespeaks adult control and self-observation, this is rather vague as the opening gambit of a specific jealousy. It sounds more like a horror at sexuality in general as contamination or overheating than at adultery in particular: the horror and disgust a child might express at discovering the truth (which so often seems like a bad joke) about its sexual origins. Just who is it that is (or was) "too hot"? And when? He and Hermione have just recalled their courtship and the "clapping" that concluded it. Only slowly does the particular accusation Leontes wants emerge, and it might as easily be a displacement resisting his own implication in acts of "mingling bloods," either as producer or as product. The play undertakes a curious "layering" of occasions from its beginning, insistently citing the kings' boyhood, their courtships, their progeny, and introducing an immediate image of the latter in Mamillius. The associative plasticity of Shakespeare's rhetoric at such moments invites us to see how many of these "stages" are caught up and addressed through the ongoing work of Leontes' fantasy.

Leontes' attitude to Mamillius throughout this "primal scene" of suspicion oscillates, not surprisingly, between identification and rejection: he hugs him ("Sweet villain! / Most dear'st! my collop!") and he spurns him ("Go play, boy, play."). His search of his son's face for signs of himself works not only in the obvious way to test and confirm paternity, but more deeply to evoke self-recognition ("yet were it true / To say this boy were like me") – and he finds himself there, not only in the nose which "they say ... is a copy out of mine," but also in the "smutch" on the nose: the boy is sullied, as he has been (but when?), sinking both suddenly and gradually "Inch thick, knee-deep, o'er head and ears." He treats his son with a kind of indulgent contempt, as if embarrassed at his own affection: the boy is a "kernel," a "squash," but also "mine honest friend" who will show how his manly spirit is being "higher rear'd" by offering to "fight," perhaps to fight him.[23] Yet he is no sooner alone with him than he sends him away in disdain, as though the thought of any relationship were greatly to his distaste. Marking this ambivalence is his use of the word "honest" ("Go play, Mamillius, thou'rt an honest man," I.ii.211), which has the ring at once of Iago on Cassio and, more oddly, of Othello on Iago. That Leontes is his own Iago is a commonplace, but it comes as more of a shock to hear him making his son one too.

Leontes' search for connection to his son thus gives him both less and more than he desires: less in that it does not seem satisfactorily to still the doubts and intimations that prompted it in the first place, more in that it revives in him thoughts and modes of thought long thought overcome or put aside – thoughts that re-emerge from the strange amalgam of childhood, friendship, rivalry, and courtship that the scene anneals. This "complex" of thought and feeling is further glossed – from a developmental perspective – by the subsequent scene between Mamillius and his mother, where a broadly similar moment of tension is about to be allayed or managed by the introduction of "a winter's tale" – a tale not only *for* winter but also *of* winter, that winter of the heart in which aggression defeats, or worse unmasks, love.

III

The centrality of Mamillius to the unfolding of *The Winter's Tale* will now be clear. But the connection of his childish "play" to Shakespeare's own has still not been fully explored. Play is what we see him doing, and what most explicitly links him to his parents in Leontes' savagely punning formulation: "Go play, boy, play. Thy mother plays, and I / Play too" (I.ii.187–8). Childish recreation, female sexuality, and male self-consciousness are yoked together in this triad, and allude in turn to the Shakespearean stage that represents them all. Before we reach the metadramatic proper, however, and the relation of Leontes' theatre of cruelty to Shakespeare's, we need first to face the question of Mamillius' play as child's play. Again, it is the emergence of Mamillius' play-story as the name also for Shakespeare's play-story (augmented into *the* winter's tale) that we are looking to explain.

There is no doubt that Shakespeare's play is interested from the outset in the question of "development," that is, as an aspect of time, and that the task of "development" – as we now speak of "childhood development" – is especially focused in Mamillius. Shakespeare seems as aware as any modern psychologist of the implications of "play" in this sense. Leontes also knows, though he uses the knowledge dismissively, that what children characteristically do, and must do as part of the business of becoming adults, is "play." But the concern with time and what it requires also goes deeper. It is the opening subject of the play. In the first scene, Archidamus and Camillo trace both the occasion of their speech and its urgent sense of economic and social indebtednesses to an earlier time when the recent difficult and attornied negotiations – now perhaps becoming a burden – were part of a simpler structure. The large register of economic language in the play noted by Cavell – all the talk of debt, payment, gift, redress, revenge, just desert, and so forth – emerges from a need to confront and reconcile differences that emerge developmentally as gaps, branches, partings, and "vasts."[24] What one party owes to another – that is, the difference between them and what to do about it (and among others what to do or say about *sexual* difference) – is an almost ubiquitous concern. Difference is the topic of the opening remark of the play, and its implications as debt are disputed in a courtly manner between Archidamus and Camillo throughout the first scene:

ARCHIDAMUS If you shall chance, Camillo, to visit Bohemia on the like
occasion whereon my services are now on foot, you shall see (as I have
said) great difference betwixt our Bohemia and your Sicilia.
CAMILLO I think, this coming summer, the King of Sicilia means to pay
Bohemia the visitation which he justly owes him.
ARCHIDAMUS Wherein our entertainment shall shame us: we will be justified in
our loves; for indeed –
CAMILLO Beseech you –
ARCHIDAMUS Verily, I speak it in the freedom of my knowledge: we cannot
with such magnificence – in so rare – I know not what to say – We will give
you sleepy drinks, that your senses (unintelligent of our insufficience) may,
though they cannot praise us, as little accuse us.
CAMILLO You pay a great deal too dear for what's given freely. (I.i.1–18)

Archidamus' sense of "difference" between their two countries here
concerns less their societies or landscapes than their resources for
discharging the great debt of hospitality. Insofar as the kings take their
names from their countries, this also suggests a network of obligation
between the friends (one also expressed by Polixenes at the opening of
the next scene). Camillo's denial of the obligation does not relieve
Archidamus of his sense of an invidious and unbridgeable "difference"
which will only be overcome by some subterfuge – whether "sleepy
drinks" or "cross'd eyes." Camillo in reply begins himself to chafe, and
denies the need to feel any burden of "insufficience" by explaining the
essential unity of the two kings from childhood friendship, a unity which
has maintained its perfectly equilibrated economy of love almost by
miracle. Within such a relationship there cannot be any question of a
difference that can "count," of any "too much." Yet the strain of this
mutual unity appears in a sense of the gigantic effort now expended to
sustain it:

CAMILLO Sicilia cannot show himself overkind to Bohemia. They were trained
together in their childhoods; and there rooted betwixt them then such an
affection, which cannot choose but branch now. Since their more mature
dignities and royal necessities made separation of their society, their
encounters (though not personal) have been royally attorney'd with interchange of gifts, letters, loving embassies, that they have seem'd to be
together, though absent; shook hands, as over a vast; and embrac'd, as it
were, from the ends of oppos'd winds. The heavens continue their loves!
(I.i.21–32)

Camillo's concluding prayer almost suggests that something more than
human will be required to maintain this stance. An immense quantity of
material and social energy is being expended to "fill up" (as Polixenes
will say) and hence in some sense to deny what is to all others a very
palpable sundering. The flaw, as Camillo expresses it, lies in the inevitable

changes of "development," of young trees "trained" together (are there two or one?), their roots intermixed but growing only to "branch." This suggests that development itself – the organic processes of life – necessitates the unraveling of primary unities into difference and separation, and that this unraveling can be traumatic, and hence generate resistance. Like Hegel's bud that contains in dialectic both the stem and the flower, time here is the engine of an unfolding that both flourishes and severs – two senses in which "affection" may "branch." Leontes and Polixenes strain ever more energetically to preserve a superseded version of their relation. And perhaps the strain is beginning to tell. It is precisely at this point that Archidamus first refers to Mamillius.

If the language of debt, gap, gulf, vast – and also "part" – emerges from this concern with ineluctable development and the management of its transforming consequences, the young Prince's task in relation to his parents – his play that is an attempt to cope with change within himself and his family – once more becomes a central focus of the tale. Change, ambivalence, the presence of contrary states of being or feeling in developmental dialectic with one another: how are these to be accommodated, processed, and represented by and to the ongoing self that mediates them? Mamillius' "sad tale ... for winter" is, we saw, an attempt to do just this, and the play takes it appropriately as a model for its own processes of adjustment and symbolization. If we understand the child's play of the ghost story to be a way of responding to his developing ambivalences at once about his parents and about his feelings towards them, Shakespeare's play will also be understood as a tale told to mediate a complex ambivalence, to respond to a developmental pressure by acting on it symbolically through the control and disposition of the energies of narrative. But what ambivalence and pressure are at issue?

The answer is surely that they are, at least in part, Leontes' sexual paranoia and hysteria, and this returns us to the relation between Mamillius as "player" and Leontes' remark that "thy mother plays and I / Play too, but so disgraced a part, whose issue / Will hiss me to my grave" (I.i.187–9). If we understand Leontes not only to be speaking of "a part" that he "plays" here in some diabolical theatre (to that implication we will return), but also to be engaged in "play" like that of Mamillius in thus rubbing the quat of his desire into a wound of delusive jealousy, what do we imply that he is doing? Precisely that his jealousy is a narrative structure with its own logic and progress under his control which covers, manages, and substitutes for something else. Leontes almost admits this very connection between his imaginings and those of child's play in a moment of outraged self-justification:

No; if I mistake
In those foundations which I build upon,
The centre is not big enough to bear
A schoolboy's top. Away with her to prison!   (II.i.100–3)

The "centre" here seems moreover to refer back obscurely to that earlier "centre" stabbed by affection at the heart of his dark feeling. Both Leontes' jealousy and Shakespeare's play provide an "intermediate area" – and they provide it in response to the same fundamental fact or fantasy: male terror at the nature and implications of sexual desire.

Leontes' behavior invites us to see him as an hysteric terrified of his own capacity and wish to inflict the aggressive pain of his sexuality on the female. So terrified in fact that, "deciding" such an inhuman (as he sees it) impulse can hardly come from himself, he "prefers" to arrange it or act it out as a fantastic scenario of *her* guilt and his justice.[25] Leontes gives himself a sleepy drink to avoid knowledge of his own "insufficience" – hence the link between his spider-poisoned cup and Archidamus' joke.[26] This allows him the vicarious and secret pleasure of acting on his aggression even while denying it, in fact while outwardly justifying it as Hermione's fault even against his own more secret "knowledge" of the untruth of this charge. Hence Leontes' extraordinary and quite uncanny tendency all through these early acts to speak directly about his situation and yet not hear himself. Over and over again, in breathtaking acts of "unsight," he shouts out the truth: "Your actions are my dreams. / You had a bastard by Polixenes, / And I but dream'd it" (III.ii.82–4).[27]

His bitter but exquisite announcement that "I play too" is therefore in part an acknowledgment of the constructing and manipulating aspect of his suspicion, of its aspects at once active and passive, exactly corresponding to his deep doubts about his sexuality – whether it is more properly "his" or something that "comes upon" him from outside, from Hermione. This split in the origin of his desire for "play" explains the sudden and overwhelming irruption of a theatrical consciousness into Leontes' world and language at just this point. As desire is both "his" and "not his," so also Leontes sees himself as both ruler and instrument, both on stage and remote manipulator/observer of the spectacle, at once (anti-)hero and playwright.

Leontes casts himself as either villain or dupe (or both) with "so disgraced a part / Whose issue will hiss me to my grave" – fatherhood becomes a demeaning, secondary role. His theatricalized consciousness even begins to bleed male suspicion out into the audience in an attempt to infect others in its own defense. The effect on an audience can be very disturbing indeed, the more so as it is difficult to shrug off:

> There have been
> (Or I am much deceiv'd) cuckolds ere now,
> And many a man there is (even at this present,
> Now, while I speak this) holds his wife by th' arm,
> That little thinks she has been sluic'd in's absence,
> And his pond fish'd by his next neighbour.   (I.ii.190–5)

This is equal parts disgust at female sexuality and comfort – even exultation – at the community of sufferers. The "it" to which the speech insistently returns is also presumably Leontes' way of referring to, without explicitly examining, the surging source of this kind of thought in a sort of primal "itness" at once of perception and feeling, his and not his. Metatheatricality is just one way of showing Leontes as half-aware of, intervening in, several levels of manipulation from this point on.

As playwright and supervisor, Leontes can assign roles himself, can arrange events to fit his fancy. This is a way to "solidify" perception by giving it at last reliable and external objects, everting it from the darker and more terrible contemplation of his own self-division: it distances comfortingly into a stance of spectation, erects a boundary between the play and audience along which a judicial and policing action can be staged. Yet that same staging must at the same time go unacknowledged, lest the spectator discover himself all along as the secret author of the piece, and therefore as implicated in its fantastic elaboration. Leontes continues to speak of himself at once as plotter and plotted against: "There is a plot against my life, my crown; / All's true that is mistrusted" (II.i.47–8) but "I am angling now, / Though you perceive me not how I give line" (I.ii.180–1) and

> the harlot king
> Is quite beyond mine arm, out of the blank
> And level of my brain, plot-proof; but she
> I can hook to me – say that she were gone....   (II.iii.4–7)

Leontes creates spectacles of Hermione ("You, my lords, / Look on her, mark her well") to keep her at arms' length, yet at the same time to control her, "hook her" to him in a terrible parody of an embrace. The trial he stages, as he says, to "openly / Proceed in justice" against one "too much belov'd" is a theatrical fiction already plotted out by him, "devis'd / And play'd to take spectators" (III.ii.36–7) as Hermione knowingly phrases it. The "flatness" of her misery, which she wishes her father could behold "with eyes of pity, not revenge" (III.ii.120–3), is the flatness of cardboard characters devised by an amateur and melodramatic imagination. And in the end the king's own sense of being trapped in a play not of his making, of being a foolish and infuriating theatrical spectacle, is part and parcel of his suspicion of his own fantasy: the only way to cast out his doubt is to make of it a finished device he can then stand aside from. Again, the impulse towards the aesthetic, towards the perception of a definite "shape" for judgment, defends against the inchoate threat of the psychological, with its implication of implication. Reading defends against being read. "Play out the play," cries Leontes, "I have much to say in the behalf of that Leontes!"

Leontes' imaginings are therefore a "theatre of cruelty" not only in that they are cruel, but also in Artaud's sense that that same cruelty is intended to be cathartic in some way – to purge passions and representations Leontes can neither disown nor acknowledge. Leontes himself speaks of prosecuting Hermione "to the guilt or the purgation" (III.ii.7), but it might as well have suited his purpose to say "the guilt *and* the purgation" since enforcing the one will accomplish, for him, the other. The courtroom drama is one devised to cover and deflect a deeper scenario of intertwined violence and desire which he cannot accept either as "his own or not his own." Unable to intuit the desire without the violence, he wishes to expropriate both. Yet this is not only or wholly a vicious strategy if we accept that an important reason why Leontes cannot accept his desire is that he finds its implications of violence towards its object at some level morally and humanly repulsive. Leontes' paranoia is scarcely an advance over Mamillius' suicide, yet it is rooted in the same impulse to refuse violence. Perhaps this sense that Leontes has the right problem but the wrong solution goes some way to explaining why the play in the end wants to recover him.[28] He has seen the spider all right – but the appropriate thing to do is to find the antidote, not smash the goblet.

IV

That versions of theatre seem to multiply in the middle acts of the play is only one way of drawing our attention to the stakes *for* theatre once Leontes has begun his pageant of calumny. *The Winter's Tale* incorporates a kind of "career in review" of the manifold dramatic modes in which Shakespeare has worked over the years. In the present case, our revulsion at the "Leontine" dramaturgy of paranoia and scandal threatens to turn itself backwards upon Shakespearean tragedy and expose it as no more than a vast and incomparably more sophisticated (but not therefore less impugnable) version of the same thing. *Hamlet, Othello, King Lear, Macbeth, Coriolanus* – all those delirious plays of female-blaming parade themselves, unwittingly indicted by Leontes' own desperately compensatory rage. Is *this* what has been at stake through those works, *The Winter's Tale* prompts us to ask? What fantasy were those plays all along managing and concealing that this play seeks at last to expose, confront, and, if possible, undo? Is the choice of Mamillius' "winter's tale" as the title of this play merely a way of denying the more apposite simulacrum in Leontes' forensic melodrama?[29] That Shakespeare should represent man's sexual impulses as a source of hysterical terror and self-alienation to men themselves is one thing. That he should go on to see this terror as hysterically refused and converted into an animus against generation in general and women in particular, and then link this gesture to the modes of his own poetic and dramatic work, suggests great depth of self-reflection.

But Leontes' theatre is not the only one made available to us, and does not exhaust the range of Shakespeare's theatrical fictions. Alternative theatres or versions of theatre multiply throughout *The Winter's Tale*, according to the developmental principle of dialectical "branching" announced by Camillo: no one theatre will serve all consciousnesses or states of mind.[30] Even as Leontes speeds on in his theatre of blame towards an inevitable appointment with the death he must refuse to acknowledge in his own desires, his messengers, Cleomenes and Dion, tell us of another spectacle and voice, and another, if rarer, auditorium. Themselves "theorists" of a certain kind of knowledge, they are also "theatrists" of certainty in knowledge – a certainty guaranteed for us by the impact they record as audience of its impress on them.[31] If Shakespeare cannot have us meet the gods directly (as he tried in *Pericles* and *Cymbeline*), he can at least suggest what an audience who felt they had might be moved to say:

> DION   ... O, the sacrifice!
> How ceremonious, solemn, and unearthly
> It was i' th' off'ring!
> CLEOMENES   But of all, the burst
> And the ear-deaf'ning voice o' th' oracle,
> Kin to Jove's thunder, so surpris'd my sense,
> That I was nothing.   (III.i.6–11)

Much of the thematic vocabulary of wonder sketched out in Chapter One appears here: the appeals to eye and ear as distinct portals of perception, the sense of imminent damage which goes hand in hand with a rush to knowledge, the apocalyptic thrust, the ambush by a superior force, all play their part in sketching in the image of a "theatre of total conversion" in which selves and their knowledges are battered and reconstituted by a divine afflatus to which they willingly accede. Yet for us this remains an echo only, an ideal perhaps of a kind of drama never to be for us, since a modern stage at least could not present it without a self-consciousness that would inevitably at some point keep us at a distance. The play's presentation of such an experience through Cleomenes and Dion offers us a limit case at once of an absolute knowledge and an absolute theatre – a theatre whose powers of skepticism have been abolished by *force majeure*, and which has therefore abolished itself as theatre. This is what principally we take to guarantee that what Apollo says – with unusual clarity for an oracle – is a truth beyond the theatre of its saying.[32]

Along with the Apollonian (anti-)theatre of absolute knowledge there is also the gelid theatre of remorse that emerges under Paulina's direction after Hermione's death. This theatre refuses all impulse of development: it remains stuck in a rocky and willed wilderness of abjection whose very unflinching severity is a punitive allegory of the stoniness of heart that brought it into being. It is also a futile performance since it cannot win the attention of the very audience it seeks:

> PAULINA   ... therefore betake thee
> To nothing but despair. A thousand knees,
> Ten thousand years together, naked, fasting,
> Upon a barren mountain, and still winter
> In storm perpetual, could not move the gods
> To look that way thou wert.   (III.ii.209–14)

This is a ghost-theatre, the permanent ossification of remorse into the posture forecast for it by Mamillius in the story of the churchyard man. Yet by being here lived instead of told, it cannot be escaped: it is a prison lacking a principle of release, of dénouement. Since the proper audience (the gods? Hermione?) is never present, it cannot fulfill itself, cannot be forgiven. It is damned to perpetual repetition: "Once a day I'll visit / The chapel where they lie, and tears shed there / Shall be my recreation" (III.ii.238–40), where the latter is also "re-creation." There is no other principle of development but this one of obsessive commemoration: any other gesture, as we are informed in Act V, is horribly shadowed by the repetitive vengefulness of its own sense of self-wrong in wronging others:

> LEONTES   Whilest I remember
> Her and her virtues, I cannot forget
> My blemishes in them, and so still think of
> The wrong I did myself; which was so much
> That heirless it hath made my kingdom, and
> Destroy'd the sweet'st companion that e'er man
> Bred his hopes out of.   (V.i.6–12)

There is no way out of such a structure. It must repeat in an older, colder key that same conjugation of Hermione's virtue and breeding, between which came Leontes' "blemishes" that killed her. Were it not for what Paulina knows in secret, she and Leontes would torment each other forever with images of Hermione's "sainted spirit," conjuring it to "Again possess her corpse, and on this stage / (Where we offenders now) appear soul-vexed" (V.i.57–9). Marriage in such a theatre is still and always linked to murder.[33] What now holds Leontes is only a moralized abreaction from his earlier contradictory intuitions about desire – this has not gone beyond them, it merely seeks to pay their price.

V

I have attempted to locate the origins of theatricality in the first half of *The Winter's Tale* in the difficult meditations of the self on its desires and in its attempts to shape responses to its intuitions about the meaning of those desires. *The Winter's Tale* is hardly exceptional among Shakespeare's plays in focusing attention on how human life copes with time and the changes it forces. Yet it does insist with unusual strength on the psychic difficulty of change, on the potential disasters that can occur. By this late stage in his career, Shakespeare's dramatic language has become an instrument subtle and searching enough to register not only the surface gestures of a character, but also the secret affections or intentions that inform those gestures. The imagination has become a layered thing, often obscure to itself, inventing its purposes moment by moment at several levels. Characters at times hardly hear what they say, so deeply can they become self-enchanted. In order to read such a language, it is sometimes necessary to extrapolate or extend an obscure inkling into an entire line of thought. In doing so, I have been employing a mode of discussion familiar to modern psychoanalysis, but I have preferred not to use the more technical vocabulary and, in particular, the shaping fantasies of that mode of interpretation. This is because it seems to me these modern fictions conceal at least as much about the pattern of Shakespearean psychology as they reveal. It is by no means certain that the mythological narratives that recent depth psychology has constructed will correspond to the inner mythography of a Shakespearean fiction. For that to be the case, one would have to posit either a universal structure not only of feeling but also of mythic transcription of that feeling, or a specific inheritance in psychoanalysis from Shakespeare (perhaps the most likely), or some common source for both.[34] That Shakespeare was a writer interested in the life and permutations of deeper fantasy, and in the possibility of curative action where fantasy was distorting personality, we have no reason to doubt. But the more pressing question for a full account of Shakespeare's psychology is the one not asked by most modern psychoanalytic critics: what are the particular mythological or narrative patterns subtending Shakespearean dramatic fictions, on which the fictions themselves are built and which they reflect? From what experience of the persistence of fantasies or fictional structures in the imagination did Shakespeare himself develop, without the benefit of modern psychology, his particular sense of their "layering," their struggle for expression, and their potential for change?

In the readings of *The Comedy of Errors* and *Pericles*, I attempted to demonstrate the workings of a dynamic of self-recognition in Shakespeare's drama, by which the poetic underpinnings of the plays are eventually brought to light and transformed. It is a curious fact about these structures that a surface influence or indebtedness often conceals a deeper one which emerges only during the course of the action. Thus the elaborately Plautine surface action of *Errors* converts itself eventually into a Biblical-Ovidian amalgam that shapes an early version of a peculiarly Shakespearean poetics I have called "incarnational." And in *Pericles*, an elaborately acknowledged indebtedness to Gower also overlies and eventually cedes to an awareness of underlying Ovidian myths – in particular those of Niobe and Narcissus. *The Winter's Tale* represents Shakespeare's fullest working-out of this pattern, and in it at last the presence of latent narrative substructures shaping action beneath acknowledged schemata is not only the method of the action but also one of its subjects. Mamillius' small tale already points us in this direction insofar as it shows surface narrative as an occasion for confronting and controlling less easily acknowledged kinds of feeling and knowing. So we are returned once more to Shakespeare's choice of title: at the level of the Shakespearean imagination what foundational myth is being confronted and metamorphosed anew by the action of dramatic composition?

Jonathan Bate's recent work on the complex relations between Shakespeare and Ovid notes of the opening act of *The Winter's Tale* that it "does not contain a single mythological reference. Everything seems to come from within Leontes' brittle psyche, nothing from the gods."[35] In fact the whole of the early part of the play having to do with Leontes is devoid of mythological or mythographic reference until very late, as though the king's "brittle psyche" had swept all clear. Yet this very brittleness and surface absence may point to a mastering myth within: there is no one so keen not to acknowledge the presence of a myth as he who is its captive. Following a suggestion variously put forward by both Stanley Cavell and Ruth Nevo, that Shakespeare's composition often moves, in Nevo's phrase, "backwards through a retrospective succession of partial recognition scenes," we should expect the relevant latency to emerge into view later in the play.[36] Bate's work points to one possible answer in his study of Perdita, the figure the play positions most forcefully opposite the dark king who governs its secret and interior undertale, and who will be eventually the corrective to his terrors. Perdita's chief mythological association in the play, as she herself announces, is with Proserpina. What Leontes throughout the opening action may be both resisting and, by the very hysterical intensity of his resistance, confirming, is the intuition of male desire as capture by death, couched in the archaic tale of the rape of Ceres' daughter.[37]

E. A. J. Honigmann proposed some time ago that Ovid's tale and Golding's translation of it in particular provide a "secondary source" for the play, and showed how traces of Golding have worked themselves back into the play in several places.[38] It is possible to go further than these verbal traces, however, if one connects the tale of Proserpina's abduction by the King of Death, a terrible figure for all his imperial dignity, with Leontes' own dark intuition of the damage lurking in sexuality. There is some evidence that the myth (with that of Narcissus, one of Shakespeare's deepest purchases from Ovid) pervades the whole play, often in unexpected places. Leontes himself directly echoes Golding's Jove in calling his child a "collop" of himself, and the whole Ovidian episode provides a mythic background for the nomination of "winter" as the mode of the play's opening, as well as for its location in Sicily, where the rape took place.[39] As far back as *A Midsummer Night's Dream*, the passage in which Ceres curses the ground of Sicily and strips it of fertility had haunted Shakespeare's imagination.[40] Now that act of abomination, and the violence of male desire that underlay it and whose inner deathliness it responds to, returns as the deeper inkling of Leontes' fantasy, and turns the play he heads from a tale "for" or "about" winter into *"The" Winter's Tale*, the tale of Winter in its mythic origin, its sexual meaning, and its psychological inflection.

In Ovid's tale, initiation into sexual life for Proserpina is the rush into a darkness never to be thrown off, a snatching by and into the embrace of a frozen shadow. Dis' sexual desire is male sexual voraciousness *as death*, deriving from and inflicting death. In Ovid, its violence is figured in the blow of the "sceptrum regale" that opens a passage for Dis through the lacerated earth into the underworld.[41] This may be the original blow that "stabs the center." In resisting the image of himself as Dis, Leontes resists all involvement in the sexual. Leontes will be Jove, judging from a distance, putting it all in order, righting the wrong his brother Dis/Polixenes has done. Paulina calls on him at last, like Ceres to Jove, to "Look down / And see what death is doing" (III.ii.148–9), to pretend no longer to the immortality of the Olympian master, but to acknowledge himself at last as the very figure of Death, the bringer of death to his wife and child. Terribly, Leontes awakes and finds it true. The "man who dwelt by a churchyard" was the man who saw himself as Dis. For him sexual desire and death have secretly shared a certain hardness, which is also that of winter – *rigor mortis* and *rigor sexualis* have been coactive.

Other aspects of the play seem likewise to root in Ovid's tale. What happens to Hermione, deprived of her children by death and abduction, is given in what happened to Ceres when she heard at last where Proserpina had been taken: "Hir mother stoode as stark as stone, when she these newes did heare, / And long she was like one that in another world had beene" (632–3). Goddesses recover more quickly than humans, and it takes Ceres much less than sixteen years to put aside "hir great amazednesse" (634). But when she does, her announcement is strikingly similar to the one with which Paulina undoes Hermione's stony captivity: "Behold our daughter whome I sought so long is found at last" (643).[42]

Even the fearful and silly bear may be an Ovidian/Leontine bear, a final emblematic product of the angry, wintry world. If he is hungry (as the Clown suggests) it may be because he has just endured – and woken from – his winter sleep. There is a strange verbal anticipation in some of Leontes' remarks that seems to conjure up the bear before his time, lurking especially within the more violent of his outbursts: "Bear the boy hence" (II.i.59); "the centre is not big enough to bear / A schoolboy's top" (II.i.102–3); "It is but weakness / To bear the matter thus" (II.iii.2–3) or "and that thou bear it / To some remote and desert place" (II.iii.175–6). This last puts the burden of bearishness on Antigonus immediately in advance of his fatal encounter.[43]

So much for the underworld of Leontes' fantasy. But a "winter's tale" is also a story told *against* the apparent devastation that surrounds: it wants to shield us from the storm of aggression, to make it bearable, to explain, protect, and deliver us from winter's intimation of universal death. Shakespeare's play, that is, may also be a tale *against* male sexual violence, not merely opposing it, but attempting to recognize and incorporate it into a larger pattern in order to rewrite or control it, as the tale by the fire offers to deliver us from the regime that howls outside of and for our death. Shakespeare's drama would then speak of Leontes' enchantment by the vision of death only eventually to cure both him and itself of captivity to that vision, a captivity once embraced as tragedy. In enacting the undoing of Leontes' fantasies, the play also works through its own relation both to Shakespearean tragedy and, even deeper, to Ovidian fictions of metamorphosis. The bear is the emblem and commencement of a general unloosing both of narrative stringency and of tragic emotion insofar as its appearance must always be, for the audience, a moment of intense self-consciousness coupled with laughter – a laughter that, as Andrew Gurr has pointed out, looses the audience by its very staginess from too literal-minded and, following Barthes, "hysterical" a bondage to tragic fiction. Gurr comments that the bear "exploits [the] base level, the hysterical reaction, and then pushes the level of audience response higher up the scale by the blatant challenge to credulity which the bear offers," and Nevill Coghill calls the bear, in its staginess "a kind of hinge . . . passing from tears to laughter."[44]

In the task of "unbinding" that the second half of the play undertakes, Perdita is the crucial figure. Where the disguised Florizel hints at a repetition of the pattern of metamorphosis and sexual betrayal, Perdita counters with a wish to go back to the play's primal deep moment of disaster and undo it, to recoup Proserpina's flowers at the very moment of their loss and by so doing bring what was dead back to life. This will be her function at the level of the family story also: she is a general solvent of overgrown rigidities.

VI

From the moment of her appearance, Perdita exhibits a profound suspicion of the various designs and theatricalities thrust upon her. Her response to Florizel's opening accolade to her "unusual weeds" that "to each part of you / Does give a life" (IV.i.1–2) is that these are "extremes" in which she has been "pranked up." In part these fears are inflected socially and address the distance between aristocrat and shepherdess, yet at the same time social distance also figures an anxiety about female vulnerability to male predation, also felt as a discrepancy in power. Perdita's response to Florizel's citation of Olympian precedents for his love, even with his added promise that "my desires / Run not before mine honor, nor my lusts / Burn hotter than my faith" (IV.iv.33–5), is distinctly skeptical:

> PERDITA   O but, sir,
> Your resolution cannot hold when 'tis
> Oppos'd (as it must be) by th' power of the King.
> One of these two must be necessities,
> Which then will speak, that you must change this purpose,
> Or I my life.   (IV.iv.35–40)

The last lines here may as easily intimate that the change will be in Perdita's life as a virgin as in her life as shepherdess, or that Florizel's changed "purpose" will be his protestation of honor. Florizel himself picks up the latter hint when he calls these "forc'd thoughts."

The scene of the presentation of flowers that follows has been commented on many times, but it is important to note that during its course Perdita at last refers directly to the myth of Proserpina I believe underpins so much of the play. Its open citation occurs here because now at last the implications of the myth are being directly confronted and resisted. Despite her doubts about the intentions inside male theatrical fictions such as Florizel's, Perdita publicly declares herself committed to active sexual expression, and to Florizel. Of all Shakespeare's young women, save perhaps Juliet, she is the most open in welcoming the biological life of the sexual body. But in order to assert this rightness of sexuality, she must somehow confront and defeat the pervasive connection between desire and death which has so far dominated the play.

For even as the play celebrates Perdita in the scene, it also hedges its account of her beauty with a male death-gaze whose implications we should by now be alive to. Perhaps jogged by her clearly expressed desire to have Florizel "breed by" her, together with her citation of the marigold "that goes to bed wi' th' sun, / And with him rises weeping" (IV.iv.105–6), Camillo's response to Perdita's beauty has wintry undertones that she quickly pinpoints and laughs away:

> CAMILLO   I should leave grazing, were I of your flock,
> And only live by gazing.
>
> PERDITA   Out, alas!
> You'ld be so lean, that blasts of January
> Would blow you through and through.   (IV.iv.109–12)

Within Camillo's image of himself as "gazing" we may descry Leontes' use of the aesthetic stance as a way of resisting human connection. Though Camillo himself does not see it, his way of putting it "freezes" both himself and Perdita into the postures of statuary. Perdita follows up the implications for sexual life of such an idolatry in order to undo them. She at once turns to Florizel and her companion shepherdesses "that wear upon your virgin branches yet / Your maidenheads growing," and it is to apprehend and gloss the moment of defloration that the thought of Proserpina's flowers springs up. The lines are famous, but for that reason often skimmed. For instance, the metrical pause at the first "daffadil" may well be a way to mark the difficulty of negotiating imaginatively the very moment of abduction and winter. The mythographic profusion, the sexual personality and reach with which the flowers are conjured from this hiatus is remarkable, and indexes the

intensity of Perdita's wish to exercise imaginative control over the choice
and meaning of sexual surrender:

> O Proserpina,
> For the flow'rs now, that, frighted, thou let'st fall
> From Dis's waggon! daffadils,
> That come before the swallow dares, and take
> The winds of March with beauty; violets, dim,
> But sweeter than the lids of Juno's eyes,
> Or Cytherea's breath; pale primeroses,
> That die unmarried, ere they can behold
> Bright Phoebus in his strength (a malady
> Most incident to maids); bold oxlips, and
> The crown imperial; lilies of all kinds
> (The flow'r-de-luce being one). O, these I lack,
> To make you garlands of, and my sweet friend,
> To strew him o'er and o'er!   (IV.iv.116–29)

Lively enjambments, especially of the sexually-charged "take" and of
"behold," give the passage great energy. The lines are infused with
metamorphic and creative power, growing out of their population by
images of reproductive potency. Jonathan Bate comments eloquently of
them that:

the undertow of allusion to the classical gods forces us to read this speech
mythologically as well as naturally. Flowers here have a metamorphic power –
daffodils can charm the wild winds of March and yellow fritillaries can signify
royalty.... And the language itself is metamorphic: "O, these I lack" comes as a
shock because in the mind's eye the flowers have been present.... Something
similar happens with the apostrophe to Proserpina: Perdita is saying that she is
not like Proserpina, because she lacks the flowers, but in realizing the flowers
linguistically she becomes Proserpina. She has picked up what her predecessor
dropped when whisked away by Dis.[45]

Yet this is not quite so: Perdita becomes not Proserpina, but the maiden
for whom Proserpina's story stands as a warning – to whom it has *not*
happened. The flowers emblematize what must not be allowed to
happen, what Perdita's strong imaginative response to the energies, even
dangers, of sexuality will war against in the name of life. It is Florizel,
like Leontes before him, who sees himself as "taken" into death by the
profusion of flower-language, who associates it not with reproduction
but with elegy: "What? like a corse?" Perdita insists that Florizel's desire
will *not* become the portal of death ("icta viam tellus in Tartara"), but
will remain forever the body of his life, the "sceptrum regale" "not to be
buried / But quick and in mine arms." Its only rigor will be hers willingly
to enjoy: "a bank for love to lie and play on," its death one to be played
out "o'er and o'er" in the dying and rising of sexual love. And suddenly

she seems to have overcome Dis, to have the very flowers she wished for: "Come, take your flow'rs."

Imaginative energy intercoupled with sexual longing have carried Perdita herself into a strangely metamorphic ambience, which she now registers with some hesitation as a version of the very theatricality over which she had earlier hesitated: "Methinks I play as I have seen them do / In Whitsun pastorals. Sure this robe of mine / Does change my disposition" (IV.iv.133–5). Sexual inventiveness, it seems, creates out of its own – human – energy a correspondent impulse into fiction and theatre. The insight, over which Perdita is in doubt, answers more surely than anything so far the rather stiff conversation on "art and nature" with Polixenes that has preceded. Sexuality spins itself a metamorphic theatricality that rushes to keep up with, express, and render for consciousness the developmental urgencies of generative process and time. Perdita's local myth of the flowers of life thus not only provides a dialectical outgrowth of her own and Polixenes' positions from the earlier dialogue on "art" and "nature," it also answers very carefully across the waste of Leontes' tragic nightmare to Mamillius' abortive allegory of his frostbitten desires.

That the moment of Perdita's triumph is full of poetic release for Shakespeare also is suggested by the extraordinary hymn to Perdita that he now finds for Florizel. It has been little noticed how the rhythm of her conjuration is sustained and answered by the drive of his. The interchange is surely motivated by the energies unleashed through Perdita's exorcism of the covering figure of sexual death. Unchained from that dark intimation, Florizel sees Perdita as the miraculously human site of a kind of endlessly mobile self-reproduction he can only apprehend as the charging of each separate moment with the force and sweetness of the whole motion – and vice versa. Perdita seen so is a force never expended and ever renewing, that resists the freezing even of aesthetic celebration. His is a strange outburst, synthesizing a kind of stop-action perception with the sense of a fluid energy and continuity, whose best formula is the abstract and motionless motion of a wave, and whose achieved rhetorical image a chiasmus wrapped around an oxymoron and prolonged into a pun, all instances of a complex tension between motion and rest at once syntactic, semantic, and lexical. It is infinitely stronger than the "grazing/gazing" gambit of old Camillo it recalls, and we can measure in that difference the transformative work done by Perdita's refiguration of desire in between. It is the crowning moment of the scene, and will be answered itself in turn in the final animation of Hermione's statue, also a greatly stilled and moving moment:

FLORIZEL   What you do
Still betters what is done. When you speak, sweet
I'ld have you do it ever; when you sing,
I'ld have you buy and sell so; so give alms;
Pray so; and for the ord'ring your affairs,
To sing them too. When you dance, I wish you
A wave o' th' sea, that you might ever do
Nothing but that; move still, still so,
And own no other function. Each your doing
(So singular in each particular)
Crowns what you are doing in the present deeds,
That all your acts are queens.   (IV.iv.135–46)

Aesthetic perception here is in constant dialectic with the vitality of the world. Florizel experiences both a desire to arrest Perdita's movement for contemplation and a counter-desire to give himself over to that movement in its unexpectedness. His formalizing impulse is constantly deferred by the worldward orientation of his love and desire. We are close here to the heart of what *The Winter's Tale* wants to make of the relation between sexuality and fiction as aspects and motives of human activity. The fictions that humans create are energetic responses to the complex and ever-metamorphic motions of desire within them. They take their shifting life in turn from the constant and developing transformations of consciousness in dialectic with what comes to it – both from within and from without. Camillo's opening principle of dialectical "branching" becomes a description of how the production of fiction must answer the needs it is called upon to translate and manage into representation. The slight rhetorical stiffness of the "carnation" dialogue on art and nature that precedes these passages represents the same issue seen more abstractly as a question of the ethics of control. The carefully positioned ironies of dramatic situation between Perdita and Polixenes, so well explored by Rosalie Colie, work in part to frame our detachment from the exchange as a recognizable "topos" or debate.[46] Perdita is suspicious of just this kind of formalizing impulse imposed on the natural object, while Polixenes' sophistical chop-logic seeks to defend the prerogatives of planned intervention. But the central issue as the play has developed it is a slightly different one, less a matter of control than of decorum or correspondence: of what "kind" is the knack that fits a fiction to the need it answers, and how can we defend ourselves and others – as Leontes could not – against our generation of fictions that destroy or deform our needs into postures of sorrow or fatality, that "crush the sides o' th' earth together, / And mar the seeds within." The Bohemian pastoral shapes an answer to this only in the impassioned exchange of mutual fictions of desire between Perdita and Florizel.

VII

Seen in this light, Leontes' jealousy and the deep Ovidian generation of *The Winter's Tale* are intimately related to each other, and both to the small moment with which we began – in which a little boy gropes for a story whose purposes he hardly knows. The connection runs through their common practice of seeing the dynamic mediation of self and world performed via an imaginative structure, a story or fantasy which puts inner and outer fields of perception in touch with each other, sometimes benignly or even in such a way as to rectify or assuage discomfort, but sometimes in disastrous misprision. As Winnicott puts it: "the task of reality-acceptance is never completed, ... no human being is free from the strain of relating inner and outer reality, and ... relief from the strain is provided by an intermediate area of experience which is not challenged (arts, religion, etc.)."[47] The case of an aberrant or dangerous fantasy of the kind that Leontes develops, the idea of which runs all through Shakespeare's work, is also described by Winnicott and again related to other modes of imaginative elaboration which we associate with artistic activity:

Should an adult make claims on us for our acceptance of the objectivity of his subjective phenomena we discern or diagnose madness. If however, the adult can manage to enjoy the personal intermediate area without making claims, then we can acknowledge our own corresponding intermediate areas, and are pleased to find a degree of overlapping, that is to say common experience between members of a group in art or religion or philosophy.[48]

The ease of movement from private to public fantasies here, and the sense of interconnection between danger and necessity in the functioning of the imagination to connect self and world, touch Shakespearean matters closely. In moments like the exchange of mutual imaginative visions between Florizel and Perdita, we see this process vividly at work as a spontaneous upwelling of imaginative apprehensions that feed at once and deeply on the needs of the self and its perceptions of the needs of the other. Florizel needs to be assured that his desire is not death-dealing, Perdita that her transformations are not self-betraying.

Janet Adelman suggests that the pastoral of Bohemia – and Perdita, its dramatic center – are a version of Winnicott's "object that survives" its destruction by the child, therefore the proof to the child's imagination of a universe outside the self that is not subject to the regime of death at the hands of the subject's aggression.[49] This complex of perceptions, I have argued, appears in the play as a doubt about the human value of sexual expression rather than as a problem in infant development *per se*, though it could no doubt be argued that the former is a translated reprise of the latter. For the play, the rural environs of Bohemia are indeed a place of survival. Leontes casts Perdita forth, as he imagines, to "some remote and desert place" (II.iii.176) only to have her return intact from the plenitude of Bohemia – a plenitude as much of fictions as of flowers. In Bohemian pastoral, the abundance of theatrical forms in apposition – songs, dances, masquing, roguery, gods, and satyrs all mixed up – the very length of the scene itself, witness a resiliency and productivity of pleasure that Leontes' absolute regime has shrunk and truncated. Even when the Leontine violence returns in the fearful images of what Polixenes will have done to those who oppose him, Camillo as playwright and Autolycus as survival's ready rogue (for whom "the red blood raigns[50] in the winter's pale") have their ways of outflanking and skewering that severity into a kind of comic impotence. From this point of view the infamous Bohemian "sea-coast" is neither a blunder nor a thumbing of the nose, but an insistence on the transgressive prerogative of the imagination in answering the needs of survival.

From this perspective too, the question of Autolycus' relation to the rest of the play becomes clear: he presents at once the necessary freedom of story to range where it will in order to find its always-variable rightness ("And when I wander here and there / I then do go most right," IV.iii.17–18), and the transgressive or resistive impulse resident within that freedom. He is a rogue always cheered by audiences because they see in him a spirit of their own energetic resistance to darker necessities, a resistance innately part of the impulse to play: Autolycus catches us grinning because in the theatre we are (or wish to be) his counterparts in imaginative ranging. His adoption – or theft – from Ovid is itself openly admitted in his name: poets take what they need and as they must.[51] The prerogatives of fiction are subject to no law except that they must answer the needs that generate them. In Autolycus, as in Perdita though in different registers, we encounter a constant self-revision figuring a Shakespearean account of the temporality of fictions. The business of fiction-making is a never-ending one, endlessly and dialectically entwined with both itself and the need from which it springs to touch and open the world. Inside Shakespeare's play lie the husks of those fictions he has himself consumed or been fertilized by, sedimented in varying layers of acknowledgment and power: Greene, Peele, Ovid. As the occasion of playing transforms, so the medium and content of the play must also develop, in part out of its own history. *The Winter's Tale*, long observed to thematize seasonal transformation and renewal, also proffers that cycle of loss and recovery as the way of its own imaginative genealogy. It is necessary to learn to imagine the absoluteness of neither life nor death in order to enter such a landscape. These are hard lessons, not learned in Leontes, who precipitates out of Polixenes' fantasy of absolute boyhood life a terrible and reactionary image of absolute death, of "nothing."

The openness with which Shakespeare acknowledges his own poetic genealogy through the play is of a piece with his whole understanding of the dynamics of composition as a version of the general dynamics of human life in time. Though the Ovidian fictions that lie inside *The Winter's Tale* – Proserpina, Arachne, Niobe, Autolycus, even Pygmalion – all unfold in *Metamorphoses* as directly or indirectly associated with challenges to the authority of the gods, Shakespeare's own writing in the end does not display such challenge and competition.[52] Harold Bloom has remarked (*Anxiety of Influence*, p.11) on what he calls Shakespeare's extraordinary ability to "swallow his precursors whole." But perhaps "eating" is less apposite here than "breeding by." It appears from *The Winter's Tale* that his assurance, so unlike that of Marlowe or Jonson, springs ultimately from an understanding of human fictions as always in need of transformation, an understanding that absorbs the lessons of metamorphosis and generation not only at the level of bodies, but also at that of fictions.[53] Time has already stripped putative precursors of the necessity they had – from age to age, from reading to reading, they are not what they are. Hence Shakespeare's recurrent insistence, as also in *Pericles*, on the audience's active role in absorbing and recirculating fictions. And hence also perhaps his apparent, and to some puzzling, unconcern about publication, again so unlike Jonson, since his own "works" must in their turn be changed to answer the world they have in part transformed by their participation in it.

The climactic scene of the play's attention to the life of fictions is the final one of Hermione's statue. By now many strands of the play have gathered to make "the statuesque" a topic that combines a number of issues. It is for that reason principally that our consideration of wonder in *The Winter's Tale*, which must inevitably take the final scene as its central meditation, has had first to traverse the entire play. For whatever energies are released, caught up, opened, or conducted by the ceremonious and ecstatic rhythms of this scene, they have been led there carefully over the long haul. Though the scene celebrates and affirms, as commentators have pointed out, the vivifying and wish-fulfilling powers of theatre, there is a sense in which it also tells us of how at some point the theatre must be given up or relinquished. Through this feeling of "letting go" of theatre, a feeling linked to the other kinds of letting go the scene does – of mourning, of recrimination, of fear – the final moments of *The Winter's Tale* resemble nothing so much as the scene of relinquishment that concludes *The Tempest*.[54] In both plays Shakespeare points to a need to move beyond theatre towards some more direct recognition which will have no need of shadows, even if the latter have been the very media by which the imagination has arrived where it is. The theatre emerges at the end of the play as a homeopathic remedy for itself – but as fantasy and purgation negate one another, so both must accordingly be given up as theatricality, and the world inhabited once more unfantasied – for the time being.[55]

VIII

The sense of undoing, of release, is almost overwhelming in the final scene of *The Winter's Tale*. Imagined most fully in the "depetrification" of the statue, it is also explicitly a verbal process sustained throughout, like saying a spell backwards. There is scarcely a line that does not deliberately tag a counterpart somewhere back in the first part of the play. Cordial for cordial, issue for issue, kiss for kiss, stain for stain, grace for grace, wooing for wooing, warmth for heat: each echo arises to its invocation as a kind of "underword," a ghost word to be laid and replaced by the strength of the scene to which it is summoned. The decision to confront the image of Hermione, and then the further attempt to recover Hermione herself from her being of stone, is a corollary of this process insofar as it reaches "underneath" the structure of likelihoods put in place by the play to the deeper rootedness of its sorrow and rupture, in order to effect an answering repair. At the same time, the scene shapes a gesture of almost direct acknowledgment to the Ovidian material that subtends so much of the earlier action, setting its Ovidian pretexts against one another, so that the myth of Pygmalion's misogyny and its overcoming is made to confront and resolve that of Proserpina's rape, the latter itself a tale of how life and time were split into antithetical halves by an abduction into an underworld realm. As a version of Shakespearean theatre and its vivifying powers, the scene also complements and negates its own internal competitors: Leontes' tragic theatre of calumny, the Bohemian pastoral of the self and its liberties, even the trumpery animal-act of the bear.[56]

This is in short a scene that risks more than perhaps any other in Shakespeare's works: no other play brings the pressure of an entire structure to bear on its conclusion in quite this way. That it succeeds so well with most critics and audiences only makes it the more difficult to account for – since it seems willfully to violate all accepted canons of construction.[57] But then the necessity of risking excess is part of the scene's point also; in this too Shakespeare has a Blake-like energy. The scene has always had powerful and moving encomiasts, but each approach to it enters a risky defile and must carefully work through the turbulent dynamics of a peculiar Scylla and Charybdis: between a credulity that believes too much and a resistance that hardens too fast.

It is in just such a "between" as this that the peculiar and overwhelming effect of the scene develops: within the ambit of powerful transactions between words now and their counterparts then, between the statue and the living body (of both actor and character), between the present fiction and its pressing analogues, between stage and audience. The risk the critic runs is that of the characters – Leontes or Hermione in particular – of negotiating the transition between impression and expression, between silence and speech, between stone and flesh, improperly. The scene is one of general trial and to venture onto its ground is dangerous. Paulina knows this very well, and how failure to negotiate this exchange may rebound disastrously on all. Hence her protestations, her stern protocols and caveats, which must be ours too in approaching the articulation of our wonder at what the scene stirs in us.

Let me begin with a remark of Leonard Barkin's that "Leontes and Hermione are not independent organisms but a pair of Shakespearean twins, two halves of a single system. The husband treats the wife lovelessly, and she becomes a stony lady."[58] This sense of the couple as entwined, even in separation, we might take to be part of the point of having their "keeper" named Paulina, pointing us back to Shakespeare's Pauline sense of marriage as a "making one flesh" – or one stone. There is indeed a deep interdependence between the imperviousness of Leontes earlier in the play and the present immobility of Hermione's statue. But we should consider carefully the multiple resonances of this mutual stoniness. Barkan points to Hermione's petrification as an image of Leontes' coldness (Cavell would say, of his skepticism), and so it is; but it is also possible to see it as a defensive manoeuver in response, and therefore at once an effect or image of what Leontes does and a reply to it. Leontes certainly sees the stone as a moralization of his cruel error, and hence as an image of the connection of their fates: "does not the stone rebuke me / For being more stone than it?" (V.iii.37–8). But for Hermione, the advantage of stone lies in its safety from attack, its impenetrability: within it she can survive, as it were, in hibernation. Hers is the gesture of Galatea discovering – at some later date – the misogyny and distrust of (female) sexuality which led Pygmalion to carve and love her in the first place.[59]

There is a further thought within this dialectical circuit: what if stone were also the fate Leontes had himself imagined to protect Hermione from the brutality and hardness of his desire for her (here we are close to Cavell's discussion of *Othello*) – even perhaps to return that hardness in some way upon him, as the statue is now "piercing to my soul"? If Pygmalion's desire, even as it turned Galatea into a living woman, had turned his love of her to a brutal and implacable hardness, he might have wished to spare her that. Here we glimpse once more Shakespeare's churchyard horror-story of heterosexual desire: that it should make men hard even as it softens women.[60] This would make of Leontes' own venture towards stone in the same scene at once a quest for Hermione's presence and experience and a homeopathic repetition of his own desire, scanning and testing it for residual blockishness and blindness (we recall the danger lurking still in his first response to Perdita, even as a simulacrum of Hermione). His impulses to kiss the statue and to become like the statue would then be counterparts in the scene's tracing of various modes of his relation to the thought of Hermione in him.

Another way of putting this would be to note that the scene undoes the making of Hermione into an object of cool aesthetic interest that we saw characterized one stage of Leontes' relation to her. Indeed it proceeds carefully backwards from the stance of the aesthete with his evaluative and technical gaze through the collapse or absorption of that distance into the more dynamic and interactive relations of the psychological, and finally the erotic. The scene insists with a fair degree of literalness on the absorption of Leontes – and to a lesser extent those around him – towards the mode of being of the statue, their sharing its stillness as a precondition of its coming to share their life. Perdita is observed "standing like stone with thee" and declares she could "stand by, a looker-on" for twenty years; Leontes' sense of the statue's life turns him to the thought of his own death ("Would I were dead but that methinks already –"); when Paulina offers to awake the image, Leontes declares "No foot shall stir," they must "all stand still," and when she moves he must "Start not" and must be told, like her, when to move and to "present your hand." The ideas of her (potential) motion and their lack of it are intertwined throughout. Only by creating a world of stilled lives can the statue be tempted to share any life.

This gradual, painful approach worked out between Leontes and the statue is not without risk. Kenneth Gross has best described what is at stake in the play's recalling other images of return (and, I would add, of artifice):

such images are like ghosts that the play must both conjure and exorcize before any further enchantment or disenchantment of the statue is possible.... The general fantasy of return is shared by many spectators; but Shakespeare allows us at least the thought that Leontes with Hermione could all too easily become like Lear with Cordelia, torn at the end of his tragedy between the deluded knowledge of his daughter's being restored to life and the absolute certainty that she is a corpse.[61]

Other ghost fates threaten as well, and not only for Leontes: other tales of animated idols press to mind, and may lie behind Paulina's apprehensions about how her conjuration may be understood, if things should go badly.[62] Paulina's image of Leontes "marring" the stone lips and "staining" his own suggests a range of partial and improper relations between feeling and representation, lover and object, reader and text. They cannot simply meet: they must first exchange properties, even become metaphors for one another: mutual desire and mutual attentiveness are alike required.[63] What does it mean to read an aesthetic object as more than just an occasion for the exercise of one's skill or force in interpretation? What does it mean to respond to a person with fully engaged human attention? What, above all, is the relation between these two questions? (And what is it about our needs as humans that we must ask it?) Paulina's answer is "It is requir'd / You do awake your faith." But faith in *what* she does not say.

Likewise deliberately evoked is a correspondence between the statue's artifice and Leontes' frozen ceremonial of grief, that "theatre of remorse" we observed before as the ash of tragedy. The similarity is made plain by Camillo:

> PAULINA   O, patience!
>   The statue is but newly fix'd; the colour's
>   Not dry.
> CAMILLO   My lord, your sorrow was too sore laid on,
>   Which sixteen winters cannot blow away,
>   So many summers dry.   (V.iii.14–22)

Camillo has perhaps noticed Leontes weeping here, but the odd image of him as painted picked up from Paulina's lines (as if his grief were make-up) also recalls Perdita's earlier objections against "painting" as falsification – even if augmenting a genuine impulse. This brings up the question once more of what fiction or form of representation can best match itself to or answer feeling. Camillo complains, albeit gently, that Leontes, in overdoing it, has only continued to damage himself, but it is enough here that Leontes' wet tears match the statue's undried color to indicate the way the two are approaching one another, mutual images or representations of artifice as a refuge from the pain of change as well as mutual figures of death in life. Art and desire front life and death in a complex dialectic of mutual combination in which each serves as the precondition of its antithesis. The structure has an inevitable temporal dynamic – a necessarily developmental impetus of binding and loosing. Each modifies the others and what one kills, its contrary vivifies.

One way to get at the way this complex motion works is to consider a key pair of terms that run through the scene: "mock" and "like." These seem chosen specifically to suggest at once modes of representation and moods of feeling, and to provide a subtle network of relations between these. Through them the scene exposes and works through the connection of perception and emotion as explicitly as it can, a connection that goes back at least as far as the problem of Leontes' "crossed eyes" and his imagined trip-wire spider, and that underlies his increasingly hysterical attempts to straitjacket complex ambivalences in the paranoid theatricality of conspiracy theory. Consider the moment of unveiling the statue:

> PAULINA   As she liv'd peerless,
> So her dead likeness, I do well believe,
> Excels what ever yet you look'd upon,
> Or hand of man hath done; therefore I keep it
> Lovely, apart. But here it is; prepare
> To see the life as lively mock'd as ever
> Still sleep mock'd death. Behold, and say 'tis well.
>   *Hermione like a statue.*
> I like your silence, it the more shows off
> Your wonder; but yet speak.   (V.iii.46–51)[64]

There is an insistent jingle here among "likeness," "look'd," "lovely," "life," "lively," and "like" which links what is "like" to what "likes" according to an ancient and true etymological connection that Shakespeare seems here to be dramatizing. Hermione's "likeness" will revive in Leontes his "liking" – not just his remorse – which in turn will lead on to her "life." A true likeness, one made as here "to the life" is, as Aristotle said of theatrical spectacle, "psychagogic": it attracts the soul. The silent response, the intensity of attention turned to the statue by its viewers, are things Paulina "likes."

And yet bracketed inside this intercourse of likeness with liking is a counterpun in which life is "mock'd": imitated, yet also made fun of as sleep makes fun of or plays games with death (Paulina knows the statue can be awakened). The specific simile here insists on the one hand that aesthetic or mimetic "mocking" of this kind is as much a heightening of "life" as it is a gaming; one might even go further and say a gaming *in order to* heighten. But it also insists on a power to humiliate or damage the living that resides in artifice (recall Hermione's sense of her trial as a "mock-trial"). Leontes will reinforce this sense of vulnerability or victimization at the hands of the statue twice, and both times the "mockery" is keyed to the statue's ability to challenge ordinary notions of what constitutes "liveliness" and what sort of emotion ought to be directed towards works of art: "The fixure of her eye has motion in't, /

As we are mock'd with art" and at last, desperately, "Let no man mock me, / For I will kiss her" (V.iii.67–8; 79–80). With Paulina's warning reply that what Leontes proposes is only a mistaken parody of the contact he seeks (like Pygmalion bedding his ivory), the scene reaches a momentary stalemate. Paulina will allow no further approach, Leontes will not let the curtain fall but stands, as his daughter says, for ever "a looker-on."

Each of these postures of response, we may feel, even this risking of indecorum and humiliation, must be passed through as stages of Leontes' "trial by mockery" before the statue can be invoked to life, according to the crucial condition "If you can behold it." Hermione's return takes place on a middle ground "between" stone and flesh onto which Leontes in particular ventures in love and danger. And the scene compares this transaction between man and stone to the complex mediations of all our forms of address to fictional objects: the emotional investment we make in them, their mode of being through that invest-ment for us, our mode of being through their challenge to us, the claims we make on them and on each other through them, and so forth.

Yet the moment of Hermione's revival remains extraordinary by any measure. Nevill Coghill has drawn attention to the length of the scene as a way of confirming for us her actual stoniness through her lack of motion, so that an audience may be "reconvinced against hope that she is a statue." This strategy is the play's own version of the deferral of Leontes' desire. Coghill demonstrates the point by reprinting the Folio text of the passage, remarking that "only at the end of the long, pausing entreaty, when the suspense of her motionlessness has been continued until it must seem unendurable, is Hermione allowed to move":[65]

PAULINA   Musick; awake her: Strike:
          'Tis time: descend: be Stone no more: approach:
          Strike all that looke vpon with meruaile: Come:
          Ile fill your Graue vp: stirre: nay, come away:
          Bequeath to Death your numnesse: (For from him,
          Deare Life redeemes you) you perceiue she stirres. . . .

The insistent and repetitive character of the lines is well caught by the look of the Folio text. Apart from " 'Tis time" – a kind of declarative command – only one utterance before Hermione's stirring is not an imperative. Each seems to punch itself into being against a resistance, a resistance registered in the strange sense of violence and blockage in the lines, as if Paulina's call had somehow to bore through or chisel away layers of deafness to reach its target ear. "Strike," she cries as though directing a blow at the statue, and an echo rebounds off it into her invitation to deliver a return blow that will "Strike all that looke vpon with meruaile," as if the statue should revenge on "the lookers-on" all the trauma of its awakening through their wonder at it. Yet Paulina's very insistence that " 'Tis time" overgoes itself, to suggest that it is in the end up to the statue to approach them rather than to be summoned. The spectators invite, would relish, would take pleasure in, nothing so much as suffering the statue's marvelous blow if it only meant their dream of life and motion had come true. Paulina's imperatives are those of entreaty, even prayer; her cry of "Come" is a version of the ancient hymn: "Veni, creator spiritus."

These lines, in their complex mixture of exultation, power, fear, and vulnerability, crystallize from the scene as a whole the typically turbulent metaphoric energy of "wonder" that is the focus of this study. All the elements of wonder reappear here, and much more vividly realized than with Cleomenes and Dion: the sense of inhabiting a borderline "between" knowledge and emotion, of a fearful power both in and beyond the spectator, an acute self-consciousness of the medium of representation which reinforces rather than drains the expectation of enlightenment. Even the recurrent sense of spectral doubles as pressing onto the scene of wonder appears, not only in the twinning of Leontes and Hermione, but also in Paulina's odd phrasing of her warning to Leontes not to "shun her / Until you see her die again, for then / You kill her double" (V.iii.105–7).[66] And as we have already seen, there is a programmatic exploration throughout of ways in which Leontes and Hermione are alike. Longinus spoke of the strange sense of readers "producing what they had only heard." Here that very sense is taken by the play to correspond to and "justify" the general desire that Hermione's recovery be real. What Paulina calls their (and our) "faith" will produce its object "if you can behold it." It is not enough here to speak of "the power of theatre" or of "art": the impact of the scene grows also from the power of a collective desire for its success which stems from its audience. It answers a general need to test what fiction can be called upon to do in the way of reparative and sustaining work for us; to justify at last, despite the pathos of his own failure, Mamillius' sense that what was needed to deliver himself and his mother safely to one another was some fiction, if only the right one could be found. The dangers of that search, its delicacies, are recalled here through Paulina's sense of her perils, of her responsibility. The one sentence in her invocation which is *not* a command must be construed as in part an offer, in case of disaster, to go down to death herself in Hermione's place: "I'll fill your grave up." This beautifully resonant line suggests that Hermione's may have been somehow an open grave all these years – or one just reopened, at great risk. The gap of the gaping grave is now to be closed, its image of sundering to be not merely denied, like that of Polixenes and Leontes with which we began ("Time as long again / Would be fill'd up ..."), but repaired. In a dialectical reversal, Hermione will die to death, bequeathing him the very "numnesse" that belongs to him. So that the fatal shadow of Dis can at last depart.

It is therefore appropriate that the play's image for the consummation of this repair, and I think its most moving moment (at any rate the one that angles for *my* eyes) should be a slow, hesitant, astonished clasping of hands – closing the gap between two bodies through their organs of most developed, most typically human feeling. And again, according to the scene's therapy of repetitive reversal, recalling that very moment of Leontes' hostility for being made a spectacle before a Hermione who would not "open thy white hand and clap thyself my love." The play deliberately draws attention to this in Paulina's urging that "When she was young you woo'd her; now, in age, / Is she become the suitor." The Folio does not give a question mark here, and this seems to me right. On stage the moment is electrifying: its element of the startling breaks forth through Leontes, our surrogate in touching the impossible, in that expressive "O," as if he had been given a shock: "O, she's warm!" The claims of imagination to deliver the world we wish, and sustain us, if anything can, from death are now specifically ratified by his proclamation: "If this be magic, let it be an art / Lawful as eating."

Yet, as long as we are in the presence of someone called Paulina, we ought to be at least careful of claims about what may and may not be eaten. For though eating *per se* is lawful, this does not imply that all eating is lawful, or even appropriate at all times. In Jacobean England, some kinds of eating were expressly forbidden. Meat in Lent, for instance, was unlawful without special dispensation (as for pregnancy). And so was theatre. Moreover, even if lawful, it is not always a good idea to eat just anything: some things are positively dangerous as foods, and some are dangerous for some people at some times. Proserpina, for instance, might have done better not to have eaten seven pomegranate seeds in the halls of Dis. And though bears may eat people when hungry, people mostly do not – unless they are really bears in disguise, or have names like Tereus and Tamora. Paulina instructs those on stage that they should their "exultation / Partake to every one" as though it were a food like the feast that ends many another comedy. But if fiction is to be our food, we should be discriminating about it, and only eat what is good for us, what is lawful, what sustains. But how shall we know it?

The answer is that we cannot, but that certain signs can make us confident and "awake our faith." One of these is the presence of a certain kind of intuitional and self-conscious surprise at a pertinence beyond the moment, a sudden waiving of the barriers to self-knowledge, what I have been describing throughout this study as an experience of "wonder." In speaking of his psychiatric work with children, Winnicott tells of the "scribble game" – an improvisation in which child and physician alternate making and interpreting scribbles on paper. Sometimes the game would yield out of its own insouciant dynamics of mutual play a moment of enlightenment, of which Winnicott remarks that "the significant moment is that at which *the child surprises himself* [*or*] *herself*. It is not the moment of my clever interpretation that is significant."[67] The emphasis on surprise here seems to me close to the use in Shakespearean drama of wonder as "the significant moment" at which the whole fiction aims through its various divagations, the precipitation out of an experience of play of a moment that addresses the world directly, not only in terms of knowledge about it but in ways that release emotion at once towards it and towards the self in it. Winnicott's surprised children come upon themselves and their stories unexpectedly, excitedly, in the scribble game. Audiences of Hermione's recovery, on stage and off, come upon themselves, though less unexpectedly, in the act of wishing her fervently back into life – and this tells them something about themselves, about their own desires, and about the uses of fictions in recognizing, enacting, and understanding those desires. This is so even for those in the audience who might *not* wish in this way, who might need, for whatever reason, to resist such a wish, to imagine some other theatre.

These considerations illuminate both why the imagination that needs to find itself in the world among other imaginations should turn to the thought of theatre to screen itself, and why that same thought of theatre must eventually be given up in its turn. As the figure of Father Time explicitly shows with his hour-glass, time is always at once both a flowing and a turning. The Time who says "I turn my glass," and presumably does so, visually embodies both. He even suggests that the flowing might itself prove a turning insofar as the sands of his glass flow back on themselves. His whole speech speaks of a process that, while it moves always forward, both "makes and unfolds error" (as if error were at times a folded thing), and can both create and "slide O'er" a "wide gap." The theatre is implicated in this "branching" process, even in the moment of its self-recognition, since Time will "make stale / The glistering of this present, as my tale / Now seems to it" (IV.i.13–15). Through the set of deep puns on "depart, parting, departure, apart, party to, partner, and, of course, bearing a part" noted by Cavell, the question of coping with Time's partitioning (and parturitioning) flow is linked to the finding of a form of play in response.[68] And this link allows us once more to see that the source of Leontes' theatrical self-awareness in Act I was of a piece with his implication in Time's flow through his growth into desire and with his resistance against the world of generation that spoke of his emasculating mortality. Against Leontes' theatre of "one self king," the play eventually ripostes another of collective desire *for* vulnerability after all, for risking the wounds alike of wonder and of love. Truth may be the daughter of Time, but her other parent is Imagination, and their marriage is that of Blake's Prolific and Devourer.

Shakespeare's elaboration of wonder as a "between" state that precipitates recognitions, that marries Time and Imagination, necessarily includes – even begins with – the actors who inhabit and enliven the play's "parts" and who actively adjust the fit between self and role moment by moment in the theatre to answer the flow of "live" performance with a new inflection here, a more sudden movement there. As actors are the ones who take on and interact most deeply with the theatrical fiction, so the final scene is, as has been often noted, charged with the heady self-consciousness of an explicitly "actorly" task: what is the actress playing Hermione doing? Playing a statue? Playing Hermione playing a statue? How long can she hold the pose without breathing, etc? Our skepticism and our pleasure at the pretenses of the theatrical meet each other in pursuing this kind of question, and the result is a tremendous influx of self-conscious excitement, so that we feel our very attentiveness to the scene, even our sense of being "mock'd," becoming part of the developing action.[69] Kenneth Gross comments: "That the closing scene allows us neither self-evident faith in magic nor the quiet comforts of disenchanted irony is where its real difficulty lies. Finally, the enchantment ... is in the willfulness of the fiction of disenchantment, the fantasy of the relinquishment of fantasy."[70] The fine balance of that formulation itself reproduces the sense of being "caught between" that the scene so carefully fosters. Bate remarks of the final scene that "It is not enough to say of the statue scene that nowhere does Shakespeare's art substitute more brilliantly for myth, nowhere is there more powerful testimony to the creative, even redemptive, power of drama, nowhere is there a creative coup more *wonder*ful. For it must also be said that the redemption is only partial, it is neither a reversal of time nor a transcendence into eternity" (pp. 238–9). It seems to me, however, that the wonder so finely caught in the first sentence draws its power precisely from the point made in the second: not its war against time, but its awareness of the temporal in the imaginative, its finely balanced sense of their balance. Fervencies of self aside, it calls on us to see the aspect of surrender inside that imaginative demythologizing Bate calls "the distinctively Shakespearian *species humanitatis*."

The ancient metaphor of the human being as an actor and life as a stage here touches a new elaboration: the making and unmaking, the composition and decomposition of the self in its fictions becomes a process of continual dialectical pulsion and response, like the actor making his performance – not in slavish obedience to the script, but in interpretive and immediate tension with it. The theatre which was a screen for Leontes' darknesses is removed to reveal another theatre. Each in its turn must be acknowledged, and given up. But if we must give up the theatre, we do so only for an interval, before its return.

As our own excitement becomes the "subject" of the final scene, even as it prepares to end itself and leave us to ourselves, so the space "between" stage and audience becomes the site of the scene's imaginative activity, in which the whole community may "participate." No doubt this sort of thing is occurring all the time in the theatre: where else is the action at any time if not between us? But we are not always made so deliberately conscious of the stakes of our "investment" in this way. When Hermione prays: "You gods, look down / And from your sacred vials pour your graces / Upon my daughter's head!" (V.iii.121–3, beautifully undoing as she does so Paulina's agonized cry to Leontes to "Look down / And see what death is doing") there is a sense in which the theatre audience are at once co-petitioners and the powers to whom the petition is being addressed. The audience contemplates the action from within and without, and stands beside older fictions invoked as gods around their latest offspring to offer it, as much as precursors can, deliberate blessing.[71] This self-conscious invocation of the audience as parties to the outcome is also presumably one point of the return, at the play's end, of the theatrical language first introduced in Leontes' fear of and resistance to the world of generation. Through Leontes' last lines, the actor seems to speak to his fellows of a get-together in the green room, with jokes about dropped cues and missing props, and how good Autolycus was tonight, and how the bear tripped up on his way offstage:

> LEONTES   Good Paulina,
> Lead us from hence, where we may leisurely
> Each one demand, and answer to his part
> Perform'd in this wide gap of time, since first
> We were dissever'd. Hastily lead away.   (V.iii.151–5)

If these last lines call upon both cast and audience to "answer to," and hence to move away from, this theatre, as though to stay in it too long might risk repetrification, the lines also insist there must be an "answer" to this theatre somewhere else, that it must take in turn a "part" in some other life. As in *Pericles*, the work of the theatre does not stop at the stage door. It prolongs itself and finds its proper answer in some future turning of Time's glass. And we should note that even inside this imagined off-stage fellowship another, more truly final scene shapes itself, where each hearer will more strictly "answer to his part" as Polixenes once saw himself answering "heaven / Boldly, 'Not guilty'." The eschatological impulse that becomes explicit at the end of *The Tempest* is also present in *The Winter's Tale*, if hidden for now behind the image of our fellowship. The gap between the two marks an interval at once of play, of reflection, and of reflection on play, since what we will be called to answer to will be the kind of part we have played – not only in our lives but in the fictions that fed, and fed on, those lives. Leontes' "wide gap of time" extends back through the two hours' traffic, the sixteen years, and all our lifetimes of "branching," to our collective distance from an ancient sundering and an all-but-forgotten Paradise where "first" we were "Not guilty." Yet though that gap admonishes, it also invites. Between this end and The End the work of poetry must go on unfolding its metamorphic task. Though fiction quails in the final analysis, in today's green room and street and by tomorrow's hearth there is still room for it to branch and bud. Hence even in foreshadowing the end of fiction, the play concedes that that end is not yet, and that the question of how this fiction has answered its part arises for us as a question about the life, death, and afterlife of fictions in the world of generation.

It is not therefore surprising to find that this scene is at once one of Shakespeare's most powerful and characteristic and at the same time one of the most saturated with the presence of other fictions, especially Ovidian ones. Just as the fantasy generating Leontes' nightmare theatre of jealousy is both repeated and overcome, so also a secret register of alternative fictions at the level of composition bodies itself forth as an open allusiveness of acknowledgment and transfiguration. In part the scene's sense of being released from constriction registers the way it both realizes and undoes its indebtedness to earlier fantasies of mortality and animation, demonstrating their corrosive power as motivating fantasies in Leontes, then forcing them to the surface and repealing them. Shakespeare transmutes the myths of both Proserpina and Galatea by confounding and contaminating them into something new. In the recurrent search for the antidote to a fiction that has become petrified and petrifies, Shakespeare looks not to a counterfiction that "confronts" but one that "answers to" and so includes its occasion. The dynamics of psychological and poetic process are analogous to each other rather than recourses from each other, and neither is properly prior. Critics have often marveled at Shakespeare's invention of a newly resonant or "deep" psychological complexity in representing character. *The Winter's Tale* makes clear that that invention and the poetic question of *inventio* are intimately linked, that is that the framing of psychological complexity goes hand in hand with a complex response to the fact of "sources and analogues" as the sites of poetic invention.[72] There is therefore no question of a final, workable distinction between art and life. Where Ovid declares Pygmalion's artistry in creating Galatea one in which "ars adeo latet arte sua" – a formulation that became a Renaissance touchstone – Shakespeare's scene of vivification insists on deliberately displaying its intimate investment in and by works of art.

The dialectic of creative absorption and conversion has important implications for a Shakespearean conception of "tradition." I argued earlier that Shakespeare was essentially conservative in artistic practice insofar as he looked to preserve and adapt from what came to him whatever could continue to serve the needs of the present. This is a specifically "dynamic" conservatism, one that insists on recognizing the Mutabilitie (as Spenser would put it) of social and psychological structures. For such a view, tradition lives and does its sustaining work most of all in the vortex of its rupture and reassembly, in the struggle at once to retain what we have known and loved and to fit it to what we know and love now. In such fires tradition burns – to re-emerge as the phoenix, or as the turtle, or in some yet unknown shape of darkness or glory. It is not a Homeric or, more to the point, Miltonic battle of giant forms in a celestial and apocalyptic eyrie. The energy of its self-overcoming is Ovidian. Tradition is like wax before the fire, waiting for the thumb to turn and mold it again.

It follows further, and last, that we should not be surprised to find Shakespeare's work unfurling a similar relation of adaptation and inclusive correction to itself. *The Winter's Tale* seems, almost alone of Shakespeare's works, to be able in the end to affirm the image of a sexually vigorous and assertive woman, both in Perdita's explicit longing for Florizel and in the final scene's emphasis on Hermione's longing for her daughter. Indeed, the tale of the play is in part that of its own desire to rescue and affirm that image from behind the screen of an anger that repeats the gestures of tragedy. The play's ability to face and face down some of the fantasy substructures that have informed Shakespearean drama itself is one of its most remarkable and moving powers. Though Shakespearean wonder arises throughout his work in the context of imagined sexual generation, of the reproduction of the world (likewise the task of drama), after *The Comedy of Errors* the maternal figure who most literally embodies and enacts such regeneration is largely withheld.[73] Adelman relates this impulse to withhold the maternal figure, to keep her locked in an Abbey, an Ephesian Temple or a "remov'd house" until the play's dénouement, to a fear of the overwhelming image of a "suffocating mother." I want here rather to extend the argument to include the dramatic occasion. What implications does the appearance of this figure have for the relations, on the one hand, between the play and the "matrix" of earlier fictions from which it springs, and, on the other, between the play and the attendant audience towards which it is directed? To return to the image of mothers and generation at the end of these plays points to an entire complex of ideas about the source and direction of imaginative energy.

I noted earlier that Shakespeare's final scenes find in themselves both the ease and the fragility of a "right" language for desire's success in the world as love. The restless metaphoric energy of Shakespeare's dramatic language is both heightened and, for a moment, stilled into a silence full of the energy of contact. In the final scene of *The Winter's Tale*, this contact is at once erotic as between characters, theatrical as between play and audience, poetic as when a metaphor finds or makes its world, and what we might call "metapoetic" as when a fiction joins hands with its fellows. The image of the mother registers origin and connection in more ways than that of developmental psychology. It emerges as Shakespeare's most charged image for the discovery of the world, that world that desire touches with a confidence that expresses the faith of an imagining self as it, we might say, "matriculates" into it. It is through the search for this contact that the notion of "incarnation" becomes so important for Shakespeare. Through "incarnation" conceptions are made acts, desires are made bodies, and scripts are made actors. Because the regimes of the imagination and of the bodily world are alike metamorphic and complex, the work of making them touch is difficult. The recovery of contact acknowledges the mutual turbulences, even while subliming them.

But we must not give in to the temptation to identify the world into which we matriculate as at once and only material and maternal. Such an identification has an ancient history, but one finally refused by Shakespeare, if not by other parts of his culture.[74] The world has its materiality, of course, but it also is composed of the residue of past words, images, and fictions, just as the imagination that meets it has "taken in" impressions we call "objects." The process is a mutual conception. To label this side "self" and the other side "mother" is to refuse to acknowledge their interfusion in a "between" space that is both and neither. As Hermione's revival shows, it is the shared "between" ground that must be ventured onto in order for the petrified world to become a presence to and of the human.

What Shakespeare offers in the last scene of *The Winter's Tale* is not the "unearthly" revelation, the "burst / And th'ear-deaf'ning voice of the oracle" that Cleomenes and Dion experience at the theatre of Apollo. Shakespeare's theatre of wonder speaks to a mortality renewed in its sense of the rightness and the vivid earthwardness of its language and desires. Language and desire meet the world not in the form of a pronouncement (a scroll or a pair of tablets) but as a human body, vulnerable and marked in time. In Shakespearean wonder, one hears not so much the great voice calling (as in Milton) as the human tongue speaking. The strenuous and fatal energies of challenge and competition are converted into aspects of a continuing, fecund dialectic of life and death, art and desire.

Conclusion

Shakespeare's interest in wonder as an element of drama begins with his earliest work. However, careful consideration of his treatment of the emotion reveals that his attitude towards it differs substantially from those of either the dramatic theorists or the more avant-garde practitioners of his day – and in particular from the version of the theatre of wonder propagated in the court masques of Inigo Jones and Ben Jonson. Rather than signing on to the fashion for the masque in his later plays, Shakespeare's employment of masque-like structures and scenes in *The Winter's Tale* and *The Tempest* frames a considered rejection of the poetic implications of masque practice at court. This may shed light on Shakespeare's failure to write for the royal forum that attracted the talents of most of the contemporary Jacobean playwrights at one time or another. For the court masque is at once complacent and coercive in its spectacular articulation, or, if it suggests conflict, carefully sublimates that conflict into a polarity between images rather than evoking it within the response of the spectators. Masques tend to tell us what we ought to see and how we ought to see it. They are even inclined to shout about it, as Silenus does in *Oberon, the Faery Prince*: "For this indeed is he, / My boys, whom you must quake at when you see."[1] Even when not so insistent, the overall "poetics of spectacle" of the masque still seeks a Neoplatonic clarity of image that smoothes the surface and points recognition all one way. The masque relies on maintaining at least the illusion of willing and general submission before an overwhelming power: indeed its usefulness as a fiction of royal supremacy depends on taking wonder's pervasive sense of force as the index of royalty's sublime prerogative to install its chosen images as the only proper objects of attention. Shakespeare's evocations of wonder, on the other hand, are profoundly transactional, delicate, and full of difficult turbulences. His plays insist on a much deeper negotiation between the subject and his or her experience, so that wonder becomes a space of much more radical flux. Shakespearean practice of wonder is not the hierarchic and settled epiphany of Jonson's masques, and is underpinned by little aesthetic theory articulated anywhere in the period. It is rather the dramaturgy of a deep psychology of metaphor that has its roots in Ovid and its later counterparts in certain aspects of Blake, in Wagner, and in Freud.

In Jonson's masques, for all his vaunted artistic independence, the intellectual content remains largely fixed by the context of patronage, and the poet's task is merely to find suitable metaphoric trappings for the evocation of a set response. But in Shakespeare's scenes of wonder, even in those that seem broadly to parallel the procedures of the masque, intellect and emotion are in intimate contact with one another in such a way that unexpected results can emerge, results that are not programmed in advance. One needs only to think of Prospero's Masque of Ceres in *The Tempest* to see how the designer's imagination becomes unexpectedly and traumatically ensnared in by-ways teased out of his own working, so that the smooth annunciation of image he desires is revealed not as a hierophantic transparency, but as a figurative recompense covering the intuition of a basic flaw. Despite his best resolution, Prospero's fabling imagination is attracted back towards the very image of sexual congress – with its intimation of inevitable death – he has exiled from the forecourt of his fancy. In revealing things of darkness he had not anticipated, the masque becomes an allegory of the poet's complexity rather than the sublime machine of transcendent revelation that he imagined it to be.

In the distance between what Prospero wants and what he actually gets from the masque that he explicitly identifies as the working of his creativity we can chart Shakespeare's distrust of his contemporaries' coercive use of the dramaturgy of wonder and his final rejection of ethical intellectualism as a basis for dramatic practice. Plays will not improve us by providing instrumental object lessons, moral pictures of what we ought or ought not to do, nor by demanding that we subscribe to their view of the world. If they affect us, they do so by revealing precisely what we did *not* know or expect, by uncovering unknown sources of joy or grief through our participation in their elaborate networks of feeling, action, and image. Where the masque embraces a ideal pictorialism with clean lineaments, Shakespeare's practice is much more implicative, collusional, and messy. Its aim is not rebuke, instruction, and redress, but interrogation and, perhaps, recompense. In this aim, the complex calculus between emotional and intellectual response that is characteristic of the theatre of wonder becomes a keen and powerful ally.

Notes

INTRODUCTION

1 My thinking here has been greatly aided by Thomas Whitaker's *Fields of Play in Modern Drama* (Princeton University Press, 1977), which refers to these two aspects of a play as the "performed action" and the "action of performance."

2 *The Winter's Tale* V.ii.16–18. All references to Shakespeare will be taken from the Riverside edition of G. Blakemore Evans (Boston: Houghton Mifflin, 1972).

3 For a collection of comments on the matter, see A. K. Abdulla, *Catharsis in Literature* (Bloomington: Indiana University Press, 1985). Recent work on the question includes Elisabeth Belfiore, *Tragic Pleasure: Aristotle on Plot and Emotion* (Princeton University Press, 1992) and the essays in A. O. Rorty, ed., *Essays on Aristotle's Poetics* (Princeton University Press, 1992).

4 Longinus' attitude to Plato is the subject of dispute among commentators. D. A. Russell argues that Longinus' work is structured as an oration, one of whose goals is "to defend Plato" ("Longinus revisited," *Mnemosyne*, 4th series 34 [1981], 72–86). However, Russell admits that Longinus' celebration of *pathos* as a mark of the sublime is at least inconsistent with Plato (p. 76). On the other hand, G. M. A. Grube maintains that Longinus is hostile to Plato ("Notes on the *peri hypsous*," *AJP* 78 (1957), 371–4), and Jonathan Lamb, following Grube, insists that Longinus treats Plato with a deconstructive irony that makes him "softly to overflow with self-mimicry" ("Longinus, the dialectic, and the practice of mastery," *ELH* 60:3 (1993), 545–67).

5 Eric Havelock's *A Preface to Plato* (Oxford: Basil Blackwell, 1963) remains the best work on Plato's relation to his poetic precursors, especially Homer.

6 Descartes, *Les Passions de l'Ame*, ed. Geneviève Rodin-Lewis (Paris: Librairie Philosophique, 1966), 109. All translations from this work are mine. Descartes here means "first" in an ontological rather than hierarchical sense, though as the passion that leads to knowledge and philosophy he both values and fears it highly.

7 Descartes, *Les Passions*, p. 116. This seems a strange and counterintuitive detail of Descartes's account, especially as he goes on to speak of the "force" of wonder. Compare especially the charged account of *admiratio* in Albertus Magnus, who compares it with fear, as quoted in J. V. Cunningham, *Tradition and Poetic Structure* (Denver: Alan Swallow, 1960), pp. 205–6; the

178

Latin text appears in Stephen Greenblatt, *Marvelous Possessions: the Wonder of the New World* (Oxford: Clarendon Press, 1991), pp. 176–7.

8   "Il est certain aussi que les objets des sens qui sont nouveaux, touchent le cerveau en certaines parties ausquelles il n'a point coustume d'estre touché, et que ces parties estant plus tendres, ou moins fermes, que celles qu'une agitation frequente a endurcies, cela augmente l'effect des mouvemens qu'ils y excitent. Ce qu'on ne trouvera pas incroyable, si on considere que c'est une pareille raison qui fait que les plantes de nos pieds estant accoustumées à un attouchement assez rude, par la pesanteur du corps qu'elles portent, nous ne sentons que fort peu cet attouchement quand nous marchons; au lieu qu'un autre beaucoup moindre et plus doux, dont on les chatoüille, nous est presque insupportable, à cause seulement qu'il ne nous est pas ordinaire." Descartes, *Les Passions*, p. 117.

9   "ce qui fait que tout le corps demeure immobile comme une statuë, et qu'on ne peut apercevoir de l'objet que la premiere face qui s'est presentée, ny par consequent en acquerir une plus particuliere connoissance." Descartes, *Les Passions*, p. 118.

10 Ibid., p. 120.

11 "une habitude, qui dispose l'ame à s'arrester en meme façon sur tous les autres objets qui se presentent.... Et c'est ce qui fait durer la maladie de ceux qui sont aveuglement curieux, c'est à dire, qui recherchent les raretez seulement pour les admirer, et non point pour les connoistre." Descartes, *Les Passions*, p. 121. The sixteenth-century habit of collecting rare and strange objects especially from distant countries and displaying them in special "wonder cabinets" comes to mind here. See Donald F. Lach, *Asia in the Making of Europe*, Volume 2: *A Century of Wonder* (Chicago: University of Chicago Press, 1970), Book 1, Ch. 1.

12 This is the end of the Third Meditation, "The existence of God," cited from the translation of John Cottingham *et al.* in *Selected Philosophical Writings* (Cambridge University Press, 1988), p. 98.

13 Descartes reasserts at the end of each subsequent meditation that God can be no deceiver (Cottingham, *Philosophical Writings*, pp. 105 and 109, 122), as though it were especially important to bear this in mind. His postulation of a "deceiver of supreme power and cunning who is deliberately and constantly deceiving me" (p. 80) performs in the *Meditations* something like the kind of blocking from true knowledge that too much wonder is said to induce in *Les Passions*. Both are Descartes's opponents, and he conquers both.

14 Sumamus, exempli causa, hanc ceram: nuperrime ex favis fuit educta; nondum amisit omnem saporem sui mellis; nonnihil retinet odoris florum ex quibus collecta est; ejus color, figura, magnitudo manifesta sunt; dura est, frigida est, facile tangitur, ac, si articulo ferias, emittet sonum; omnia denique illi adsunt quae requiri videntur, ut corpus aliquod possit quam distinctissime cognosci. Sed ecce, dum loquor, igni admovetur: saporis reliquiae purgantur, odor expirat, color mutatur, figura tollitur, crescit magnitudo, fit liquida, fit calida, vix tangi potest, nec jam, si pulses, emittet sonum. Remanetne adhuc eadem cera?

Latin text quoted from George Heffernan, ed., *Meditationes de prima Philosophia* (Notre Dame: University of Notre Dame Press, 1990), p. 108. English translation is my own.

15   Here I am following a recent suggestion of John Hollander that the world
      being purged is not only that of the senses and the imagination in general,
      but specifically an Ovidian imagination resident in the *topos* of wax.
      Descartes was by his own admission an avid reader of poetry. See Hollander,
      "The philosopher's cat: examples and fictions" in *Melodious Guile: Fictive
      Pattern in Poetic Language* (New Haven: Yale University Press, 1988), esp.
      pp. 216–19.
16   Andrew Ford, "Katharsis: the ancient problem," in the collection *Performa-
      tivity and Performance*, ed. Andrew Parker and Eve Kosofsky Sedgwick
      (New York: Routledge, 1995), forthcoming.
17   Ibid.
18   Greenblatt, *Marvelous Possessions,* and see Gordon Braden's review,
      "Greenblatt's trajectory," in *Raritan* 13:1 (1993), 139–50.
19   See "Literary pleasure and historical understanding" in Greenblatt's
      Learning to Curse: Essays in Early Modern Culture (New York: Routledge,
      1990), pp. 9–11.
20   Susan Sontag, *Against Interpretation* (New York: Farrar, Strauss & Giroux,
      1961), p. 14.

1 THEORY OF WONDER; THEATRE OF WONDER

1   Francis Sparshott's comments are apposite: "What is fruitful is not to
     impose on Aristotle a distinction he did not make but ... to explore all the
     kinds of *katharsis* a fourth-century mind could have envisaged, and all the
     ways they might be involved in the structure and experience of what Aristotle
     thought of as tragedy." See Sparshott, "The riddle of *katharsis*" in Eleanor
     Cook *et al.*, eds., *Centre and Labyrinth: Essays in Honour of Northrop Frye*
     (Toronto: University of Toronto Press, 1983), p. 28.
2   Aristotle links the two explicitly in the *Topica*: "for astonishment is generally
     regarded as excessive wonder" (δοκεῖ γὰρ ἡ ἔκπληξις θαυμασιότης εἶναι
     ὑπερβάλλουσα, *Topica* IV.v.126.b14). Usage both in Aristotle and Plato
     bears out the relation. D. W. Lucas also notes in his edition of the *Poetics*
     that ἔκπληξις "is aroused by τὸ θαυμαστόν" (Oxford University Press, 1968,
     p. 236). Greek quotations of the *Poetics* are from Lucas's edition. Other
     quotations of classical texts are taken from the relevant volume of the Loeb
     Classical Library unless indicated otherwise. The English text of the *Poetics*
     is from the very literal translation of Kenneth Telford (Chicago: Gateway,
     1961), with occasional alterations.
3   Lucas, *Poetics*, p. 257. See also Stephen Halliwell, *Aristotle's Poetics*
     (London: Duckworth, 1986). Halliwell's work has been of great use to me in
     developing this account: pp. 74–8 provide in many ways my occasion.
4   The various proposals of Bernays, Else, Golden, and Nicev are discussed
     in Sparshott, "The riddle of *katharsis*," *passim*. See, in addition to
     Sparshott, S. H. Butcher, *Aristotle's Theory of Poetry and Fine Art*,
     reprint of 4th ed. of 1907 (New York: Dover Publishing, 1951);
     E. Schaper, "Aristotle's catharsis and aesthetic pleasure," *PQ* 18 (1968),
     131–43; L. Golden, "Epic, tragedy and catharsis," *Classical Philology* 71
     (1976), 77–85; Elisabeth Belfiore, "Pleasure, tragedy and Aristotelian

psychology," *Classical Quarterly* 35 (1985), 349–61 and the references in note 3 to the Introduction.

5   Sparshott, "The riddle of *katharsis*," p. 21, paraphrasing *Republic* 605b–606d.

6   For a related account of Aristotle's notion of wonder (but one which lays less emphasis on its divided character) and of its history and transmission to Renaissance England, see J. V. Cunningham's very useful synthetic review "Wonder" in *Tradition and Poetic Structure*, pp. 188–231. For a broader account of the critical afterlife of the *Poetics*, see Halliwell, *Aristotle's Poetics*, Ch. 10.

7   English quotations from Plato are taken from *The Collected Dialogues*, ed. Edith Hamilton and Huntington Cairns (Princeton University Press, 1961).

8   See 306e.4; 276d.3, 4, and 274a.3; 276d.4; 283a.7, b.1, c.1; 286c.3; 288a.6; 289e.4; 294a.4; 295a.5; 303c.2, 4. Note however the use of the term by Socrates to indicate genuine philosophical leanings at 279e.1.

9   Similar language is not infrequently used elsewhere of spurious argument or impressive rhetorical display lacking in substance, as in *Symposium* 198a.6 of Agathon's florid peroration.

10 Coleridge is speaking of *Romeo and Juliet* I.i.178–84. The passage appears as epigraph to this chapter, from Collier's notes to Coleridge's lecture, *Lectures 1808–19 on Literature*, ed. R. A. Foakes, vol. 5:1 of *The Collected Works of Samuel Taylor Coleridge* (Princeton University Press, 1987), p. 311.

11 Plato shortly after has Socrates apologize for the "poetical" quality of his language, claiming it was to please Phaedrus (257a), but the latter says it has filled him with "admiration" (θαύμασας, 257c).

12 Note also the link to logical reasoning assumed in the discussion of our interpretive acts at *Poetics* 4, 1448b.16. The nature of the "syllogisms" performed here is worth exploring: the dual criteria of "necessary *or* probable" suggests that these are not specifically rigorous logically demonstrable relations, but that rhetorical enthymemes will do as well. This possibility opens up *mimesis* to the world of persuasion, and therefore of the social and ideological in ways that Aristotle is at times anxious about (as for example in Chapter 16 over the modes of recognition). For a particularly useful discussion of these issues and their continued liveliness, see Christopher Prendergast, *The Order of Mimesis* (Cambridge University Press, 1986), esp. Chs. 1 and 7.

13 Aristotle's definition of pleasure is at *Rhetoric* 1369b.37–9: "Let it be assumed that pleasure is a certain movement of the soul [κίνησίν τινα τῆς ψυχῆς], a sudden and perceptible settling down into its natural state, and pain the opposite." This concept of pleasure has had a powerful influence. Associated with the economy of sexual excitation, from which it perhaps derives, it reappears on the opening page of Freud's *Beyond the Pleasure Principle*, in James Strachey, ed. and trans., *Standard Edition of the* [...] *Works of Sigmund Freud*, 24 vols. (London: Hogarth Press, 1955), vol. XVIII. Freud, however, goes on to explore other instances of apparent pleasure that oppose this narrative, for instance, the attraction of deferral. This latter model may recall the impulse to deferral and narrative disruption in Plato's *Phaedrus*.

14   St. Thomas Aquinas spots the difficulty, and lays it out in his usual careful
     fashion in the *Summa Theologiae*. Like Aristotle, Aquinas escapes from the
     apparent contradiction of a pleasure derived from difficulty and blockage on
     the "path to truth" by defining the affect prospectively with reference to its
     resolution in knowledge ("Est autem admiratio desiderium quoddam
     sciendi"), and the corresponding present desire for that knowledge. But
     again, though he emphasizes the forward, unimpeded movement of knowl-
     edge, the definition that allows the argument for pleasure proceeds as an
     anticipated back-formation, finding the pleasure of wonder to be dependent
     on the expectation of another retrospective pleasure resolving wonder into
     knowledge. But Aquinas also discusses the relation of wonder to fear at
     Summa, 1a.2ae. 41.4, where he divides wonder into several species to solve
     the problems arising from contradictions in its simultaneous connection to
     fear (and hence evil) and philosophical knowledge (good). All references to
     the *Summa* are to the Blackfriars edition and translation, 60 vols., general
     editors Thomas Gilby and T. C. O'Brien (London: Eyre & Spottiswoode,
     1963–75).

15   Φύσει γάρ πως ὑπὸ τἀληθοῦς ὕψους ἐπαίρεταί τε ἡμῶν ἡ ψυχὴ καὶ γαῦρόν
     τι ἀνάστημα λαμβάνουσα πληροῦται χαρᾶς καὶ μεγαλαυχίας, ὡς αὐτὴ
     γεννήσασα ὅπερ ἤκουσεν. Text and translation from the edition of
     W. Rhys Roberts (Cambridge: Cambridge University Press, 1935). Longinus
     uses ἔκπληξις and related words on numerous occasions to describe the
     reader's response to ὕψος. See especially 1.4 (with θαυμάσιον in the next
     line), 12.5 (Roberts translates "enthralled"), 15.2 ("enthrallment"), 15.11
     ("dazzling"), 35.4 (along with ἀξιοθαυμαστότερον = "a greater marvel"
     two lines later – the whole passage exploits the vocabulary).

16   Over against this, we might set the recurrent images of enslavement and
     liberation, such as the reference to broken bonds in Chapter 15. For
     discussion of these aspects of Longinus, see Neil Hertz, "A reading of
     Longinus" in *The End of the Line* (New York: Columbia University Press:
     1985), pp. 1–20; Paul Fry, *The Reach of Criticism* (New Haven: Yale
     University Press, 1983), Ch. 2, and Kimberley Benston in his unpublished
     dissertation "The shaping of the Marlovian sublime" (Yale University,
     1980), Ch. 1. On later transformations, see also Thomas Weiskel, *The
     Romantic Sublime* (Baltimore: Johns Hopkins University Press, 1976), who
     appropriates it to a psychoanalytic model.

17   Fry, *Reach of Criticism*, p. 49. For Wimsatt's remarks, see William K.
     Wimsatt and Cleanth Brooks, *Literary Criticism: A Short History*, 2 vols.
     (Chicago: University of Chicago Press, 1978), vol. 1, 97–111. See also the
     extended commentary of D. A. Russell in his edition (Oxford University
     Press, 1964) and the same author's "Longinus revisited," 72–86.

18   Since it is probably never a good idea to assume that a particular emotion
     was construed or even experienced by the Greeks in the same way as by us
     (Aristotle, for example, insists that there can be no fear if there is no hope
     of safety, which now seems counterintuitive, *Rhet.* 1383a.5–8), this detour
     has the second purpose of displaying the concrete imagery from which the
     Greek understanding of these experiences departs. The etymologies here
     follow Liddell and Scott's *Lexicon* (pp. 785–7, 517); Julius Pokorny,

Indogermanisches etymologisches Wörterbuch (Bern: Francke, 1959); E. Boisacq, *Dictionnaire étymologique de la langue grecque* (Heidelberg: Carl Winter, 1950) and especially P. Chantraine, *Dictionnaire étymologique de la langue grecque* (Paris: Editions Klincksieck, 1970).

19   E.g. *Iliad* 13.99 – Ajax on the Trojan attack; 5.725 – Hera's chariot; *Odyssey* 9.190 – of Polyphemus; 11.287 – of a beautiful woman. The abstract sense is uncommon in epic (*Od.* 10.326), but well developed in drama.

20   Chantraine (vol. 2, p. 425) remarks that "Un certain lien sémantique est senti en grec entre θέα, etc., et θαῦμα, etc."

21   The marked emphasis on the visual here contradicts Stephen Greenblatt's assertion that "The experience of wonder was not initially regarded as essentially or even primarily visual," nor was it true that in antiquity "the marvelous was principally theorized as a textual phenomenon" (Greenblatt, "Resonance and wonder" in *Learning to Curse*, p. 178). Though Aristotle does not specifically associate wonder with spectacle in the *Poetics* (but he hardly attends to the latter at all), etymology reveals a deeply visual orientation. A cursory examination of medieval histories also reveals the aliveness of the medieval observer to marvelous sights: comets, portentous births, etc.

22   Though the etymology of the English "wonder" is obscure, it may be related to "wound," which would accord with the Greek notion of ἔκπληξις. If this were the case, we would have the odd but appropriate situation of the modern predominantly visual meaning bearing within it the undertone of its own violence. Note also the implication of disabling or paralysis in associated words such as "amaze," "astonish," "stupefy," "stun," "dumbfound." One might also consider the arresting use of "Behold" in English in Biblical prophecy ("Behold I tell you a mystery") and narrative ("... and Behold a voice out of the cloud ..."). See also OED under "lo."

23   Hertz, *The End of the Line*, p. 78. We might compare this with Lacan's conceit of the "mirror stage" which allows the observing infant to assemble a perception of himself as a unitary body only through the mediation of an encountered image. Hertz seems to be suggesting that something like this process is repeated in the arena of the sublime.

24   Here we need to recall the deep link between the "theorist" as the archetype of the knower (especially in contemporary literary studies) and as the spectator at a theatrical event "about" knowledge: the religious ritual. The θεωρός was originally an envoy sent to consult an oracle or attend a religious rite, perhaps therefore someone who had seen that which the gods chose to reveal. The word may indeed be related to θαῦμα and θέατρον (see Chantraine, *Dictionnaire*, vol. 2, pp. 433–4). In Shakespeare's *Winter's Tale*, Cleomenes and Dion are "theorists" sent to Apollo's oracle (III.i). Our more abstract meaning is itself a product of the struggle between poetry and philosophy we are tracing here: it originates with Plato.

25   The dramaturgic habit in nineteenth-century melodrama of concluding an act with a sudden revelation and a "Tableau" before a quick curtain seems to be a vulgar literalization of this strategy, which registers the visual appeal and the sense of spatial "arrest," and imposes a definite "break" before the action recommences.

26 A similar remark appears in Chapter 14 (1453b.1–9): "Now the fearsome and piteous may arise from the spectacle, but they may also arise from the construction of the incidents itself, and this way is prior and belongs to the better poet. For the plot ought to be constructed so that, even ... those who hear [it] will shudder and pity. ... To render this through spectacle is more inartistic [ἀτεχνότερον] and needs the office of the *choregos*."

27 This despite the fact that Aristotle awards primacy to tragedy over epic for, among other reasons, its use of spectacle (Ch. 26 1462a.16). In the same chapter, however, he has to fend off charges that tragedy is vulgar in being open to all comers and in relying on performance: one of his grounds for defense is the dispensability of performance for its impact (1462a.11–14).

28 I owe this example, itself a Longinian wonder, to G. K. Hunter.

29 See the review by Alexander Nehamas ("Dangerous pleasures") of Halliwell, *Aristotle's Poetics*, in *The Times Literary Supplement*, Jan. 9, 1987, pp. 27–8.

30 Trans. David Grene in *Sophocles I* of *The Complete Greek Tragedies*, ed. David Grene and Richmond Lattimore, 9 vols. (Chicago: University of Chicago Press, 1954), p. 62. Greek text is quoted from the edition of R. D. Dawe (Cambridge University Press, 1982).

31 A student of mine once commented that Jocasta swinging from the ceiling reminded her of an enwombed foetus with its umbilical cord, an insight that cuts many ways at once in a way characteristic of this radically unhinged moment. On the diction of this speech, see the commentary of Thomas Gould in his translation (New Jersey: Prentice-Hall, 1970), esp. pp. 46–8, 140–51, 156 and also the remarks of Fry, *The Reach of Criticism*, Ch. 1.

32 The locution of "orbs" or "wheels" for "eyes" is found elsewhere in Sophocles, at *Philoctetes* (line 1354) and *Oedipus at Colonus* (line 705), but Dawe's comment (p. 226) that the phrasing refers to "simply eyes (sc. that can swivel)" seems to me to miss the point of the echo.

33 See below, Ch. 2.

34 On Cusanus and Descartes as "Renaissance" figures, see Gordon Braden and William Kerrigan, *The Idea of the Renaissance* (Baltimore: Johns Hopkins University Press, 1989), Chs. 5 and 8.

35 See e.g. Frances Yates, *Astraea: the Imperial Theme in the Sixteenth Century* (London: Routledge & Kegan Paul, 1975); Stephen Orgel, *The Illusion of Power: Political Theater in the English Renaissance* (Berkeley: University of California Press, 1975).

36 Relevant work on English Renaissance drama includes Eugene Waith, *The Herculean Hero in Marlowe, Chapman, Shakespeare and Dryden* (New York: Columbia University Press, 1962), esp. pp. 49–59; Reuben A. Brower, *Hero and Saint: Shakespeare and the Greco-Roman Heroic Tradition* (Oxford University Press, 1971) and Richard S. Ide, *Possessed with Greatness* (Chapel Hill: University of North Carolina Press, 1980). See also David M. Bergeron, *Pageantry in the Shakespearean Theater* (Athens: University of Georgia Press, 1985); Christopher Pye, *The Regal Phantasm: Shakespeare and the Politics of Spectacle* (New York: Routledge, 1990), and David Thurn, "Sights of power in *Tamburlaine*," *English Literary Renaissance* 19:1 (1989), 3–21.

37 Baxter Hathaway, *Marvels and Commonplaces: Renaissance Literary Criticism* (New York: Random House, 1968).

38 Hathaway, *Marvels*, and esp. Bernard Weinberg, *A History of Literary Criticism in the Italian Renaissance*, 2 vols. (Chicago: University of Chicago Press, 1961). Also relevant are J. E. Gillet, "A note on the tragic 'admiratio'," *Modern Language Review* 13 (1918), 233–8 and Marvin T. Herrick, "Some neglected sources of *admiratio*," *Modern Language Notes* 62 (1947), 222–6.

39 Patrizi's odd treatise, which seems to have irritated even the indefatigable Weinberg, is discussed in the latter's *History of Literary Criticism*, pp. 765–86. It is the only work of its day to make substantial use of Longinus.

40 Sidney, *A Defence of Poetry*, ed. John Van Dorsten (Oxford University Press, 1966), p. 67.

41 My discussion of Robortello here is based on Weinberg's essay "Robortello on the *Poetics*" in *Critics and Criticism, Ancient and Modern*, ed. R. S. Crane (Chicago: University of Chicago Press, 1952), pp. 319–48, as well as the sources in note 38 above.

42 Weinberg, "Robortello on the Poetics," p. 343. The attempt at synthesis between Aristotle and Horace is very evident here.

43 Weinberg, *History*, pp. 649–51.

44 Weinberg, "Castelvetro's theory of poetics" in Crane, ed., *Critics and Criticism*, pp. 349–71. See also Weinberg, *History*, *passim*.

45 See Stephen Orgel, "The poetics of spectacle," *New Literary History* 2:3 (1971), 372–6. In the debates of practical criticism over particular poems the role of the marvelous also bulked large, as in the lengthy tussle over Ariosto (see Weinberg, *History*, pp. 954–1073).

46 Stephen Orgel, "The play of conscience," in Parker and Sedgwick, eds., *Performativity and Performance*, forthcoming.

47 Baxter Hathaway, *The Age of Criticism: the Late Renaissance in Italy* (Ithaca: Cornell University Press, 1962), p. 206. Hathaway's discussion (pp. 205–300) is the most extensive.

48 Orgel, "Play of conscience." Hathaway associates the first two of these postures with the work of Robortello and Maggi respectively, and shows that the third is a later elaboration. It should also be noted that not all theorists agreed on either the existence or the value of *catharsis*. Both Castelvetro and Scaliger, for instance, refused Aristotle's authority on the point.

49 See Stephen Orgel, "Shakespeare and the kinds of drama," *Critical Inquiry* 6:1 (1979), 118; Weinberg, *History*, p. 658.

50 Quoted from Weinberg, *History*, p. 625.

51 Ibid., pp. 691–92.

2 VISION AND VOCATION IN THE THEATRE OF GOD

1 Mervyn James, "Ritual, drama and social body in the late medieval English town," *Past and Present* 98 (1983), 3–29. On the feast of Corpus Christi and the various associated traditions, see Clifford Davidson, "Thomas Aquinas, the feast of Corpus Christi and the English cycle-plays," *Michigan Academician* 7:1 (1974), 103–10; Darwell Stone, *A*

History of the Doctrine of the Holy Eucharist, 2 vols. (London: Longmans, 1909), pp. 319–34, 344–56; C. Lambot, "L'office de la Fête-Dieu. Aperçus nouveaux sur ses origines," *Revue Bénédictine* 54 (1942), 396–8. A most important work on the history and anthropology of the Eucharist in the late Middle Ages is Miri Rubin, *Corpus Christi. The Eucharist in Late Medieval Culture* (Cambridge University Press, 1991), esp. pp. 164–212 and 271–87. The liturgy for the feast appears in Vol.15 of St. Thomas Aquinas, *Opera Omnia*, 25 vols. (New York: Musurgia Publ., 1948–50), pp. 233–8. On the procession/pageants, see M. L. Spencer, *Corpus Christi Pageants in England* (New York: Baker and Taylor, 1911); Hardin Craig, "The Corpus Christi procession and the Corpus Christi play," *JEGP* 13 (1914), 589–602; Merle Pierson, "The relation of the Corpus Christi procession to the Corpus Christi play in England," *Transactions of the Wisconsin Academy of Arts and Letters* 18 (1915), 110–65, and Alan Nelson, *The Medieval English Stage: Corpus Christi Pageants and Plays* (Chicago: University of Chicago Press, 1974). Many towns later varied the date of performance, especially to Whitsunday. See e.g. Peter Travis, *Dramatic Design in the Chester Cycle* (Chicago: University of Chicago Press, 1982), Ch. 2.

2   James, "Social body," 13, 15. The "social body" has had a good run recently. For the medieval period, see Ernst Kantorowicz, *The King's Two Bodies: A Study in Medieval Political Theology* (Princeton University Press, 1957). A brief overview is given by Jacques Le Goff, "Head or heart: the political use of body metaphors in the Middle Ages" in *Fragments for a History of the Human Body, Part 3*, ed. Michel Feher (New York: Zone, 1989), 12–26.

3   For Hugh, see the translation of Jerome Taylor (New York: Columbia University Press, 1961); for Bonaventura, that of Sr. Emma T. Healy (New York: Bonaventure College, 1940). Glending Olson, *Literature as Recreation in the Later Middle Ages* (Ithaca: Cornell University Press, 1982) discusses *theatrica* briefly on pp. 64–75.

4   See Rosemary Woolf's discussion in *The English Mystery Plays* (Berkeley: University of California Press, 1972), Ch. 5.

5   The best account of these matters remains V. A. Kolvé's *The Play Called Corpus Christi* (Stanford University Press, 1966), esp. pp. 101–23. Robert Weimann's *Shakespeare and the Popular Tradition in the Theater*, ed. and trans. Robert Schwartz (Baltimore: Johns Hopkins University Press, 1978) illuminates performance technique, especially relations between styles of acting and their articulation in *platea* and *locus*. Matters of staging remain hotly debated. An attempt at summation is in *The Revels History of English Drama*, vol. 1, ed. A. C. Cawley *et al.* (London: Methuen, 1983), pp. 1–66.

6   We should recall here the treatment of the whole ritual of the Mass as a sacred (if fragmentary) drama of Christ's Passion, apparently first proposed by Amularius of Metz and current in the fifteenth century: see Stone, *History*, pp. 210–16.

7   On different analyses of the Sacrament, see Stone, *History*, Ch. 8, and William Barden's volume of the *Summa Theologiae* (vol. 58, 3a.73–8). About

the general theory of sacraments (Blackfriars, *Summa*, vol. 56) there was broad agreement.

8 Rubin, *Corpus Christi*, pp. 334–5.

9 See *The English Drama and Stage under the Tudor and Stuart Princes, 1543–1664*, ed. W. C. Hazlitt (London: Roxburghe Library, 1869; reprinted New York: Burt Franklin, n.d.), pp. 73–95. The document has also been edited by Clifford Davidson, *A Middle English Treatise on the Playing of Miracles* (Washington: University Press of America, 1981), with an introduction reviewing the document's polemic context.

10 Hazlitt, ed., *English Drama and Stage*, pp. 74–5.

11 When theological matters became explosive in the middle of the sixteenth century, contest and confusion over the sacramental emerged intimately linked to fear and disorder in the social body, and the flashpoint was not infrequently the presentation of plays. Kett's rebellion in East Anglia is the most famous example, though there is no good evidence on the relation of the play – on St. Thomas à Becket – to the disturbance that ensued. There was also unrest at York on at least one occasion associated with a play. See Anthony Fletcher, *Tudor Rebellions* (London: Longman, 1983), pp. 54–68, and Harold C. Gardiner, *Mysteries End* (New Haven: Yale University Press, 1946), pp. 49–50.

12 Anne Righter, *Shakespeare and the Idea of the Play* (London: Penguin, 1967; repr. from Chatto & Windus, 1962), pp. 15–24. The spear episode is from Thomas Beard's *Theatre of God's Judgments*. See also Harry Berger Jr., "Theatre, drama and the second world: a prologue to Shakespeare," *Comparative Drama* 2 (1968–9), 3–20, in which the presence of God provides an "encircling horizon" which "embraces past and future history, the fiction, the actors and the audience."

13 On the relations between the Church and "the marvelous," see Jacques Le Goff, "The marvelous in the medieval West" in *The Medieval Imagination*, trans. Arthur Goldhammer (Chicago: University of Chicago Press, 1988), pp. 27–44. Though he notes that the marvelous was sometimes "one form of resistance to the official ideology of Christianity" (p. 32), Le Goff also comments on the tension between the two as sources of wonder: "For medieval man what was astonishing about marvels was that they were tolerated by the Church" (p. 36).

14 Of other known cycles, Norwich and Beverley certainly had this play. Newcastle may have had it, and Coventry probably did not. See Norman Davis, ed., *Non-Cycle Plays and Fragments*, EETS ss 1 (Oxford University Press, 1970), pp. xxix–xxx, xliii; Kolvé, *Corpus Christi*, pp. 50–1; Hardin Craig, ed., *Two Coventry Corpus Christi Plays*, second edn., EETS es 87 (Oxford University Press, 1967), pp. xv, xviii. For comparison and evaluation of the four plays see Woolf, *English Mystery Plays*, pp. 105–13, and esp. R. W. Hanning, " 'You have begun a parlous pleye': the nature and limits of dramatic mimesis as a theme in four Middle English 'Fall of Lucifer' cycle-plays," in Clifford Davidson, C. J. Gianakaris, and John H. Stroupe, eds., *The Drama of the Middle Ages: Comparative and Critical Essays* (New York: AMS Press, 1982), pp. 40–68. Hanning outlines the plays' use of theology, especially Augustine (*De Civitate Dei*, XI.15 and XII.6) and Aquinas

(*Summa*, Ia.63, esp. Art 3), and shows how they adopt or diverge from traditional exegesis. None of the plays uses the "war in Heaven" of Revelation 12.7–9.

15   Cited by Hanning, "You have begun," p. 164, from *De Civitate Dei*, XII.6. Hanning insists that the York Lucifer also attempts such a mimesis of God (p.154 and n.) though there is no such indication in the text. The usurpation, as Hanning points out, is not a part of Augustine's interpretation of the event.

16   Texts used for the cycles are: K. S. Block, ed., *Ludus Coventriae*, EETS es 120 (Oxford University Press, 1922) crosschecked against the more recent edition of Stephen Spector, *The N-Town Play*, 2 vols., EETS ss 11 & 12 (Oxford University Press, 1991); George England and A. W. Pollard, eds., *The Towneley Plays*, EETS es 71 (London: K. Paul, Trench, Truebner & Co., 1897) and Lucy Toulmin Smith, ed., *York Plays* (orig. publ. 1885; repr. New York: Russell and Russell, 1963). In quotation, I have regularized thorn spellings to "th".

17   From Old English and Old Norse, respectively, cf. l. 85. See *MED* Vol. N, pp. 952 and 956. See also Richard J. Collier, *Poetry and Drama in the York Corpus Christi Play* (Hamden: Archon Books, 1978), esp. pp. 20–3, 26–30, 94–6.

18   Hanning, "You have begun," pp. 158–60.

19   One might invoke here Harold Bloom's proposal of Lucretius' "clinamen" or "swerve" by which a belated imagination claims the right to an originary force. See *The Anxiety of Influence*, pp. 19–45. Bloom allegorizes this creative swerve precisely as the fall of Satan, making it the first of his "revisionary ratios."

20   See *MED* under "mark." The phrase "markid and made" seems to have been a conventional alliterative pairing in the fifteenth century, as here in l. 58 in the "mightefull maker that markid us and made us." But the York author has Lucifer drive a wedge between making and marking, production and reception.

21   "Similis ero Altissimo" (Isaiah 14.14).

22   Hanning ("You have begun," p. 160) assumes that Lucifer's fault was repeated by each of the angels independently, which is possible but not stated in the play.

23   On the inspirational acquisition of knowledge in the prophets and writers of scripture, see Aquinas, *Summa*, 2a.2ae.171–3 and 175.2 (Blackfriars vol. 45, ed. Roland Potter). On knowledge of God see *Summa*, 1a.12, and on human knowledge in general, 1a.79 and 84ff.

24   See *New Catholic Encyclopedia*, vol. 14, pp. 243–5, also the commentaries on the synoptic Gospel narratives (Matthew 17.1–9; Mark 9.2–9; Luke 9.28–36) in the *Interpreter's Bible* (New York: Abingdon Press, 1951), vol. 7, pp. 458–60, 774–7; vol. 8, pp. 173–6.

25   There is some evidence that Aquinas' position is incorporated into the play – it was no doubt a standard exegesis – in the speeches of Helyas and Moyses, who refer to their respective representation of paradise and hell, future and past.

26   There is no indication in the MS as to whether or not the Father in the cloud

is directly visible to the audience. The stage-direction reads "Hic descendunt nubes" and the speech prefix "Pater in nube" (Smith reads this as a single stage-direction). Either presentation is possible, though a God who is audible only is closer to the Biblical passage. In any case God is certainly audible to the audience and neither visible nor audible to the disciples.

27 I have been able to find no authority or parallel for the York version of the disciples' experience here. In the Gospels they give no indication of not having understood. It is true that they are greatly fearful, are mistaken about the two figures (Peter offers to build Tabernacles for all three) and are "gravati ... somno" even while "vigilantes" in Luke (9.32), but in none of the Gospels do they fail to perceive the Father's voice, the more so as its main injunction is to "Hear."

28 Travis, *Dramatic Design*, p. 201.

29 "... siche myraclis pleyinge зyveth noon occasioun of verrey wepynge and nedeful, but the wepyng that fallith to men and wymmen by the siзte of siche miraclis pleyinge, as thei ben not principaly for theire oune synnes ne of their gode feith withinne sorye, but more of their siзt withoute sory, is not alowable byfore God, but more reprovable," Hazlitt, ed., *English Drama*, p. 82. (I have repunctuated the last sentence slightly where Hazlitt misinterprets the syntax.) The proto-Protestant character of the writer's position here is particularly clear.

30 The cycles choose between the various Gospel versions of the Resurrection events and have a problem reconciling the roles of Mary Magdalene. In general they have her told of the Resurrection early, but maintain her mourning into the gardener episode. Sometimes, as in Chester, this is rather awkward. York (Play 38, ll. 253–8) and N-Town (Play 37, l. 7) make her continued mourning a consequence of her desire to see Jesus bodily, unsatisfied with the mere announcement. This is also the solution employed in the highly lyric, late plays of Christ's Burial and Resurrection (Bodleian MS E Museo 160, ed. Davis, *Non-Cycle Plays*).

31 See Clifford Davidson, "The Digby *Mary Magdalene* and the Magdalen cult of the Middle Ages," *Annuale Medievale* 13 (1972), 70–87; Marjorie M. Malvern, *Venus in Sackcloth: the Magdalene's Origins and Metamorphoses* (Carbondale: Southern Illinois University Press, 1975), esp. Ch. 6.

32 Even the MS seems uncertain what evidence and testimony ought to be sufficient to convince, and there are signs of attempted revision to give news of a direct encounter. See Block, ed., *Ludus Coventriae*, p. 331.

33 See the MS facsimile published as *The N-Town Plays: a Facsimile of British Library Ms Cotton Vespasian D VIII* (Leeds: University of Leeds, 1977), fol.199ᵛ.

34 Such moments still occur in plays where one character remains ignorant of an approaching threat or answer to a problem. One sees them especially clearly in forms of children's theatre where a character invites the spectators to call out when some other character appears, and then claims not to be able to understand them. The audience at such moments are of course very self-conscious about their participation.

35 It also adds the puzzling direction "spectans." Block's edition displaces this word to the right margin. In the MS layout it looks as in the quotation just

given. Its meaning is not clear. It is presumably not spoken. Perhaps it is a direction to Mary to look at Jesus at this point, as seems indicated in John. Has she then had her back to him throughout the preceding dozen lines? In any case it seems to indicate a renewed emphasis on seeing here, at the moment of recognition.

36   Towneley theologizes: "Mary, thou sekys thy god, and that am I" (l. 585); York sympathizes: "Marie, of mournyng amende thy moode, / And beholde my woundes wyde" (ll. 62–3); Chester turns it into a rather peculiar polite inquiry: "Woman, is not thy name Marye?" (l. 8 of Appendix ID).

3 COMPOUNDING *"ERRORS"*

1   Of general studies dealing with the transition, I have found particularly useful those of David Bevington, *From "Mankind" to Marlowe: Growth of Structure in the Popular Drama of Tudor England* (Cambridge: Harvard University Press, 1962); F. P. Wilson, *English Drama 1485–1585*, ed. G. K. Hunter (Oxford University Press, 1968); Weimann, *Popular Tradition*, and Walter Cohen, *Drama of a Nation* (Ithaca: Cornell University Press, 1985).

2   This is not to imply that the enterprise was not organized by hierarchies of participation, inclusions, and exclusions – after all, there had to be audiences at least. But the whole process expressed and involved community structures as instruments of logistic management.

3   For the economic downturn in provincial municipalities at this time, see P. Clark and P. Slack, *English Towns in Transition, 1500–1700* (Oxford University Press, 1976) and Charles Phythian-Adams, "Urban decay in late-medieval England" in Philip Abrams and E. A. Wrigley, eds., *Towns in Societies: Studies in Economic History and Historical Sociology* (Cambridge University Press, 1978), pp. 159–85.

4   Emrys Jones, *The Origins of Shakespeare* (Oxford University Press, 1977), Ch. 2, pp. 31–84.

5   Based on figures from Henslowe's diary tabulated in Carol Rutter, ed., *Documents of the Rose Playhouse* (Manchester University Press, 1984). This high rate seems to be more typical of the earlier period, when the theaters were still building up a repertory of reliable hits. See also Andrew Gurr, *The Shakespearean Stage 1574–1642*, 3rd edn. (Cambridge University Press, 1992), pp. 103–4.

6   See E. K. Chambers, *The Medieval Stage*, 2 vols. (London: Oxford University Press, 1903), vol. 2, pp. 379–83. The longer performances were held at Clerkenwell before huge crowds of nobility and commoners, usually in the middle of the year and especially at the Feast of St. John. Smaller-scale plays and saints' plays were performed by various bodies of clerks and laymen at other sites, especially for saint's-day celebrations. There were also performances for city guild feasts. It is likely that not all of these plays were religious in nature, as C. R. Baskerville has demonstrated ("Some evidence for early romantic plays in England," *MP* 14 [1916], 229–51, 467–512). It is worth noting that "the acting of Christ's Passion" was undertaken as late as the 1610s in Ely House "at which there were thousands present" (Chambers, *Medieval Stage*, p. 382). Stephen Mullaney has lately speculated extensively

on "the place of the stage" in London, though to my mind his reading of the theatre as unavoidably "liminal" and therefore transgressive because of its place in "the liberties" over-reads those parts of the City, which also housed both Whitehall and the Law-courts – hardly sites of transgression. See Steven Mullaney, *The Place of the Stage: License, Play and Power in Renaissance England* (Chicago: University of Chicago Press, 1988), esp. Ch. 1.

7   Some critics have argued the contrary. A recent example is R. Chris Hassell Jr., *Renaissance Drama and the English Church Year* (Lincoln: University of Nebraska Press, 1979).

8   Besides studies on Marlowe, which have necessarily to grapple with his iconoclasm, several critics have emphasized the theatre's adoption of a posture of "cultural criticism." See e.g. Margot Heinemann, *Puritanism and Theatre* (Cambridge University Press, 1980), Jonathan Dollimore, *Radical Tragedy* (Chicago: University of Chicago Press, 1984), and Graham Bradshaw, *Shakespeare's Scepticism* (Ithaca: Cornell University Press, 1990).

9   C. L. Barber, *Shakespeare's Festive Comedy* (Princeton University Press, 1959). Barber's work remains important in orienting us on the connections between dramatic form and social custom even if he occasionally cuts the cloth to fit the argument, as with his discussion of the ending of *Twelfth Night*. It is precisely Shakespeare's impulse to revise or criticize the social forms he incorporates into comedy that Barber tends to downplay.

10 It is worth remembering in this context that the number of people in an average theatre audience was roughly comparable to the number of people in Elizabethan Stratford, so that it was at least a plausible imaginative leap to think of the Globe as a brief, nonce Stratford. See Samuel Schoenbaum, *William Shakespeare: A Compact Documentary Life* (Oxford University Press, 1987), p. 26; A. M. Nagler, *Shakespeare's Stage* (New Haven: Yale University Press, 1958), p. 107.

11 On Jonson see David Riggs, *Ben Jonson: A Life* (Cambridge: Harvard University Press, 1989). Jonson, of course, made fun of the Shakespeare coat of arms awarded in 1596 and himself claimed descent from Carlisle gentry. That Shakespeare's petition was on behalf of his father is worth thinking about. Even to a cynical eye, it indicates a desire to be seen as a dutiful son (says Lear's Fool: "He's a mad yeoman who sees his son a gentleman before him").

12 See John Pocock, *The Ancient Constitution and the Feudal Law*, rev. edn. (Cambridge University Press, 1987), pp. 34–8, 274–5, and more recently Richard Helgerson, *Forms of Nationhood* (Chicago: University of Chicago Press, 1992), Ch. 2.

13 See Gardiner, *Mysteries End*; R. W. Ingram, "1579 and the decline of civic religious drama in Coventry" in *The Elizabethan Theatre VIII*, G. R. Hibbard ed. (Ontario: P. D. Moany, 1980), pp. 114–28. Max W. Thomas discusses Will Kemp's famous dance marathon from London to Norwich in related terms: "*Kemps Nine Daies Wonder*: dancing carnival into market" *PMLA* 107:3 (May, 1992), 511–23.

14 *STC* 25752, sig. F7v-F9r. Quoted in Wilson, *English Drama*, pp. 76–7. Willis later objects by contrast to the corrupting influence of more recent plays.

15 See Schoenbaum, *Compact Documentary Life*, pp. 115–17.

16 Louis A. Montrose, "The purpose of playing: reflections on a Shakespearean anthropology," *Helios* 7 (1980), 51–74 at p. 64.

17 Francis Fergusson, *The Idea of a Theater* (Princeton University Press, 1949), Ch. 4, esp. pp. 114–19; O. B. Hardison, *Christian Rite and Christian Drama* (Baltimore: Johns Hopkins University Press, 1965), pp. 287–92.

18 Montrose, "Purpose," p. 63.

19 See the pertinent reflections of Geoffrey Hartman on this question in *Beyond Formalism* (New Haven: Yale University Press, 1970), pp. 42–60 and 356–86.

20 This connection between religious and theatrical uses of the language of "incarnation" needs more extensive investigation. Though critics as diverse as Sigurd Burckhardt, Muriel Bradbrook, Graham Hough, and Murray Krieger, along with Montrose, have all used the term to describe Shakespeare's dramatic language, there has been no sustained attempt to follow its implications. This is the more strange in that the term is clearly one of central historical significance in the period. See Burckhardt, *Shakespearean Meanings* (Princeton University Press, 1968); Bradbrook, *The Rise of the Common Player* (London: Chatto and Windus, 1962); Hough, "The allegorical circle," *Critical Quarterly* 3 (1961), 199–209; Krieger, *A Window to Criticism: Shakespeare's Sonnets and Modern Poetics* (Princeton University Press, 1964).

21 Hollander, *Melodious Guile*, p. 13.

22 For ideological criticisms of various stripes, including Marxism and some versions of "New Historicism," this element of self-consciousness has been a stumbling-block, since ideological criticism is heavily invested in the notion that the work has an "unconscious" which the critic uncovers. This difficulty has recurrently given rise to the notion of an "internal distance from ideology" by which poetry enjoys a special status as cultural production. See for instance Pierre Macherey, *A Theory of Literary Production*, trans. Geoffrey Wall (London: Routledge and Kegan Paul, 1978), pp. 90–101; Terry Eagleton, *Criticism and Ideology* (Atlantic Highlands: Humanities Press, 1976), pp. 89–101, and Stephen Greenblatt, *Shakespearean Negotiations* (Oxford: Clarendon Press, 1987), pp. 125–8. Greenblatt in particular puts the matter strongly when he comments (p. 127) that in the "complex, limited institutional independence" of Shakespeare's theatre, "this marginal and impure autonomy, arises not out of an inherent, formal self-reflexiveness but out of an ideological matrix in which Shakespeare's theatre is created and re-created." I am suspicious of that "not/but." Reflexiveness can also operate on the "ideological matrix," including inherited ideologies bound up in the forms of fiction.

23 Most recently, John D. Cox in *Shakespeare and the Dramaturgy of Power* (Princeton University Press, 1989), p. 64, arranges columns on his page to divide Egeon from his sons once more. But the play is highly suspicious of partitions like this, and always moves to break them down.

24 See T. W. Baldwin, *On the Compositional Genetics of* The Comedy of Errors (Urbana: University of Illinois Press, 1965). Baldwin demonstrates that

Shakespeare used Lambinus' edition of Plautus of 1576 with its commentary, along with T. Cooper's 1565 *Thesaurus* to gloss unfamilar terms in Plautus or Lambinus. It is therefore unlikely that the translation of Plautus' play by "W. W." (1595) was directly related to Shakespeare's composition.

25   The relevant lines are 37 "happy," 38 "hap," 65 "hope," 103 "helpful," 113 "hap," 120 "mishaps," 135 "hopeless," 138 "happy," 140 "Hapless," 141 "mishap," 151 "help," 157 "Hopeless and helpless." The pattern is striking once remarked. It recurs to some extent at the play's end.

26   Baldwin, *Genetics*, p. 207.

27   The name, in the form Dromo, is a common servant name in Terence, but not in Plautus. One of the servants in Lyly's *Mother Bombie* is called Dromio, which is no doubt where Shakespeare gets his name from. Lyly's Dromio does not enact his name, however.

28   Baldwin (*Genetics*, p. 116) points out that period Bibles contained maps of St. Paul's journeys, so that a visual element of mapping and lines may well have been part of the imaginative process of composition.

29   Lars Engle, personal communication. Note that it is not necessary for this to have been noticeable to either audience or readers: it is more like a deep schema confirming the play's concern with linearity as a narrative design. It is even, conceivably, a happy accident. Cf. Patricia Parker, "Elder and younger: the opening scene of *The Comedy of Errors*," *Shakespeare Quarterly* 34 (1983), 325–7. Parker also notes some of the Biblical references with which I will shortly be concerned, and there are a good many others. In part I hope here to remedy her description of these as "still largely uninterpreted."

30   The image of Odysseus bound to that other mast to hear the Sirens' singing is relevant here.

31   The obscure joke about the parrot may go to the breakdown of linguistic mediation here: a parrot repeats its words without intending or knowing their meanings, and therefore can be (in)opportune automatically: it has its jokes thrust upon it, as it were. Here hanging and whipping is all one.

32   II Cor. 11.14: "And no marvell: for Satan himself is transformed into an Angel of light" (Geneva Bible, 1560; "Angell of light" is the page-heading on Y.Y.ii^r). Unless otherwise indicated, all Biblical quotations will be from the Geneva Bible.

33   Echoes of Ephesians turn up in the most unlikely places: as for example when Dromio says of Nell that "If my breast had not been made of faith, and my heart of steel, / She had transformed me to a curtal dog" (III.ii.145–6), echoing Ephes. 6 just after the more often cited passages on marriage. Here an interesting question arises: are Shakespeare's characters to be understood as Christians or pagans? In accordance with a movement towards the sacramental for which I will argue shortly, they seem to move across a border during the play, beginning in the crypto-pagan ambience of romance and thence becoming more and more involved with a Christian vocabulary. "Salvation" in a strict theological sense is not the issue of the play, but the redemption of a viable community is (the impulse the play shares with medieval drama); hence the language of the play draws increasingly on Christian sources.

34   Rev. 20.1–3: "And I saw an angel come downe from heauen, hauing the kye of the bottomles pit, and a great chaine in his hand./ And he toke the dragon, that olde serpe[n]t, which is the deuil and Satan, and he bounde him a thousand yeres,/ And cast him into the bottomles pit, and he shut him vp, and sealed the dore."

35   See Baldwin, *Genetics*, pp. 47–56. We should also remember that Paul wrote to Ephesus while in prison in Rome as the Gospel's "ambassadour in bondage," and his letter uses a language of death and liberation surely not unrelated to the death sentence he always expected. Cf. his speech to the Elders of Ephesus in Acts 20, esp. vv. 22–3.

36   Cf. Ephesians 14.4: "That we hence forth be no more children, wauering & caryed about with euerie winde of doctrine. ..."

37   See Baldwin, *Genetics*, Ch. 12. Also Jonathan Crewe, "God or the good physician: the rational playwright in *The Comedy of Errors*," *Genre* 15 (1982), 209–10. Crewe's alternatives, focusing on the "rational" playwright, exclude one who relies on less rational means. A sacramentality that might mediate between the theological and the therapeutic is not discussed as a model for the action.

38   That Shakespeare was familiar with the scene of the "devil-porter" at the Gate of Hell we know from *Macbeth*. Again, I am not suggesting an allegorical reading here. It is more a question of the trains of thought and association producing the particular texture of the action. The scene is of course more immediately taken from Plautus' *Amphitruo*, but to confound a medieval echo of Hell's gates with the more classical obvious source would be characteristic of the method of this play.

39   Cf. Acts 12.11.

40   Though it is impossible that this is a recollection of Longinus' hull that saves the Homeric sailors from drowning, it is remarkable that Antipholus' erotic wonder at Luciana should come up with the same image of imminent yet screened dissolution.

41   A few lines earlier these same two tangents of "Error" had been brought within sight of one another:

>   Lay open to my earthy, gross conceit,
>   Smothered in errors, feeble, shallow, weak,
>   The folded meaning of your words' deceit.
>   Against my soul's pure truth why labor you,
>   To make it wander in an unknown field?   (III.ii.34–8)

We should recall also the strange epithets used of this Antipholus in the Folio: "Antipholus Erotes" (I.ii.s.d.) and "Antipholis Errotis" (II.ii.s.d.). These may have developed from a suggestive confounding (*contaminatio*) of Plautus' *meretrix* "Erotium" with error and errancy: see Evans's note, *Riverside Shakespeare*, p. 85. The notion of love as a kind of fruitful misprision pervades Shakespeare's work. Are these traces of his "small Latin"?

42   Ephes. 5.28–31, a passage linking the estate of marriage to the mystical body of the Church, which is Christ's "owne flesh." Luciana has earlier (II.i) used other sections of this passage to argue for the supremacy of husbands, as has frequently been remarked, but the deeper poetics of the sacramental body in the play's use of the passage have been less noted.

43 Two relevant connections can only tease us at this point: first that Ephesus was the site of the Great Temple of Diana the Mother in classical times (this was common knowledge, but also particularly available through the tale of Apollonius of Tyre that underlies *Pericles*); second that the Third General Council at Ephesus (A.D. 431) declared as doctrine, contrary to the assertion of Nestorius and his followers, that Christ did develop as a human child in Mary's body, and that she was consequently *theotokos*, the bearer of God. Whether this is design or happy accident on Shakespeare's part we cannot know, but once more we discover the confounding of a classical with a Christian motif in the play. The coincidence of Virgin and Mother in Ephesus is also relevant to *Pericles*.

44 The opening scene suggests the twins are only 23. See Baldwin, *Genetics*, pp. 107–9.

45 Lest this seem overly ingenious for such a standard "round figure," there is the page in the Bishops' Bible titled "The order of times," showing the timetable of Paul's evangelical career: its first entry gives the figure "xxxiii" as "The yeres of Christes incarnation." Before this comes a map of "the peregrination or iourney of Saint Paul" (Geneva has one of these also), and after, the opening of Romans. See Bishops' Bible, 1569, sig. K2^v.

46 Gosson, *Plays Confuted in Five Actions,* quoted in Leo Salingar, *Shakespeare and the Traditions of Comedy* (Cambridge University Press, 1974), p. 73.

47 Just these connections are revisited in an even more daring fashion in *Twelfth Night*, where the sense of wavering boundary is also present ("Do I stand there?") as though, as in love, the steady "wal" of the self could no longer be policed, and where the reminiscence of a recognition effected by tokens is made marvelously redundant ("My father had a mole upon his brow"), given that the fact of the answering *body* supersedes all symbols: "An apple cleft in twain is not more twin than these two creatures." The daring oscillation of gender identity in that play adds an extra pleat to the dialectic.

48 Antipholus (usually spelled "Antipholis" in the Folio text until II.ii.110) is probably a metathesis for Antiphilos, a Greek masculine to parallel Latin Antiphila, a name to which Shakespeare had access, and whose gloss as a "significant" name was available, in the learned editions of Terence – e.g. 1552 Paris – perhaps taught to Shakespeare in school. Antipholus thus presumably implies something like "mutual affection." Baldwin remarks (pp. 100–1) that "Shakespeare evidently expected his Antipholi to signify *amor … reciprocus*, 'reciprocal love.'"

49 That the pair "feared/embraced" should correspond with the class distinction between a kitchen wench and a gentle matron is indicative of how Shakespeare's language remains open to some kinds of transformation but not others. Still, even Nell becomes "a fat friend" at the last.

50 The feast that failed outside Antipholus' door in III.i opens with a friendly dispute over whether "flesh" or "words" make the successful social occasion (ll. 19–29). Only the play's end brings them together. On the importance of eating in the play, see Joseph Candido, "Dining out in Ephesus: food in *The Comedy of Errors*," *SEL* 30 (1990), 217–41.

51 From respectively: *A Midsummer Night's Dream, Macbeth, Othello, Troilus*

and Cressida, Twelfth Night, Much Ado about Nothing, Hamlet. Shakespeare's attraction to paradox, though it is not the first thing that strikes us since his paradoxes are not pointed in an astringently intellectual way, brings him closer to company with Donne and other emergent poets of the 1590s than we might have thought. The difference seems to be in his conception of the ontology of language in general, so that it feels a very different thing in his hands: it is not so much a set of suasive or heuristic tools, still less a suite of ornaments or a pack of social cards (though he can use it in any of these ways), as a capacious surface on which the soul's currents work themselves into expression.

52 Rosalie Colie's marvelous book on the Renaissance tradition of paradox, *Paradoxia Epidemica* (Princeton University Press, 1966), discusses Shakespeare's use of paradox mostly in the context of "affirming what is 'not'" (Ch. 7) or "reason in madness" (Ch. 15). The sense of affirmation behind apparent contradiction which can often be felt in comedy is less canvassed.

4 *PERICLES*; OR, THE PAST AS FATE AND MIRACLE

1 Nancy C. Michael, in "The relationship between the 1609 quarto of *Pericles* and Wilkins' *Painfull Adventures*," *Tulane Studies in English* 22 (1977), 51–68, gives evidence that Wilkins's book is based in part on the play as observed at the Globe. Wilkins's title-page declares over its woodcut of Gower that it is "The True History of the Play of Pericles." The illustration may therefore be a sketch of the Globe actor.

2 An account of this dramatic device is given in Walter F. Eggers Jr., "Shakespeare's Gower and the role of the authorial presenter," *PQ* 54 (1975), 434–43.

3 All quotations of *Pericles* are taken from F. David Hoeniger's New Arden edition (London: Methuen, 1963).

4 Mullaney, *Place of the Stage*, p. 149.

5 Ibid., p. 149.

6 Ibid., p. 147.

7 Though Hoeniger gives "marriage-pleasures" in line 34, I prefer the above reading of the Quarto's "marriage pleasures," both for sense and rhythm.

8 G. Wilson Knight takes this position, arguing that the scene presents "a moral on the dangers of visual lust" (*The Crown of Life*, 4th edn. [London: Oxford University Press, 1957], pp. 38–9). But Pericles is not intended to be a saint: these are the risks sexual desire runs insofar as it is part of a world of natural mortality. Lust is very differently presented by Shakespeare, for example in Act IV. Other commentators pick other aspects of Pericles' fortunes for their strictures. John P. Cutts, "Pericles' downright violence" (*Shakespeare Studies* 4 [1969], 275–93), makes him guilty for coming to Antioch at all. For a useful refutation of various "sinner" theories, see Peggy Ann Knapp, "The Orphic vision of *Pericles*," *Texas Studies in Language and Literature* 15 (1974), 615–26, at pp. 616–18.

9 This is the Quarto reading of the lines. Since Collier "sayd" has often been emended to " 'say'd," that is "assayed" (so Hoeniger). "Said," however,

does give a plausible if difficult meaning in the light of the play's concern with narration, speaking, and, eventually, therapy. The daughter would then be wishing Pericles to emerge from the linguistic trap unscathed.

10   That this episode constitutes a "primal scene" of this kind for the play has to my knowledge only been noted by John Pitcher, "The poet and taboo: the riddle of Shakespeare's *Pericles*" in Suheil Bushrui, ed., *Essays and Studies* (London: Methuen, 1982), pp. 14–28.

11   The first pun is often noted by commentators – e.g. Hoeniger, p. 14. The second is more doubtful, but contributes to an association of female characters with containers through the play: Thaisa in her casket, and Marina with "the glass of her virginity." (The latter may also suggest a moralizing function, where the "glass" is a kind of "mirror for magistrates," specifically for Lysimachus.)

12   Wilson Knight, *The Crown of Life*, p. 40.

13   John P. Cutts claims to hear an echo of Sidney's *Arcadia* in Pericles (= Pyrocles) as the "mean knight" ("Pericles in rusty armour and the Matachine dance of the competitive knights at the court of Simonides," *YES* 4 [1974], 49–51). Howard Felperin in *Shakespearean Romance* (Princeton University Press, 1972), p. 67 finds the feast "quite like a scene in Spenser," and Wilson Knight (p. 50) makes a similar but more general point.

14   See Mary Judith Dunbar, " 'To the judgment of your eye': iconography and the theatrical art of *Pericles*" in Kenneth Muir, ed., *Shakespeare: Man of the Theater* (Newark: University of Delaware Press, 1983), pp. 86–97.

15   I use Hoeniger's cited anonymous emendation of "for" for "by."

16   See also Felperin, *Shakespearean Romance*, p. 68 and Wilson Knight, *Crown of Life*, p. 49.

17   See e.g. Hoeniger, p. 75; Wilson Knight, *Crown of Life*, p. 52.

18   See Hoeniger, p. 4. That the earlier name survives in *Pericles* as the name of the child's mother is typical of the play's impulse to retain but surpass the history of its own telling.

19   As Malone pointed out, this "belching whale" is echoed from *Troilus and Cressida* (V.v.23), where, devourer but not restorer, it is Nestor's description of Hector: "anon he's there afoot, / And there they fly or die, like scaled sculls / Before the belching whale." The appearance of "Nestor" as a servant two lines later in *Pericles* confirms the reminiscence. Connection between II.i and III.i is evidence for Shakespeare's authorship of both. See James O. Wood, "Shakespeare and the belching whale," *ELN* 11 (1973), 40–4.

20   See Michael, "Relationship," on Wilkins's transcription of the scene.

21   The technical use of "water" for the grading of jewels plays into Shakespeare's hands here as metaphor, linking deliquescence and hardness, clarity and fluidity in a way that looks back to Helena.

22   "Pleasure" in line 41 is the Q reading, which I prefer given the importance of "pleasure" in the play. Hoeniger, following Stevens and others, emends to "treasure."

23   For another view of the erotic element in Shakespeare's language, see Stephen Greenblatt, "Fiction and friction" in his *Shakespearean Negotiations*.

24   Terry Eagleton, *William Shakespeare* (Oxford: Basil Blackwell, 1986), Ch. 6.

25   Shakespeare uses this term in such a syntax suggestively at the close of *Twelfth Night*, where Sebastian both defuses and ratifies Viola's wonder by affirming that he is a spirit, "grossly clad" in a medium "which from the womb I did participate" (V.i.237–8). This usage is very close to one in contemporary sacramental theology, and marks again a point at which the languages of theatre and religion touch each other. I owe this observation to an unpublished paper by Anthony Dawson.

26   Marina's behavior in the brothel is connected with her victory over Pericles' melancholy by Inga-Stina Ewbank in " 'My name is Marina': the language of recognition," in Philip Edwards *et al.*, eds., *Shakespeare's Styles* (Cambridge University Press, 1980), pp. 111–28.

27   Marina's apostrophe to the gods before Lysimachus suggests that she sees herself in a position analogous to Philomela's: she prays "That the gods / Would set me free from this unhallowed place, / Though they did change me to the meanest bird / That flies i'th'purer air!" (IV.vi.98–101).

28   Mullaney, *Place*, pp. 143–5.

29   There are other reasons for having Marina not tell her story: its inclusion would greatly weaken the scene between Marina and Pericles, not only because we would have heard it before, but because the crucial fact of a *mutual* revelation in the latter scene would be lost. Marina's reticence about her past is insisted upon, and only put aside in the face of Pericles' own, apparently greater, need.

30   See *OED* under "recover, recovery." The more modern, specifically medical meaning is there first cited from *Troilus and Cressida*.

31   A song is recorded in Twine and Wilkins at this point, but as these differ from the play in their treatment of this scene, it is of little authority.

32   The stage direction for the shove is not in the Quarto, though the text – and Wilkins – affirm that it occurs. Hoeniger's placing it at this point seems correct. Pericles later (l. 127) says he did it "when I perceived thee."

33   On the role of riddles in the play, see Phyllis Gorfain, "Puzzle and artifice: the riddle as metapoetry in *Pericles*," *Shakespeare Survey* 29 (1976), 11–20.

34   As Hoeniger points out, such a paradox appears elsewhere in Shakespeare: in *Antony and Cleopatra* II.ii.241–2, *Hamlet* I.ii.144–5, and *Sonnets* 75. 9–10. All are in erotic contexts, and the parallel in *Antony* is especially suggestive in view of the sexualization of seeing and hearing in that play.

35   The following lines from Ovid are especially crucial:

> ... corpus putat esse, quod umbra est.
> adstupet ipse sibi vultuque inmotus eodem
> haeret, ut e Pario formatum marmore signum. ...
> credule, quid frustra simulacra fugacia captas?
> quod petis, est nusquam ...
> ista repercussae, quam cernis, imaginis umbra est.   (III.417–19; 432–4)

36   On the use of music in the play, see Catherine M. Dunn, "The function of music in Shakespeare's romances," *Shakespeare Quarterly* 20 (1969), 391–405; William A. McIntosh, "Musical design in *Pericles*," *ELN* 11 (1973), 100–6; Knapp, "Orphic Vision," and Wilson Knight, *Crown of Life*, p. 56 and *passim*. Knight's reading remains one of the more sensitive to the remarkable combination of simplicity and intellect at work here. See also

Marjorie B. Garber, *Dream in Shakespeare* (New Haven: Yale University Press, 1974), pp. 150–7.

37 On this and similar scenes in Shakespeare's late work see Richard Paul Knowles, "'The more delay'd, delighted': theophanies in the last plays" *Shakespeare Studies* 15 (1982), 269–80; and Garber, *Dream*, pp. 155–6.

38 A similar effect appears between Viola and Sebastian at the end of *Twelfth Night* in a section of antiphon-like patterned dialogue (V.i.241–8), where the truth of pattern is both the pleasure and the point.

39 Terence Cave, *Recognitions: a Study in Poetics* (Oxford University Press, 1988), p. 288.

40 Ibid., p. 291.

41 By an utterly uncanny accident, Jonson's famous barb that *Pericles* is a "mouldy tale" has its Shakespearean match in the play's use of the word to describe just those processes that are at the heart of Shakespeare's poetics: "by the loss of maidenhead / A babe is moulded" (III.Pro.10–11).

42 That the opening group of *Sonnets* concerns itself with precisely this question seems in this light much more than a response to local occasions, and might well throw in doubt once more the wisdom of any attempt to locate a specific "addressee" for the sequence.

43 Shakespeare seems deliberately to have heightened the role of Diana as the sponsoring deity of *Pericles*. In Gower the dream is of "the hie god" and Twine uses an angel messenger.

44 It would be possible to argue here for the image of Queen Elizabeth as Virgin-Mother as lying behind this current of Shakespeare's work, yet it seems to me more plausible to see Elizabeth herself as drawing on the same nexus. To trace all such imagery back to a political origin seems to me to reduce the complex interplay among facets of a shared cultural vocabulary in the period.

45 The figure even appears allusively at the very moment the stolen sons of Cymbeline are revealed to him. Even in *The Tempest* we may note a figure of motherhood (though this time a more tragic and threatening one) deeply buried in Prospero's farewell to his magic, which echoes Golding's version of Ovid's Medea, whose maternity was too formidable and violent a magic, but whose rhetorical power again undergirds the resolution of the play (cf. *Cymbeline*, V.v.368–70).

5 *THE WINTER'S TALE*; OR, FILLING UP THE GRAVES

1 I note also that the 1623 Folio gives the phrase as "rais'd the Tempest" (*The First Folio of Shakespeare*, ed. Charlton Hinman, p. 34), though it is not unusual to find nouns capitalized like this. My sense that we are close to allegorical and metadramatic talk here is also reinforced by what seems a hidden picture of a human in the passage – one with a "head," "charm," and "spirits" who "goes upright." The famous Oedipal riddle may also be somewhere close by: though it is late in the day, human time still has his two legs and all his charming faculties. In particular this suggests Prospero as designer of the entire enterprise. (Caliban, of course, slouches under his many burdens.)

2 Other title-allusions are, as with Prospero, given to major or principal characters: Helena in *All's Well*, the Duke in *Measure for Measure* (V.i.411). More remote cases are Rosalind in the epilogue to *As You Like It*, the Princess in *LLL* (V.ii.520), Don Pedro in *Much Ado* (II.iii.57) and Hortensio at the very end of *Shrew*.

3 "Mamillius" has no precise meaning (perhaps that is part of the boy's problem), but suggests at once mother, breast, and littleness, as though he were a kind of diminutive or (more strongly) dependent of his mother's body. For an interpretation that makes this relation the central issue of the play, see Janet Adelman, *Suffocating Mothers: Fantasies of Maternal Origin in Shakespeare's Plays* (New York: Routledge, 1992), pp. 220–38. I read Adelman's account of the play after mine was already drafted, but note several points of similarity between us, especially a shared sense that the work of D. W. Winnicott has much to say to it.

4 Freud's description of the game of "fort-da" he watched his grandson play with a toy he interpreted as representing the child's mother is relevant here. See *Beyond the Pleasure Principle*, pp. 14–17. Even more so is D. W. Winnicott's discussion of "transitional phenomena" and the developmental process of "illusion–disillusion" throughout his *Playing and Reality* (New York: Basic Books, 1971).

5 Stanley Cavell, *Disowning Knowledge in Six Plays of Shakespeare* (Cambridge University Press, 1987), pp. 194–5.

6 My emphasis, but the meter supports it.

7 At the same time, the very literality and solidity of the Leontes who now enters, with his own history and agenda, marks a crucial difference in representational strategy between the Shakespearean mode and that of the allegory that seems imminent yet avoided here. Consider how our reading of the scene would differ if it were to take place in *The Faerie Queene*. In Shakespeare, an allegorical relation is registered yet overgone by a preference for "personation" or what I have been calling "incarnational" translation. Yet though this difference is crucial for the definition of Shakespearean representation, the play as a whole remains aware of Spenser in a spectral, perhaps sponsoring way. Other contacts include the baby-and-bear conjunction in III.iii, so teasingly reminiscent of *Faerie Queene* VI.iv, and the location of the final scene in a Spenserian chapel/gallery where a statue comes to life and invokes the gods (cf. Britomart's dream in Isis Church in *F. Q.* V, yet there the image is not living flesh). Such resemblances suggest a deeper relation between the epic and the dramatic poet than is usually claimed. The most extensive exploration remains W. B. C. Watkins, *Shakespeare and Spenser* (Princeton University Press, 1950).

8 Cavell, *Disowning Knowledge*, p. 194.

9 Oscar Wilde's wry homoerotic joke that a man's tragedy is that he does not become like his mother is queerly apposite here. At this point we should also reveal that a dying Camillo confessed that Mamillius did not die at all, but was transported to the sea-coast of Denmark, where he was adopted as the King's son and re-christened "Hamlet" after him. A scrambled echo of his former name remained nonetheless, and he later had a recurrence of the "old tale": Leontes returned in a dream disguised as the Danish King's ghost to

make the same old accusations about his "brother." Mamillius/Hamlet thereupon himself became the man who dwelt by a churchyard and finally accomplished the protracted self-murder he had forgotten how to seek, while using on the "harlot king" Camillo's old poison-cup, which had made the voyage with him in his childhood bundle.

10   Freud's concept of the "primal scene" of parental copulation might be invoked here, though my reading does not depend on it. Freud's sense of the child as perceiving an act of violence performed by the father brings the two models into particularly close alignment. Freud's interest in this fantasy first appears in *The Interpretation of Dreams* (Standard Edition, vols. IV and V, 1905), though it is not until the "Wolf Man" case study (1918) that the term "primal scene" is specifically applied. The theatrical resonance of the idea of a "scene" is especially relevant to my argument later – note that Freud did not insist that the "scene" should actually have been witnessed, but rather thought it could be compiled phantasmatically through hints and inferences. See also J. Laplanche and J-B. Pontalis, *The Language of Psychoanalysis*, trans. D. Nicholson-Smith (New York: Norton, 1973) under "Primal Phantasies" pp. 331–3 and "Primal Scene" pp. 335–6.

11   Winnicott, *Playing and Reality*, p. 12. The whole of Winnicott's conception of the transitional nature of "play" is acutely relevant to Shakespeare's dramatic fable, insofar as both are concerned with the vicissitudes and dangers of growth and "development," whose deformation in the play deeply illuminates the relation between sexuality, fantasy, and dramatic mimesis.

12   On *Othello* from this perspective, see both Cavell, *Disowning Knowledge*, Ch. 3 and Peter Stallybrass, "Patriarchal territories; the body enclosed," in Margaret W. Ferguson, Maureen Quilligan and Nancy Vickers, eds., *Rewriting the Renaissance* (Chicago: University of Chicago Press, 1986), pp. 123–42.

13   This apparent change of subject that may hide a clue to the real direction of the play may be compared with the similar moment in the opening scene of *King Lear*, where Kent responds "Is not this your son, my lord?" to Gloucester's remark of Albany and Cornwall that "curiosity in neither can make choice of either's moi'ty" (I.i.6–8). The "curiosity of nations," as Edmund calls it, in choosing their proper heirs will be precisely the source of Gloucester's problem.

14   Between Hermia and Helena in *Midsummer Night's Dream* for instance, or Rosalind and Celia in *As You Like It*, and perhaps Marina and Philoten in *Pericles*.

15   This line might be stressed "... when *you* were boys" to emphasize the child's presence.

16   One might compare here Angelo's fudging of the similar issue of whether he or Isabella is to blame for his desires when he speaks of "the strong and swelling evil / Of my conception" (II.iv.1–7; this just after we have seen the pregnant Juliet catechized by the Duke in prison). The tactic is still unfortunately familiar in contemporary legal proceedings on rape and sexual assault.

17   "Screen" here should be understood in the senses both of concealing

("screen from view") and revealing ("screen a film"). Compare Freud's concept of a "screen memory."

18   This linking of clothing with wounding rather recalls the discovery of Duncan's body in *Macbeth* (both the embroidered corpse and the grooms' daggers "unmannerly breeched with gore"), and suggests there may be a further pun on Leontes the boy as "unbreached" – that is not yet wounded with that master-biting dagger.

19   We might also consider whether the identification of father and son here (and the connection of this scene with II.i) suggests that within the adult's discovery of his wife and friend as secret adulterers lies a dim and difficult memory of discovering his own parents as partners in a sexual "crime" that also excluded him. This might well have been Freud's reading, but the play is not quite explicit about it. Of course, Leontes is not quite explicit about his mental processes either.

20   Cavell (*Disowning Knowledge*, pp. 190–1) sees a similar strategy of "deferred representation" as shaping the final scenes of several of Shakespeare's plays, among them *The Winter's Tale*.

21   Here we may note an important *difference* between Leontes' jealousy and that of Othello. Where Othello's torments generate a heightened sense of the sexual appeal of Desdemona, most horribly played out in the "brothel" scene, in Leontes there is no such sense of any residual attraction to his wife. Yet as though a powerful feeling of "heat" were being fiercely imagined somewhere, his thoughts seem to run a great deal on the literal fire with which he will consume Hermione and the bastard child.

22   Stephen Orgel has recently discussed this passage and its difficulties under the heading of "The poetics of incomprehensibility," *Shakespeare Quarterly* 42:4 (1991), 431–8. Orgel's warnings on the dangers of forcing meanings on the passage or others like it in the play are salutary. I would note however that the fact that this sort of speaking is very frequent in *The Winter's Tale* is something about which a critic might legitimately frame questions: why would a play deliberately, as it seems, cultivate obscurity as an aspect of its texture? What is the dramatic function of this sense of sense as veiled or layered in too much possibility?

23   Leontes' references to Mamillius as a "kernel" and a "squash" continue the submerged sexuality of his line of thought, especially the latter, aptly glossed in G. B. Harrison's edition (London: Penguin, 1947, p. 131) as a "peapod before the peas have swelled." Cf. Bottom's joke to Peaseblossom: "Commend me to Mistress Squash, your mother, and to Master Peascod [cf. Codpiece] your father" (*MND* IV.i.186–7).

24   On the economic register of the play, in addition to Cavell, see Michael Bristol, "In search of the bear: spatiotemporal form and the heterogeneity of economies in *The Winter's Tale*," *Shakespeare Quarterly* 42:2 (1991), 145–67.

25   These verbs must remain in quotation marks to indicate that they are not quite mental acts, but nor are they quite "unconscious." They are rather "overlooked" or "ignored." But perhaps the latter is a closer characterization of what is often called "unconscious" thought.

26   The link goes right through the crossed eyes again, since Leontes has now "seen the spider." Hence too the more ghastly pun on the "cordial" poison-

cup he wishes to have Polixenes given that will give him "a lasting wink," as if in parodic revenge for his duplicitous carnality. Note that the word "cordial" returns when Leontes looks upon the statue: "For this affliction has a taste as sweet / As any cordial comfort" (V.iii.75–6).

27   A similar point is made by Ruth Nevo, *Shakespeare's Other Language* (New York: Methuen, 1987), p. 115.

28   That this be not thought merely a sentimentality, I note that the reason Hermione is restored to Leontes is *not* because of his long repentance, but because he was persuaded not to have Perdita "consumed with fire" in Act II. This persuasion in turn seems to stem from Leontes' desperate need to refuse the image of himself as a man of violence, the same need that lies together with violence at the heart of his intuition about desire.

29   Recent feminist criticism has described Shakespearean drama, and especially the tragedies, as produced by just such a paradigm of scandal and blame, generated out of male anxiety. See, among others, Madelon Gohlke, "'I wooed thee with my sword': Shakespeare's tragic paradigms" in Murray Schwartz and Coppelia Kahn, eds., *Representing Shakespeare* (Baltimore: Johns Hopkins University Press, 1980), pp. 170–87; Coppelia Kahn, *Man's Estate: Masculine Identity in Shakespeare* (Berkeley: University of California Press, 1981); Adelman, *Suffocating Mothers. The Winter's Tale* is at one level an acknowledgment of the strength of this critique, yet also frames an attempt to look further, to how the knot might be loosed.

30   On the proliferation of theatres and the defiance of orderly generic expectations by the play, see esp. Rosalie Colie's account in *Shakespeare's Living Art* (Princeton University Press, 1974), pp. 265–83.

31   On the etymology of "theorist" alluded to here, see Chapter One above. It is always possible to cast doubt on such reports, as Howard Felperin has recently attempted to do. Casting doubt is one of the things theatre is for, but also a thing represented here in Leontes himself as autist and skeptic. It seems truer to say that the play here reads the critic than vice versa. But this is a danger we all run. See Felperin, "The deconstruction of presence in *The Winter's Tale*" in *The Uses of the Canon* (Oxford University Press, 1990), Ch. 1.

32   It is worth pondering the choice of Apollo as the play's sponsoring deity (that Shakespeare followed Greene in this is neither here nor there: he *chose* to do so where he need not have). The choice is justified in particular by the play's concern to show Leontes as involved with questions of poetic composition through his deliberate "scripting" of Hermione's infidelity. The change made to Greene in having Leontes deny the truth of the oracle not only heightens the dramatic moment through the blasphemy, but frames a concealed instance of an "agon" of the poets, in which Leontes plays Marsyas to Apollo's oracle. Leontes attempts to outscript the god by calling the divine plot "mere falsehood" – a piece of business, a red herring. As usual, Apollo is quick to punish challenges not only to his divinity, but to his poetic pre-eminence. The god knows an overweening rival when he sees one. The punishment of child-deprivation might even be compared to that of Niobe, who boasted she had excelled Apollo's mother in fecundity – she ended up, of course, frozen and petrified in grief.

33 The link between this play and *Hamlet* appears again in the curious echo of Paulina's proposing to appear as Hermione's ghost, to "shriek, that even your ears / Should rift to hear me, and the words that follow'd / Should be 'Remember mine.' " (V.i.65–7). The combination of second marriage, mourning, and murder is presumably part of the trigger here, but the connections go deeper, as I have already suggested.

34 As a result of its dependence on recent myth, psychoanalytic criticism of *The Winter's Tale* has for the most part been forced to import sooner or later into its reading a symbolic transcription of Shakespearean psychological tokens into Freudian or post-Freudian ones. A particular popular instance has been Leontes' "spider in the cup." Some recent critics have translated this into a fearful fantasy of the overwhelming pre-Oedipal mother poisoning the maternal milk, while others have preferred to see the ravenously sexual Oedipal mother of a later stage of development. The basic insight here – developmental ambivalence towards the residues of infantile dependence – is hardly a modern instance, but these particular translations have a decidedly arbitrary feel. The play is, I would argue, deliberately occluding the spider from transcription, and that blockage is what needs to be noted – the more so as Leontes *thinks* he is expounding an image for the acquisition of (infected) knowledge. For this reason, such readings cannot help feeling to me distinctly partial at this point: insofar as they do not explore the contours of a particularly Shakespearean psychic mythology, they can read the historical dimension of Shakespeare's work only imperfectly, and cannot incorporate the question of his theatre and its self-awareness into the psychological dynamic. For my part, it seems to me more likely that the spider is Arachne – who competed with Athena for pre-eminence by weaving a tapestry of divine rapes. Arachne's tapestry figures via *Pandosto* in Florizel's later catalogue of divine metamorphoses (IV.iv.25–31). See esp. the citations gathered in Adelman, *Suffocating Mothers*, p. 354, n. 54.

35 Jonathan Bate, *Shakespeare and Ovid* (Oxford University Press, 1993), p. 222.

36 Nevo, *Shakespeare's Other Language*, p. 41. For Cavell, see above, n. 20.

37 See Bate, *Shakespeare and Ovid*, pp. 230–3. Bate is, of course, not the only commentator to identify the story of Proserpina as relevant to the play: see the next note.

38 See Honigmann, "Secondary sources of *The Winter's Tale*," in *PQ* 34 (1955), 27–38. Ovid is only one of three proposed "sources," and the pervasiveness of traces of Golding especially is not followed out in the brief note. Honigmann is following up a suggestion originally made by W. F. C. Wigston in 1884. Honigmann's complaint that work up until the time of writing "failed to bring the Proserpine-myth into the discussion" no longer applies, as the Ceres–Proserpina story has become a regular discussion point. See esp. Carol Thomas Neely, "Women and issue in *The Winter's Tale*," *PQ* 57 (1978), 181–94 (revised in *Broken Nuptials in Shakespeare's Plays*, New Haven: Yale University Press, 1985, pp. 198–9); Adelman, *Suffocating Mothers*, p. 360. The tale is now usually cited in discussing the mother–daughter axis of the play, without inquiring into its image of male sexuality or the role of that image in the play, or indeed of the deeper aspects

of an Ovidian "source" generally. Yet if one is dealing with questions of "issue" or "origin," it seems important to ask where and how the question of "poetic source" obtrudes.

39 Honigmann ("Secondary sources," p. 37) was the first to suggest the connection between the Sicily of Ceres' curse and the location of Shakespeare's play. It explains Shakespeare's otherwise puzzling reversal of the locales from Greene. Bate incorrectly (*Shakespeare and Ovid*, p. 232n) attributes the word "collop" to Golding's Ceres. That this echo is not a coincidence is suggested by the fact that both Leontes and Jove are asserting their part in their offspring against a challenge: Ceres has just begged that Jove "have not lesser care / Of hir (I pray) bicause that I hir in my bodie bare." But for Leontes, the challenge comes from himself, and may turn on precisely such questions as lie within Ceres' entreaty. See Golding's translation printed as *Shakespeare's Ovid*, ed. W. H. D. Rouse (Carbondale: Southern Illinois University Press, 1961), p. 114, ll. 641–2.

40 Following out this suggestion, we might re-envision Oberon as a kind of middle figure between Dis and Leontes – a dark and jealous spirit who wishes to capture and manage female sexual expression. Like Leontes, Oberon wishes to wrest a boy from his spouse, and occupies himself creating images of the monstrosity of her desire ("ounce or cat or bear / pard or boar with bristled hair"). We might also recall Oberon's epithet "King of shadows" (*MND* III.ii.347), which closely translates Ovid's "rex ... silentum" (V.356), and his ancient kinship with Alberich and the Nibelungen tribe of earth-dwellers. Ceres' curse in Golding is also worth scanning with Titania's account of the recent weather in mind (*MND* II.i.88ff.):

> But bitterly above the rest she banned Sicilie,
> In which the mention of her losse she plainly did espie.
> And therefore there with cruell hand the earing ploughes she brake,
> And man and beast that tilde the ground to death in anger strake.
> She marrde the seede, and eke forbade the fieldes to yeelde their frute.
> The plenteousnesse of that same Ile of which there went such brute
> Through all the world, lay dead: the corn was killed in the blade:
> Now too much drought, now too much wet did make it for to fade.
> The stars and blasting winds did hurt, the hungry foules did eat
> The corn in grounde: the Tines and Briars did overgrow the Wheate,
> And other wicked weedes the corne continually annoy,
> Which neyther tylth nor toyle of man was able to destroy.
>
> (*Shakespeare's Ovid*, ed. Rouse, p. 113)

41 The relevant lines in Ovid follow the vain attempt of the pool-nymph Cyane to invoke the proper course of courtship and to stop Dis. They are among the more horrible pictures of rape in classical literature:

> haud ultra tenuit Saturnius iram
> terribilesque hortatus equos in gurgitis ima
> contortumque valido sceptrum regale lacerto
> condidit, icta viam tellus in Tartara fecit
> et pronos currus medio cratere recepit.   (*Metam.* V.420–4)

Latin citations of Ovid are from the edition of William S. Anderson (Leipzig: Teubner, 1977). Golding translates these lines (ll. 525–8) as:

His hastie wrath Saturnus sonne no lenger then could stay.
But chearing up his dreadfull Steedes did smight his royall mace
With violence in the bottom of the Poole in that same place.
The ground streight yeelded to his stroke and made him way to Hell,
And downe the open gap both horse and Chariot headlong fell.

42   Likewise the Paulina who takes the newborn girl to Leontes *in loco matris*, insisting that "We do not know / How he may soften at the sight o' th' child" may recall Golding's Ceres, who avows to Jove: "I hither come if no regard may of the mother be, / Yet let the child hir father move." The episode is not in Greene.

More remotely, the image of Hermione in Antigonus' dream (III.ii), where her eyes become "two spouts," resembles in wateriness the fate of Cyane, the nymph who attempts to prevent Dis from abducting Proserpina, and whose grief at her failure and his abuse of "her fountaines priviledge" causes her to dissolve "so that nothing now remained whereupon / Ye might take hold, to water all consumed was anon" (ll. 542–3). In Ovid, Cyane seems to stand for the deep, inarticulate grief alike of mother and daughter at the violence of the rape, as Cyane directly witnesses the blow of Dis' "royall mace." Martin Mueller argues for the additional presence of some version of the Alcestis myth in the play's final scene ("Hermione's wrinkles, or, Ovid transformed: an essay on *The Winter's Tale*," *Comparative Drama* 5:3 [1971], 226–39). Though a narrative of descent into death and return is covered both in the Proserpina myth and in the Orphic frame of the Pygmalion story in Ovid, the (non-Ovidian) Alcestis tale may also be relevant.

43   The Old Shepherd later calls authority "a stubborn bear" (IV.iv.802). For the bear as an Ovidian beast, see also Bate, *Shakespeare and Ovid*, pp. 224–7. The inchoate shape of bear-cubs made them especially apt as metamorphs, of course. I note also that the title pages of the first three editions of Golding's Ovid (*STC* 18956, 57, and 58, dated respectively 1567, 1575, and 1584) all sport the emblem of a bear muzzled, chained down and leaning on a dead tree stump. Shakespeare had already associated bearishness with the violence of a man's desires, both to himself and others, in the Count Orsino ("Bearlet") of *Twelfth Night*, who begins the play speaking of himself as hunted (though as "an hart" not a bear) and ends it threatening to kill others out of frustration. Bear-baiting also figures several times in the play, and an Ovidian context is provided by Orsino-as-Actaeon, and perhaps Malvolio-as-Narcissus "practicing behavior to his own shadow." Bristol, "In search of the bear," has more information on bears and bear-lore.

44   Andrew Gurr, "The bear, the statue and hysteria in *The Winter's Tale*," *Shakespeare Quarterly* 34 (1983), 420–5 at p. 424; Nevill Coghill, "Six points of stagecraft in *The Winter's Tale*," *Shakespeare Survey* 11 (1958), 31–41 at p. 35. Barthes' "hysterical" reader who takes the text as literal truth is the lowest in a hierarchy to be found in *Le Plaisir du texte* (Paris: Editions Tel Quel, 1973), pp. 99–100. Gurr does not connect the bear and its moment of hysterical "resolution" with the character of Leontes and the tragic theatre of transferred blame which has dominated the preceding acts. It remains also to consider whether taking the stage action for "true" at some level is entirely so primitive a response as Gurr (and Barthes) seem inclined to claim.

This is an issue which will be addressed most fully in the closing scene of the play.

45 Bate, *Shakespeare and Ovid*, pp. 231–2.

46 Colie, *Living Art*, pp. 274–7.

47 Winnicott, *Playing and Reality*, p. 13.

48 Ibid., p. 14.

49 Adelman, *Suffocating Mothers*, pp. 231–2 and 358–60.

50 This is the Folio spelling which suggests "reigns in," "reins in," and "rains in" all at once.

51 The question of "thievery" that emerges with Autolycus also connects with the insistent economic language of the play. On Autolycus' Ovidian roots, see Bate, *Shakespeare and Ovid*, pp. 228–9.

52 The sequence of stories involving Proserpina, Niobe, and Arachne is told in Ovid's Books V and VI, in a framework set of "mortals competing with gods." The set begins with the Pierides' challenge to the Muses, against whom Calliope sings the tale of Proserpina, which victory prompts Minerva to think of Arachne's challenge, whose unhappy destiny fails to instruct her friend Niobe, whose fate in turn reminds her townsmen of that of Marsyas, the final and most disastrous example. Not only is Autolycus born in the competition between Mercury and Apollo to impregnate Chione, his mother, but she in turn is killed for boasting against Diana of her motherhood (*Metam.* Book XI). Pygmalion's decision to sculpt a bride stems from his disgust at the whoredom of the Propoetides, their punishment for refusing to acknowledge Venus (Book X). On the latter, see also Leonard Barkan, "Living sculptures: Ovid, Michelangelo, and *The Winter's Tale*," *ELH* 48 (1981), 639–67, esp. p. 644.

53 Barkan ("Living sculptures") suggests that an element of competition emerges not at the level of authors or authority, but at that of artistic media through the tradition of the *paragone* or contest among the arts, which Shakespeare incorporates into the end of the play when he compares the incredible narrations of the Gentlemen in V.ii against first the silence of sculpture in Hermione's statue and finally the "living statues" of the theatre when she descends. Barkan points out (p. 663) that "the ultimate destination of the *paragone* ... is the rivalry of art and life." Even here, however, competition evaporates into the more complex dialectic of what Barkan calls (p. 664) "the mutual triumph of art and nature." But at this point the competitive language of "triumph" begins to get in the way and might be abandoned in favor of some other relation, such as the complementary or the dialectical.

54 See also the remarks on this point of Mueller, "Hermione's wrinkles," 236–7.

55 Here once again, Cavell's account of the return of Hermione as the recovery of "the ordinary" against the forces of both cynical skepticism and excessive enchantment is pertinent. I have also found the discussions of "the statuesque" by Barkan ("Living statues") and especially by Kenneth Gross illuminating and suggestive. See Gross, "Moving statues, talking statues" in *Raritan* 9:2 (1989), 1–25 and expanded in *The Dream of the Moving Statue* (Ithaca: Cornell University Press, 1992).

56   On the statue scene and the bear scene as counterparts in self-consciousness, see Gurr, "The bear, the statue and hysteria." This time, however, the challenge offered to the audience is precisely to credit and embrace what Gurr identifies as an "hysterical" reaction: that the action is literally taking place – an actor is no longer pretending to be a statue – and that the faith and pleasure in that trick legitimately stand for deeper repairs of trust and enlivenings of story. At this level, the play insists on the reality of its theatricality as a force of truth-telling, and opposes its therapeutic "hysteria" of "faith" to the pathological and misplaced hysteria of Leontes' skepticism.

57   See the brief citations given by Barkan, "Living sculptures," p. 664, n.1 and the editorial strictures cited by Coghill, "Six points," *passim*.

58   Barkan, *The Gods Made Flesh* (New Haven: Yale University Press, 1986), p. 284. See also Cavell's remarks on the couple's relation, on how "For her to return to him is for him to recognize his relation to her; in particular to recognize what his denial of her has done to her, hence to him. So Leontes recognizes the fate of stone to be the consequence of his particular scepticism" (*Disowning Knowledge*, p. 125). But I wonder whether Hermione's part in the transaction must be as passive as this suggests. What does Leontes' attack mean for her, and how is stone *her* response to it?

59   Bate's claim that the tale of the Propoetides is "not relevant" to the scene (*Shakespeare and Ovid*, p. 234) seems to me wrong-headed. That prehistory of misogynist disgust forms a close parallel, which Shakespeare transforms by fusion with the Dis abduction story. Both the fate of the Propoetides and that of Proserpina, incidentally, stem in Ovid from a parallel refusal to acknowledge Venus: "Pallada nonne vides iaculatricemque Dianam / abscessisse mihi? Cereris quoque filia virgo, / si patiemur, erit" (V.375–7).

60   Shakespeare had first represented such an antithesis and interrelation in *The Rape of Lucrece*, where Tarquin's desire and Lucrece's vulnerability are explicitly linked (though the poem does not suggest any softening of desire in her): "His ear her prayers admits, but his heart granteth / No penetrable entrance to her plaining: / Tears harden lust, though marble wear with raining" (558–60); cf. Lucrece's lament: "For men have marble, women waxen minds, / And therefore are they form'd as marble will" (1240–41), where "they" refers to both men and women, linked by the shaping of a hardened "will" at once noun and verb, mental act and physical implement. Mentation migrates and hardens into the erection itself, and becomes insensible.

61   Gross, "Moving statues," p. 17.

62   In the case of *Lear* it is those around him that Lear accuses of having been turned into "men of stones" by the deadness they confront, as if it exposes or creates a deadness in them. Apart from the "monumental alabaster" that Othello makes of Desdemona, there are also Viola's spectral self who "sat like Patience on a monument" and the "marble-breasted tyrant" Olivia, the Mariana who warrants her truth by offering herself as a "marble monument" in its guarantee (V.i.230–3), the Marina who looks "like Patience gazing on kings' graves," and, in her own monument, the Cleopatra who declares herself "marble-constant" (V.ii.240). Some of these return to life and some do not, but all are images of the survival of female will in its chosen posture

beyond the power of onlookers to get at it. That Coriolanus of the crystalline will who advances on Rome like a revenging robot is another, more alarming image of the animate idol. See Barkan, "Living statues," p. 665 n. 2 and Honigmann, "Secondary sources." Gross, *The Dream of the Moving Statue*, discusses the larger issues in detail. The *topos* of animation survives into modern fiction of course – my own favorite instance of how *not* to wake a statue occurs in C. S. Lewis's *The Magician's Nephew*.

63 I have in mind here W. H. Auden's description of love as an "intensity of attention" which seems to me highly relevant to this scene. It may be worth noting that another forum for such intense attention is that of the inquisitor, which Leontes has already adopted in default of love. Paulina's deliberate "slowing down" of Leontes' desire here, forcing it to attend to the right moment, may be a counterspell to the terrible haste of Dis in the Ovidian story, a hotness of libidinal sight which was nevertheless blind in every other way to its object: "paene simul visa est dilectaque raptaque Diti: / usque adeo est properatus amor" (V.395–6).

64 I have given here the Folio readings of "Louely" and the stage direction. Most modern editors expand the latter and emend the former to "Lonely." Either reading is possible: one emphasizes the power of the statue's "likeness" to stir love – a key thread of the scene; the other prefigures the discovery of life and emotion in the statue itself, since it makes little sense to speak of a statue as *per se* "lonely."

65 Coghill, "Six points," p. 40. Coghill also notes that this passage is "the most heavily punctuated passage I have found in the Folio," which points to the way it makes visually clear its interest in (the difficulty of) getting from one moment to the next, an interest we should compare to Florizel's encomium of Perdita discussed above. (The lines are V.iii.98–103 in Riverside.)

66 This strange sense of alternative or "ghost" figures of other versions of the play being present at its end is found in other final scenes of wonder in Shakespeare. In particular there is the darkening pressure exerted by that "other" and happier Claudio and Hero at the end of *Much Ado about Nothing* in Hero's words upon her unveiling: "And when I liv'd, I was your other wife, / And when you lov'd, you were my other husband" (V.iv.60–1). When the Friar counsels all to "let wonder seem familiar" (l. 70), we may wonder how much his words point to the unexorcised, "familiar" ghosts of a less shadowed matrimony.

67 Winnicott, *Playing and Reality*, p. 51, emphasis in original. For particular, often very moving, examples of these sessions, see also Winnicott, *Therapeutic Consultations in Childhood* (New York: Basic Books, 1971).

68 Cavell, *Disowning Knowledge*, p. 200. He continues: "That last phrase, saying that parts are being born, itself suggests the level at which theater … is being investigated in this play; hence suggests why theater is for Shakespeare an *endless* subject of study; and we are notified that no formulation of the ideas of participation and parturition in this play will be complete that fails to account for their connection with theatrical parts[.]"

69 There is a comparable moment of metadramatic fun at the end of *Henry IV, Part One* when (the actor playing) Falstaff makes fun of (the actor playing) Hotspur for obeying the rules about being dead on stage. An audience's

recurrent, and enjoyable, cynicism about "dead" actors ("I can see him breathing!") is thereby incorporated into the play's gaming with itself, just as here. Rosalie Colie's remarks on "tragicomedy" as a genre of various "mixings" and of the "between" are also relevant here (*Living Art*, pp. 278–83).

70 "Moving statues," p. 20.

71 A similar double movement out to the immediate audience and up to the gods as a second ring of spectators is explored by Harry Levin for the Player's Speech in *Hamlet* in his *The Question of Hamlet* (New York: Oxford University Press, 1959), pp. 139–64.

72 As so often, William Empson anticipates this way of putting it in his reflections on the importance to *Hamlet* of the existence of a previous hit play on the same subject. See Empson, *Essays on Shakespeare*, ed. David B. Pirie (Cambridge University Press, 1986), Ch. 3.

73 A partial but powerful exception to this is the persistent association of Titania with motherhood (and with the mortality that so frequently attends it), so that the scenes with Bottom take on a peculiar blithe confidence and indulgence, with Bottom in part "his Majesty the Baby" in delicious and beguiling fantasy. Only from without, and from the perspective of aristocratic disdain, are these scenes called disgusting. Within them they have an amplitude of mutual enchantment untouched by anxiety that has come to be an index of the Shakespearean dramatic imagination itself. That Oberon regards this with vengeful loathing is important, but not conclusive.

74 Adelman bases her identification of "fantasies of maternal origin" in part on a review of early modern views of childbirth and nursing that saw "matter" as "Mater." See Adelman, *Suffocating Mothers*, pp. 1–10 and 239–45. And though Shakespeare consistently identified this aspect of the world, what I am calling its "matriculation" of us, as female, there seems no essential or inherent need for that function in fact to be performed only by females.

CONCLUSION

1 Cited from Stephen Orgel, ed., *Ben Jonson: the Complete Masques* (New Haven: Yale University Press, 1969), p. 169.

Bibliography

Abdulla, A. K., *Catharsis in Literature* (Bloomington: Indiana University Press, 1985).

Adelman, Janet, *Suffocating Mothers: Fantasies of Maternal Origin in Shakespeare's Plays* (New York: Routledge, 1992).

Aquinas, Thomas, *Opera Omnia*, 25 vols. (New York: Musurgia Pub., 1948–50).

Summa Theologica, 60 vols., gen. eds. Thomas Gilby and T. C. O'Brien, (London: Eyre & Spottiswoode, 1963–75).

Baldwin, T. W., *On the Compositional Genetics of* The Comedy of Errors (Urbana: University of Illinois Press, 1965).

Barber, C. L., *Shakespeare's Festive Comedy* (Princeton University Press, 1959).

Barkan, Leonard, "Living sculptures: Ovid, Michelangelo, and *The Winter's Tale*," *ELH* 48 (1981), 639–67.

The Gods Made Flesh (New Haven: Yale University Press, 1986).

Barthes, Roland, *Le Plaisir du Texte* (Paris: Editions Tel Quel, 1973).

Baskerville, C. R., "Some evidence for early romantic plays in England," *MP* 14 (1916), 229–51, 467–512.

Bate, Jonathan, *Shakespeare and Ovid* (Oxford University Press, 1993).

Belfiore, Elisabeth, "Pleasure, tragedy and Aristotelian psychology," *Classical Quarterly*, 35 (1985), 349–61.

Tragic Pleasure: Aristotle on Plot and Emotion (Princeton University Press, 1992).

Benston, Kimberley, "The shaping of the Marlovian sublime" (Ph.D. thesis, Yale University, 1980).

Berger, Harry Jr., "Theatre, drama and the second world: a prologue to Shakespeare," *Comparative Drama* 2 (1968–9), 3–20.

Bergeron, David M., *Pageantry in the Shakespearean Theater* (Athens: University of Georgia Press, 1985).

Bevington, David, *From "Mankind" to Marlowe: Growth of Structure in the Popular Drama of Tudor England* (Cambridge: Harvard University Press, 1962).

Block, K. S., ed., *Ludus Coventriae* EETS es 120 (Oxford University Press, 1922).

Bloom, Harold, *The Anxiety of Influence* (Oxford University Press, 1973).

Boisacq, E., *Dictionnaire étymologique de la langue grecque* (Heidelberg: Carl Winter, 1950).

Bonaventura, St., *De Reductione Artium ad Theologiam*, trans. Sr. Emma T. Healy (New York: Bonaventure College, 1940).

Bradbrook, Muriel, *The Rise of the Common Player* (London: Chatto and Windus, 1962).

Braden, Gordon, and William Kerrigan, *The Idea of the Renaissance* (Baltimore: Johns Hopkins University Press, 1989).

Braden, Gordon, "Greenblatt's trajectory," *Raritan* 13:1 (1993), 139–50.

Bradshaw, Graham, *Shakespeare's Scepticism* (Ithaca: Cornell University Press, 1990).

Bristol, Michael, "In search of the bear: spatiotemporal form and the heterogeneity of economies in *The Winter's Tale*," *Shakespeare Quarterly* 42:2 (1991), 145–67.

Brower, Reuben A., *Hero and Saint: Shakespeare and the Greco-Roman Heroic Tradition* (Oxford University Press, 1971).

Burckhardt, Sigurd, *Shakespearean Meanings* (Princeton University Press, 1968).

Butcher, S. H., *Aristotle's Theory of Poetry and Fine Art*, reprint of 4th edn. of 1907 (New York: Dover Publishing, 1951).

Candido, Joseph, "Dining out in Ephesus: food in *The Comedy of Errors*," *SEL* 30 (1990), 217–41.

Cave, Terence, *Recognitions: a Study in Poetics* (Oxford University Press, 1988).

Cavell, Stanley, *Disowning Knowledge in Six Plays of Shakespeare* (Cambridge University Press, 1987).

Cawley, A. C. *et al.*, eds., *The Revels History of English Drama*, vol. 1 (London: Methuen, 1983).

Chambers, E. K., *The Medieval Stage*, 2 vols. (London: Oxford University Press, 1903).

Chantraine, P., *Dictionnaire étymologique de la langue grecque* (Paris: Editions Klincksieck, 1970).

Clark, P. and P. Slack, *English Towns in Transition, 1500–1700* (Oxford University Press, 1976).

Coghill, Nevill, "Six points of stagecraft in *The Winter's Tale*," *Shakespeare Survey* 11 (1958), 31–41.

Cohen, Walter, *Drama of a Nation* (Ithaca: Cornell University Press, 1985).

Coleridge, S. T., *Lectures 1808–19 on Literature*, ed. R. A. Foakes, Vol. 5:1 of *The Collected Works of Samuel Taylor Coleridge* (Princeton University Press, 1987).

Colie, Rosalie, *Paradoxia Epidemica* (Princeton University Press, 1966).
Shakespeare's Living Art (Princeton University Press, 1974).

Collier, Richard J., *Poetry and Drama in the York Corpus Christi Play* (Hamden: Archon Books, 1978).

Cox, John D., *Shakespeare and the Dramaturgy of Power* (Princeton: Princeton University Press, 1989).

Craig, Hardin, "The Corpus Christi procession and the Corpus Christi play," *JEGP* 13 (1914), 589–602.

Craig, Hardin, ed., *Two Coventry Corpus Christi Plays*, 2nd edn., EETS es 87, (Oxford University Press, 1967).

Crewe, Jonathan, "God or the good physician: the rational playwright in *The Comedy of Errors*," *Genre* 15 (1982), 209–10.

Cunningham, J. V., *Tradition and Poetic Structure* (Denver: Alan Swallow, 1960).

Cutts, John P., "Pericles' downright violence," *Shakespeare Studies* 4 (1969), 275–93.

"Pericles in rusty armour and the Matachine dance of the competitive knights at the court of Simonides," *YES* 4 (1974), 49–51.

Davidson, Clifford, "The Digby *Mary Magdalene* and the Magdalen cult of the Middle Ages," *Annuale Medievale* 13 (1972), 70–87.

"Thomas Aquinas, the feast of Corpus Christi and the English cycle-plays," *Michigan Academician* 7:1 (1974), 103–10.

A Middle English Treatise on the Playing of Miracles (Washington: University Press of America, 1981).

Davis, Norman, ed., *Non-Cycle Plays and Fragments*, EETS ss 1 (Oxford University Press, 1970).

Descartes, René, *Les Passions de l'ame*, ed. Geneviève Rodin-Lewis (Paris: Librairie Philosophique, 1966).

Selected Philosophical Writings, ed. and trans. John Cottingham *et al.*, (Cambridge University Press, 1988).

Meditationes de prima Philosophia, ed. George Heffernan (Notre Dame: University of Notre Dame Press, 1990).

Dollimore, Jonathan, *Radical Tragedy* (Chicago: University of Chicago Press, 1984).

Dunbar, Mary Judith, " 'To the judgment of your eye': iconography and the theatrical art of *Pericles*," in Kenneth Muir, ed., *Shakespeare: Man of the Theater* (Newark: University of Delaware Press, 1983), pp. 86–97.

Dunn, Catherine M., "The function of music in Shakespeare's romances," *Shakespeare Quarterly* 20 (1969), 391–405.

Eagleton, Terry, *Criticism and Ideology* (Atlantic Highlands: Humanities Press, 1976).

William Shakespeare (Oxford: Basil Blackwell, 1986).

Eggers, Walter F., Jr., "Shakespeare's Gower and the role of the authorial presenter," *PQ* 54 (1975), 434–43.

Empson, William, *Essays on Shakespeare*, ed. David B. Pirie (Cambridge University Press, 1986).

England, George, and A. W. Pollard, eds., *The Towneley Plays*, EETS es 71 (London: K. Paul, Trench, Truebner & Co., 1897).

Ewbank, Inga-Stina, " 'My name is Marina': the language of recognition," in Philip Edwards *et al.*, eds., *Shakespeare's Styles* (Cambridge University Press, 1980), pp. 111–28.

Felperin, Howard, *Shakespearean Romance* (Princeton University Press, 1972).

The Uses of the Canon (Oxford University Press, 1990).

Fergusson, Francis, *The Idea of a Theater* (Princeton University Press, 1949).

Fletcher, Anthony, *Tudor Rebellions* (London: Longman, 1983).

Ford, Andrew, "Katharsis: the ancient problem," in Andrew Parker and Eve Kosofsky Sedgwick, eds., *Performativity and Performance* (New York: Routledge, 1995).

Freud, Sigmund, *Beyond the Pleasure Principle*, in James Strachey, ed. and trans., *Standard Edition of the Complete Psychological Works of Sigmund Freud*, 24 vols. (London: Hogarth Press, 1955–74), Vol. XVIII.

Fry, Paul, *The Reach of Criticism* (New Haven: Yale University Press, 1983).

Garber, Marjorie B., *Dream in Shakespeare* (New Haven: Yale University Press, 1974).

Gardiner, Harold C., *Mysteries End* (New Haven: Yale University Press, 1946).

Gillet, J. E., "A note on the tragic 'admiratio'," *Modern Language Review* 13 (1918), 233–8.

Gohlke, Madelon, " 'I wooed thee with my sword': Shakespeare's tragic paradigms," in Murray Schwartz and Coppelia Kahn, eds., *Representing Shakespeare* (Baltimore: Johns Hopkins University Press, 1980), pp. 170–87.

Golden, L., "Epic, tragedy and catharsis," *Classical Philology* 71 (1976), 77–85.

Gorfain, Phyllis, "Puzzle and artifice: the riddle as metapoetry in *Pericles*," *Shakespeare Survey* 29 (1976), 11–20.

Greenblatt, Stephen, *Shakespearean Negotiations* (Oxford: Clarendon Press, 1987).

   Learning to Curse: Essays in Early Modern Culture (New York: Routledge, 1990).

   Marvelous Possessions: the Wonder of the New World (Chicago: University of Chicago Press, 1991).

Gross, Kenneth, "Moving statues, talking statues," *Raritan* 9:2 (1989), 1–25.

   The Dream of the Moving Statue (Ithaca: Cornell University Press, 1992).

Grube, G. M. A., "Notes on the *peri hypsous*," *AJP* 78 (1957), 371–4.

Gurr, Andrew, "The bear, the statue and hysteria in *The Winter's Tale*," *Shakespeare Quarterly* 34 (1983), 420–5.

   The Shakespearean Stage 1574–1642, 3rd edn. (Cambridge University Press, 1992)

Halliwell, Stephen, *Aristotle's Poetics* (London: Duckworth, 1986).

Hanning, R. W., " 'You have begun a parlous pleye': the nature and limits of dramatic mimesis as a theme in four Middle English 'Fall of Lucifer' cycle-plays," in Clifford Davidson, C. J. Gianakaris, and John H. Stroupe, eds., *The Drama of the Middle Ages: Comparative and Critical Essays* (New York: AMS Press, 1982), pp. 40–68.

Hardison, O. B., *Christian Rite and Christian Drama* (Baltimore: Johns Hopkins University Press, 1965).

Hartman, Geoffrey, *Beyond Formalism* (New Haven: Yale University Press, 1970).

Hassell, R. Chris, Jr., *Renaissance Drama and the English Church Year* (Lincoln: University of Nebraska Press, 1979).

Hathaway, Baxter, *The Age of Criticism: the Late Renaissance in Italy* (Ithaca: Cornell University Press, 1962).

   Marvels and Commonplaces: Renaissance Literary Criticism (New York: Random House, 1968).

Havelock, Eric, *A Preface to Plato* (Oxford: Basil Blackwell, 1963).

Hazlitt, W. C., ed., *The English Drama and Stage under the Tudor and Stuart Princes, 1543–1664* (London: Roxburghe Library, 1869; reprinted New York: Burt Franklin, n.d.).

Heinemann, Margot, *Puritanism and Theatre* (Cambridge University Press, 1980).

Helgerson, Richard, *Forms of Nationhood* (Chicago: University of Chicago Press, 1992).

Herrick, Marvin T., "Some neglected sources of *admiratio*," *Modern Language Notes*, 62 (1947), 222–6.

Hertz, Neil, *The End of the Line* (New York: Columbia University Press, 1985).

Hinman, Charlton, ed., *The First Folio of Shakespeare* (New York: Norton, 1968).

Hollander, John, *Melodious Guile: Fictive Pattern in Poetic Language* (New Haven: Yale University Press, 1988).

Honigmann, E. A. J., "Secondary sources of *The Winter's Tale*," *PQ* 34 (1955), 27–38.

Hough, Graham, "The allegorical circle," *Critical Quarterly* 3 (1961), 199–209.

Ide, Richard S., *Possessed with Greatness* (Chapel Hill: University of North Carolina Press, 1980).

Ingram, R. W., "1579 and the decline of civic religious drama in Coventry," in G. R. Hibbard, ed., *The Elizabethan Theatre VIII* (Ontario: P. D. Moany, 1980).

James, Mervyn, "Ritual, drama and social body in the late medieval English town," *Past and Present* 98 (1983), 3–29.

Jones, Emrys, *The Origins of Shakespeare* (Oxford University Press, 1977).

Jonson, Ben, *Ben Jonson: the Complete Masques*, ed. Stephen Orgel (New Haven: Yale University Press, 1969).

Kahn, Coppelia, *Man's Estate: Masculine Identity in Shakespeare* (Berkeley: University of California Press, 1981).

Kantorowicz, Ernst, *The King's Two Bodies: A Study in Medieval Political Theology* (Princeton University Press, 1957).

Knapp, Peggy Ann, "The Orphic vision of *Pericles*," *Texas Studies in Language and Literature* 15 (1974), 615–26.

Knight, G. Wilson, *The Crown of Life*, 4th edn. (London: Oxford University Press, 1957).

Knowles, Richard Paul, " 'The more delay'd, delighted': theophanies in the last plays," *Shakespeare Studies* 15 (1982), 269–80.

Kolvé, V. A., *The Play Called Corpus Christi* (Stanford University Press, 1966).

Krieger, Murray, *A Window to Criticism: Shakespeare's Sonnets and Modern Poetics* (Princeton University Press, 1964).

Lach, Donald F., *Asia in the Making of Europe*, Volume 2: *A Century of Wonder* (Chicago: University of Chicago Press, 1970).

Lamb, Jonathan, "Longinus, the dialectic, and the practice of mastery," *ELH* 60:3 (1993), 545–67.

Lambot, C., "L'office de la Fête-Dieu. Aperçus nouveaux sur ses origines," *Revue Bénédictine* 54 (1942), 396–8.

Laplanche, J. and J-B. Pontalis, *The Language of Psychoanalysis*, trans. D. Nicholson-Smith (New York: Norton, 1973).

Le Goff, Jacques, *The Medieval Imagination*, trans. Arthur Goldhammer (Chicago: University of Chicago Press, 1988).

"Head or heart: the political use of body metaphors in the Middle Ages," in *Fragments for a History of the Human Body, Part 3*, ed. Michel Feher (New York: Zone, 1989), 12–26.

Levin, Harry, *The Question of Hamlet* (New York: Oxford University Press, 1959).
Longinus, *On the Sublime*, ed. W. Rhys Roberts (Cambridge University Press, 1935).
　On the Sublime, ed. D. A. Russell (Oxford University Press, 1964).
Lucas, D. W., ed., *Aristotle's Poetics* (Oxford University Press, 1968).
McIntosh, William A., "Musical design in *Pericles*," *ELN* 11 (1973), 100–6.
Macherey, Pierre, *A Theory of Literary Production*, trans. Geoffrey Wall (London: Routledge and Kegan Paul, 1978).
Malvern, Marjorie M., *Venus in Sackcloth: the Magdalene's Origins and Metamorphoses* (Carbondale: Southern Illinois University Press, 1975).
Michael, Nancy C., "The relationship between the 1609 quarto of *Pericles* and Wilkins' *Painfull Adventures*," *Tulane Studies in English* 22 (1977), 51–68.
Montrose, Louis A., "The purpose of playing: reflections on a Shakespearean anthropology," *Helios* 7 (1980), 51–74.
Mueller, Martin, "Hermione's wrinkles, or, Ovid transformed: an essay on *The Winter's Tale*," *Comparative Drama* 5:3 (1971), 226–39.
Mullaney, Steven, *The Place of the Stage: License, Play and Power in Renaissance England* (Chicago: University of Chicago Press, 1988).
Nagler, A. M., *Shakespeare's Stage* (New Haven: Yale University Press, 1958).
Neely, Carol Thomas, "Women and issue in *The Winter's Tale*," *PQ* 57 (1978), 181–94.
　Broken Nuptials in Shakespeare's Plays (New Haven: Yale University Press, 1985).
Nehamas, Alexander, "Dangerous pleasures," in *The Times Literary Supplement*, Jan. 9, 1987, pp. 27–8.
Nelson, Alan, *The Medieval English Stage: Corpus Christi Pageants and Plays* (Chicago: University of Chicago Press, 1974).
Nevo, Ruth, *Shakespeare's Other Language* (New York: Methuen, 1987).
The N-Town Plays: a Facsimile of British Library Ms Cotton Vespasian D VIII (Leeds: University of Leeds, 1977).
Olson, Glending, *Literature as Recreation in the Later Middle Ages* (Ithaca: Cornell University Press, 1982).
Orgel, Stephen, "The poetics of spectacle," *New Literary History* 2:3 (1971), 372–6.
　The Illusion of Power: Political Theater in the English Renaissance (Berkeley: University of California Press, 1975).
　"Shakespeare and the kinds of drama," *Critical Inquiry* 6:1 (1979), 107–23.
　"The poetics of incomprehensibility," *Shakespeare Quarterly* 42:4 (1991), 431–8.
　"The play of conscience," in Andrew Parker and Eve Kosofsky Sedgwick, eds., *Performativity and Performance* (New York: Routledge, 1995).
Ovid, *Metamorphoses*, ed. William S. Anderson (Leipzig: Teubner, 1977).
Parker, Patricia, "Elder and younger: the opening scene of *The Comedy of Errors*," *Shakespeare Quarterly* 34 (1983), 325–7.
Phythian-Adams, Charles, "Urban decay in late-medieval England," in Philip Abrams and E. A. Wrigley, eds., *Towns in Societies: Studies in Economic History and Historical Sociology* (Cambridge University Press, 1978), pp. 159–85.

Pierson, Merle, "The relation of the Corpus Christi procession to the Corpus Christi play in England," *Transactions of the Wisconsin Academy of Arts and Letters* 18 (1915), 110–65.

Pitcher, John, "The poet and taboo: the riddle of Shakespeare's *Pericles*," in Suheil Bushrui, ed., *Essays and Studies* (London: Methuen, 1982), pp. 14–28.

Plato, *The Collected Dialogues*, ed. Edith Hamilton and Huntington Cairns (Princeton University Press, 1961).

Pocock, John, *The Ancient Constitution and the Feudal Law*, rev. edn. (Cambridge University Press, 1987).

Pokorny, Julius, *Indogermanisches etymologisches Wörterbuch* (Bern: Francke, 1959).

Prendergast, Christopher, *The Order of Mimesis* (Cambridge University Press, 1986).

Pye, Christopher, *The Regal Phantasm: Shakespeare and the Politics of Spectacle* (New York: Routledge, 1990).

Riggs, David, *Ben Jonson: A Life* (Cambridge: Harvard University Press, 1989).

Righter, Anne, *Shakespeare and the Idea of the Play* (London: Chatto & Windus, 1962, repr. Penguin, 1967).

Rorty, A. O., ed., *Essays on Aristotle's Poetics* (Princeton University Press, 1992).

Rouse, W. H. D., ed., *Shakespeare's Ovid* (Carbondale: Southern Illinois University Press, 1961).

Rubin, Miri, *Corpus Christi. The Eucharist in Late Medieval Culture* (Cambridge University Press, 1991).

Russell, D. A.,"Longinus revisited," *Mnemosyne*, 4th series, 34 (1981), 72–86.

Rutter, Carol, ed., *Documents of the Rose Playhouse* (Manchester University Press, 1984).

Salingar, Leo, *Shakespeare and the Traditions of Comedy* (Cambridge University Press, 1974).

Schaper, E., "Aristotle's catharsis and aesthetic pleasure," *PQ*, 18 (1968), 131–43.

Schoenbaum, Samuel, *William Shakespeare: A Compact Documentary Life* (Oxford University Press, 1987).

Shakespeare, William, *Works*, ed. G. Blakemore Evans (Boston: Houghton Mifflin, 1972).

    Pericles, Prince of Tyre, ed. F. David Hoeniger (London: Methuen, 1963).

    The Winter's Tale, ed. G. B. Harrison (London: Penguin, 1947).

Sidney, Sir Philip, *A Defence of Poetry*, ed. John Van Dorsten (Oxford University Press, 1966).

Sontag, Susan, *Against Interpretation* (New York: Farrar, Strauss & Giroux, 1961).

Sophocles, *Oedipus the King*, trans. David Grene, in *Sophocles I* of *The Complete Greek Tragedies*, ed. David Grene and Richmond Lattimore (Chicago: University of Chicago Press, 1954).

    Oedipus the King, trans. Thomas Gould (New Jersey: Prentice-Hall, 1970).

    Oedipus Tyrannos, ed. R. D. Dawe (Cambridge University Press, 1982).

Sparshott, Francis, "The riddle of *katharsis*," in Eleanor Cook *et al.*, eds., *Centre and Labyrinth: Essays in Honour of Northrop Frye* (Toronto: University of Toronto Press, 1983).

Spector, Stephen, ed., *The N-Town Play*, 2 vols., EETS ss 11 & 12 (Oxford University Press, 1991).

Spencer, M. L., *Corpus Christi Pageants in England* (New York: Baker and Taylor, 1911).

St. Victor, Hugh of, *Didascalion*, trans. Jerome Taylor (New York: Columbia University Press, 1961).

Stallybrass, Peter, "Patriarchal territories; the body enclosed," in Margaret W. Ferguson, Maureen Quilligan, and Nancy Vickers, eds., *Rewriting the Renaissance* (Chicago: University of Chicago Press, 1986).

Stone, Darwell, *A History of the Doctrine of the Holy Eucharist*, 2 vols. (London: Longmans, 1909).

Telford, Kenneth, trans., *Aristotle's Poetics* (Chicago: Gateway, 1961).

Thomas, Max W., "*Kemps Nine Daies Wonder*: dancing carnival into market," *PMLA* 107:3 (May, 1992), 511–23.

Thurn, David, "Sights of power in *Tamburlaine*," *English Literary Renaissance*, 19:1 (1989), 3–21.

Toulmin Smith, Lucy, ed., *York Plays* (orig. publ. 1885; repr. New York: Russell and Russell, 1963).

Travis, Peter, *Dramatic Design in the Chester Cycle* (Chicago: University of Chicago Press, 1982).

Waith, Eugene, *The Herculean Hero in Marlowe, Chapman, Shakespeare and Dryden* (New York: Columbia University Press, 1962).

Watkins, W. B. C., *Shakespeare and Spenser* (Princeton University Press, 1950).

Weimann, Robert, *Shakespeare and the Popular Tradition in the Theater*, ed. and trans. Robert Schwartz (Baltimore: Johns Hopkins University Press, 1978).

Weinberg, Bernard, "Robortello on the *Poetics*," in *Critics and Criticism, Ancient and Modern*, ed. R. S. Crane (Chicago: University of Chicago Press, 1952), pp. 319–48.

"Castelvetro's theory of poetics," in *Critics and Criticism, Ancient and Modern*, ed. R. S. Crane, pp. 349–71.

A History of Literary Criticism in the Italian Renaissance, 2 vols. (Chicago: University of Chicago Press, 1961).

Weiskel, Thomas, *The Romantic Sublime* (Baltimore: Johns Hopkins University Press, 1976).

Whitaker, Thomas, *Fields of Play in Modern Drama* (Princeton University Press, 1977).

Wilson, F. P., *English Drama 1485–1585*, ed. G. K. Hunter (Oxford University Press, 1968).

Wimsatt, William K. and Cleanth Brooks, *Literary Criticism: A Short History*, 2 vols. (Chicago: University of Chicago Press, 1978).

Winnicott, D. W., *Playing and Reality* (New York: Basic Books, 1971).

Therapeutic Consultations in Childhood (New York: Basic Books, 1971).

Wood, James O., "Shakespeare and the belching whale," *ELN* 11 (1973), 40–4.

Woolf, Rosemary, *The English Mystery Plays* (Berkeley: University of California Press, 1972).

Yates, Frances, *Astraea: the Imperial Theme in the Sixteenth Century* (London: Routledge & Kegan Paul, 1975).

Index

acting companies, social institution of, 64–5, 70, 88, 190n 5, 191n 6
Adelman, Janet, 158, 173, 200n 3, 203n 29, 204n 34, 210n 74
admiratio, 36–7, 38, 40–1, 178n 6
l'admiration, 6–11
Aeschylus, 33; *Agamemnon*, 33; *Persians*, 33
aesthetics, and psychology, 136, 146, 154, 163, 173
Albertus Magnus, 4, 178n 6
antitheatricalism, 43, 45–6, 66
Aquinas, St. Thomas, 4, 43–5, 47, 54, 87, 182n 14, 188n 25
Ariosto, Lodovico, 185n 45
Aristotle, 3, 4, 5, 6, 10, 11, 14, 17–21, 29–30, 31, 32, 33, 34, 38, 39, 40, 44, 47, 60, 100, 115, 117, 165, 185n 42, 185n 48; *Metaphysics*, 26–8, 32, 32, 36; *Poetics*, 10, 11, 14, 17–21, 25, 27, 28, 30, 32, 33, 34, 36, 60, 180n 6, 181n 12, 182n 14, 183n 21, 184n 26, 184n 27; *Politics*, 41; *Rhetoric*, 27–8, 181n 13, 182n 18; *Topica*, 180n 2
art/nature debate, 15, 74, 156–7, 164, 167, 175, 207n 53
Artaud, Antonin, 146
astonishment, 7, 18–19, 20, 22, 40, 98, 180n 1
Auden, W. H., 209n 63
audience, emotion in, 33, 36, 165; imagination of, 67, 104, 167, 170–1
audition, 32–3, 34, 47, 53, 55, 57, 60, 62, 113, 147
Augustine, St., 48, 187n 14, 187n 15
authorship, early modern, 95, 121

Baldwin, T. W., 76, 191n 24, 193n 28, 194n 35, 195n 48
Barber, C. L., 66–7, 191n 9
Barkan, Leonard, 162, 207n 53
Barthes, Roland, 153, 206n 44
Bate, Jonathan, 150, 155, 170, 204n 37, 205n 39, 206n 43, 208n 59

Blake, William, 13, 161, 170, 177
Bloom, Harold, 160, 188n 19
Bonaventura, St., 43
bondage, 79–83, 85, 86, 88, 114, 153, 182n 16, 194n 35; and the erotic, 86; metaphor as, 80
Buonamici, Francesco, 40
Buontalenti, Bernardo, 39

Castelvetro, Lodovico, 38, 185n 48
castration, 100, 113, 137–9
catharsis, *see* katharsis
Cave, Terence, 119–20, 121, 122
Cavell, Stanley, 127, 130–1, 141, 150, 162, 169, 202n 20, 207n 55, 208n 58, 209n 68
Chester cycle, 48, 69, 189n 30, 190n 36
childhood, 128, 169; innocence in, 128, 134; sexual knowledge in, 130–3, 135, 139, 141, 202n 19
Cicero, 36
Cinthio, Giraldi, 38
Coghill, Nevill, 153, 166
Coke, Sir Edward, 67, 69
Coleridge, S. T., 22
Colie, Rosalie, 157, 196n 52, 210n 69
contaminatio, 15, 86, 172, 194n 41
Coventry cycle, 69; *Shearmen and Taylors' play*, 46
Cradle of Security, The, 69–70
Crewe, Jonathan, 194n 37
cultural criticism, Elizabethan, 66
Cunningham, J. V., 28–9, 181n 6
cycle-plays, relation to later drama, 63–4, 190n 6; social character of, 66, 69; structure of, 42, 46, 54, 58, 62–4, 190n 2

danger, 33–5, 99, 138, 165
De Reductione Artium ad Theologiam, 43
death, 75–6, 80, 82–4, 85, 88, 97, 99, 101, 119, 122–3, 131–2, 136, 138, 151–2, 155, 159–60, 167–8, 172, 175, 177, 194n 35

delivery, as childbirth, 88–9, 114, 117, 133,
    210n 74; as liberation, 116, 167–8
Denores, Giason, 40
Descartes, René, 4, 6–11, 15, 24, 37;
    Meditationes, 8–10, 179n 13; *Les
    Passions de l'Ame*, 6–8, 178n 6, 178n 7;
    and Ovid, 180n 15
desire, 16, 97, 98, 129, 143, 149, 163, 175,
    196n 8
development, human, 134, 141–3, 147, 149,
    157, 158, 169, 172, 174, 201n 11
Didascalion, 43
Donne, John, 196 n51

Eagleton, Terry, 108
ekplexis, 18, 19, 21, 29, 31, 33, 180n 1,
    183n 22
Empson, William, 210n 72
Engle, Lars, 79, 193n 29
Enough is as Good as a Feast, 125
erotic, in art, 16, 22–4, 25, 86, 91–2, 97, 104,
    108, 113, 115, 118, 156–7, 163–5,
    174–5, 194n 40, 194n 41, 198n 34
Eucharist, social character of, 42–5, 58, 62,
    72–3, 84, 87, 89, 90–1, 187n 11, 194n 37
Euripides, 33

Fantasy, 15, 52, 57, 124, 129, 132, 134, 135,
    139–40, 144–5, 147, 149–50, 152, 158,
    160, 172, 173, 201n 11
father, 96–9, 103–4, 118, 122, 129, 131–2,
    140, 201n 10, 202n 19
Felperin, Howard, 203n 31
Fergusson, Francis, 71
flux, semiotic, 47, 51, 86, 115, 117, 119; in
    nature, 83–6, 90, 102, 104, 156
Ford, Andrew, 10
Freud, Sigmund, 177, 181n 13, 200n 4, 201n
    10, 202n 17, 202n 19, 204n 34
Fry, Paul, 30

gestation, 88–91, 109, 113, 121, 131–2, 173
Golding, Arthur, 151, 199n 45, 204n 38,
    205n 39, 205n 40, 206n 41, 206n 42
Gosson, Stephen, 66, 67, 89
Greenblatt, Stephen, 12, 192n 22
Greene, Robert, 68, 72, 159, 203n 32, 205n
    39, 206n 42
Gross, Kenneth, 163, 170
Gurr, Andrew, 153, 206n 44, 208n 56

Hanning, R. W., 48, 53
Hardison, O. B., 71, 72
Hathaway, Baxter, 37, 38, 39
Hertz, Neil, 31, 183n 23
Hesiod, 22

Hollander, John, 73, 180n 15
Homer, 5, 173, 178n 5, 183n 19
Honigmann, E. A. J., 151, 204n 38
Horace, 36, 185n 42
hubris, 27
hysteria, 153, 208n 56; male sexual, 130,
    143–4, 147, 151, 203n 29

incarnation, 14, 15, 47, 72–3, 84, 87–8, 89,
    94, 101, 114, 118, 121–2, 150, 170, 174,
    192n 20, 200n 7
incest, as metaphor, 96

James, Mervyn, 42–3
Johnson, Samuel, 2
Jones, Emrys, 64
Jones, Inigo, 39, 176
Jonson, Ben, 67, 68, 72, 102, 121, 160, 177,
    191n 11, 199n 41; *Bartholomew Fair*,
    67; *Oberon*, 176–7
katharsis, 5, 11, 18–19, 36, 38, 39, 40, 41,
    146, 160, 180n 1, 185n 48
Knight, G. Wilson, 100, 196n 8, 198n 36
knowledge, 4–8, 13, 26, 35, 40, 41, 54, 56–7,
    89–90, 97, 99–100, 112, 118, 120, 127,
    135, 136, 139, 144, 147–8, 177, 178n 6,
    179n 13, 182n 14, 188n 23

Lacan, Jacques, 183n 23
Levin, Harry, 210n 71
Lewis, C. S., 209n 62
Like Will to Like, 125
Longinus, 5, 6, 14, 29–32, 51, 52, 62, 167,
    178n 4, 182n 15, 182n 16, 185n 39,
    194n 40
Lucas, D. W., 18, 19, 180n 2

Marlowe, Christopher, 41, 66, 88, 160, 182n
    16, 191n 8
marriage, 74, 86–7, 89, 91–2, 103, 107–8,
    116, 149, 162
masque, 176–7
metaphor, 23, 25, 29–30, 32, 34, 35, 50, 67,
    80, 86, 88, 89, 91–2, 110, 115–17, 118,
    164, 167, 174
Milton, John, 173, 175
mimesis, 5, 28, 37, 44, 48, 165, 181n 12,
    187n 15, 201n 11
Minturno, Antonio, 38
misogyny, 99, 133, 144, 147, 162
mother, 88, 91, 108–9, 122, 123, 124,
    128–31, 152, 173–4, 195n 43, 197n 18,
    199n 44, 199n 45, 200n 4, 204n 34,
    204n 38, 206n 42, 210n 73, 210n 74
Montrose, Louis A., 71–2
Mount Tabor, 69–70

Mullaney, Steven, 95, 111, 121, 190n 6

N-Town cycle, 48, 189n 30; *Resurrection*
    sequence, 14, 47, 58–62, 189n 35
naming, 25, 52, 55, 61, 62, 79, 81–2, 83, 96,
    105, 111, 116, 121, 125, 194n 27, 197n 18
narrative, 28–35, 40, 75, 93–4, 104, 119,
    126–7; Aristotle and, 18–19, 33; as
    cause and effect, 5, 19, 76, 82, 132; as
    cultural transmission, 95, 102, 111,
    122–3; as defence, 150, 152; deferral in,
    23, 25, 32, 61, 117–18, 181n 13; as
    human practice, 94, 104, 107, 116, 168;
    linearity in, 13, 15, 18, 77, 78–9, 80, 84,
    85, 86, 118, 193n 28, 193n 29; as play,
    128–9, 141, 144; as reproduction, 104,
    107–8, 116, 118, 132; sociality of, 43,
    63, 74–5, 79, 87, 94–5, 108, 112, 120;
    temporality of, 75–78, 82–4, 88, 118;
    and theft, 85, 97, 159, 206n 51; and
    therapy, 95, 113, 117, 120, 128, 149,
    160–1, 167–8, 172, 197n 9
Nevo, Ruth 150

Orgel, Stephen, 39, 202n 22
Ovid, 10, 88, 115, 150–6, 158–60, 161, 168,
    172–3, 177, 180n 15, 198n 35, 199n 45,
    204n 38, 205n 39, 205n 40, 206n 41,
    206n 42, 206n 43, 207n 52, 208n 59,
    209n 63; *Metamorphoses*, 115, 160

paradox, 89, 91–2, 117, 121, 196n 52,
    198n 34
paralysis, 112–13, 116, 148, 183n 25
parody, in cycle-plays, 46, 48, 65
participation, 108, 118, 198n 25
pastoral, 102, 134, 156–7, 158–9
pathos, 4, 21, 27, 33–4, 178n 4
Patrizi, Francesco, 38, 185n 39
Paul, St., 75, 82, 83, 86, 87, 88, 89, 193n 33,
    194n 35
Peele, George, 159
platea, and *locus* staging, 61
Plato, 3, 4, 5, 14, 17, 21–6, 29, 31, 36, 89,
    187n 11, 183n 24; *Euthydemus* 21;
    Letter VII, 25; *Phaedrus*, 22–4, 25, 29,
    30, 89, 181n 13; *Symposium*, 24–6, 181n
    9; *Republic*, 20, 21, 25; *Theaetetus*,
    21–2, 25
Plautus, 15, 74–5, 81, 89, 193n 24, 194n 41;
    Menaechmi, 76–7; *Amphitruo*, 194n 38
play, 133, 135, 140–1, 143–4, 169, 172,
    201n 11
pleasure, 29, 38, 40–1, 94, 97, 99, 107, 113,
    118, 122, 144, 170, 181n 13, 182n 14
Proclus, 36

Prynne, William, 66
Puttenham, George, 92

rape, male desire and, 137–8, 144, 151–5,
    201n 16, 203n 28, 205n 40, 206n 42
reason, 3, 4, 5, 7, 8, 14, 196n 52
recognition, 5, 19, 23, 32, 33, 48, 61–2, 73,
    89–91, 112, 114–15, 120–1, 123, 137,
    150, 169–70, 176, 181n 12, 190n 35,
    195n 47, 198n 29
recovery, 15–16, 93–4, 104, 117–19, 159,
    167, 198n 30
recreation, 43, 107, 141, 148
riddles, 25, 96, 98–9, 111, 114, 199n 1
Righter, Anne, 46, 47
ritual, in drama, 43, 65, 66, 71–2, 94, 186n 6
Robortello, Francesco, 36, 38, 185n 48
Rubin, Miri, 45

sacrament, semiotics of, 43–5, 65, 72, 84, 87,
    91, 193n 33; and the erotic, 86, 194n 42
St. Victor, Hugh of, 43
Scaliger, Julius Caesar, 38, 185n 48
Schlegel, Friedrich, 73
self-consciousness, in art, 12, 31, 35, 47, 50,
    52, 57, 62, 73–4, 91–2, 107, 123, 126, 133,
    144–5, 160, 164, 167, 170–1, 204n 34
Shakespeare, William, *passim*; and Bible,
    87–8, 150, 193n 29, 195n 45;
    conservatism in, 15, 66–68; and
    psychoanalysis, 149–50, 204n 34;
    skepticism in, 63, 73–4, 90, 98, 162;
    relation to Stratford-on-Avon, 68,
    191n 10; and tradition, 15, 74, 94–6,
    102–3, 121, 123, 173, 191n 9
    Works: *All's Well that Ends Well*, 114,
    126, 200n 2; *Antony and Cleopatra*,
    198n 34, 208n 62; *As You Like It*, 125,
    200n 2, 201n 14; *The Comedy of Errors*,
    13, 14–15, 63–91, 125, 150, 173, 192n
    24, 193n 29; *Coriolanus*, 146, 209n 62;
    Cymbeline, 147, 199n 45; *Hamlet*, 70,
    71, 111, 196n 51, 198n 34, 204n 33,
    210n 71, 210n 72; *Henry IV Part One*,
    11, 209n 69; *Henry V*, 67, 125; *Henry
    VI Part Two*, 64; *Julius Caesar*, 125;
    King Lear, 2, 74, 102, 163, 191n 11,
    201n 13, 208n 62; *Love's Labours Lost*,
    70, 125; *Macbeth*, 41, 194n 38, 195n 51,
    202n 18; *Measure for Measure*, 41, 108,
    114, 200n 2, 201n 16; *A Midsummer
    Night's Dream*, 92, 104, 106, 112, 141,
    195n 51, 201n 14, 205n 40, 210n 73;
    Much Ado about Nothing, 74, 108, 125,
    138, 196n 51, 200n 2, 209n 66; *Othello*,
    133, 140, 162, 195n 51, 202n 21,

Shakespeare, William, Works (*cont.*)
  208n 62; *Pericles, Prince of Tyre*, 15,
  93–123, 147, 150, 160, 171, 195n 43,
  196n 8, 197n 18, 197n 19, 198n 29,
  199n 41, 199n 43, 201n 14, 208n 62;
  The Phoenix and the Turtle, 91; *The
  Rape of Lucrece*, 208n 60; *Richard II*,
  72–3; *Richard III*, 11; *Sonnets*, 198n 34,
  199n 42; *The Taming of the Shrew*,
  200n 2; *The Tempest*, 108, 122, 126,
  160, 172, 176, 177, 199n 45, 199n 1;
  Twelfth Night, 65, 66, 191n 9, 195n 47,
  196n 51, 198n 25, 199n 38, 206n 43,
  208n 62; *Troilus and Cressida*, 195n 51,
  197n 19; *The Winter's Tale*; 2, 15, 74,
  124–75, 176, 183n 24, 202n 19, 292n 22,
  203n 29, 205n 39; economic language
  in, 141–2, 202n 24, Proserpina myth in,
  151–6, 161, 172, 204n 37, 204n 38, 206n
  42, 207n 52
spectacle, 14, 30–3, 39, 57, 63, 96, 102, 145–7
Sparshott, Francis, 20, 180n 1
Snow White, 2
Sontag, Susan, 16
Sophocles, 71; *Oedipus the King*, 27, 32,
  34–6, 61, 184n 31, 184n 32
skepticism, 60–1, 66, 74, 90, 148, 162, 170,
  203n 31, 208n 56, 208n 58
Sidney, Sir Philip, 38
Spenser, Edmund, 9, 67, 68, 173; *Faerie
  Queene, The*, 68, 200n 7
statues, 7, 15, 101, 152, 154, 161–7, 170,
  200n 7, 203n 26, 207n 53, 208n 56,
  209n 64
Stubbes, Philip, 66, 68

Tasso, Torquato, 38
Towneley cycle, 48, 190n 36, *Second
  Shepherds' Play*, 11, 46, 65, 73
Travis, Peter, 58
time, 75–8, 80, 83, 84, 85, 88–9, 105, 141–3,
  149, 160, 169–70, 172
Treatise of Miraclis Pleyinge, 45–6, 58
Twine, Lawrence, 111

unreasonable, the, 20–1, 29

violence, 30–1, 32, 33–5, 46, 77–8, 81, 98,

110, 112–13, 131, 133, 138, 141, 146,
  166, 201n 10, 206n 42
virginity, 109, 112, 121–2, 123, 124, 153–4,
  195n 43, 197n 11, 199n 44
visual in theatre (*opsis*), 32–3, 39, 47,
  58, 60–1, 96, 98–9, 106, 113, 135,
  182n 21
Vitruvius, 39

Wagner, Richard, 177
Weimann, Robert, 186n 5
Weinberg, Bernard, 38
Wilde, Oscar, 200n 9
Wilkins, George, 94–106, 196n 1
Willis, Ralph, 69–70
Wimsatt, William K., 30
Winnicott, D. W., 132, 138, 158, 169, 200n
  4, 201n 11
winter, 141, 143, 151–2, 164
wonder, 22, 31; and blockage, 9, 20, 28, 31,
  57, 114, 118, 166, 176, 179n 13, 182n
  14, 183n 25; definition, 3, 73, 147, 167;
  and difficulty, 23, 28–9, 38, 113;
  doubleness in, 20, 49, 53, 89–90, 92, 98,
  112, 114, 118, 137, 167; dynamic of, 3,
  16, 22, 29, 30, 31, 32, 47, 63, 73, 74, 92,
  113, 117, 123; as emotion, 5, 6–11, 14,
  15, 23, 73, 92, 121, 167, 182n 18; as
  epiphanic moment, 20, 35, 36, 47, 57,
  88, 92, 118, 169; etymology of, 30–1,
  182n 18, 183n 22; and fear, 28–9, 46,
  96, 101, 160, 167, 182n 14, 184n 26;
  force in, 6, 15, 27, 55, 57, 73, 101, 113,
  118, 148, 167, 176, 178n 7; liminal
  character of, 6, 19, 31, 41, 58, 84, 86,
  92, 112, 115, 118, 162, 165, 167–8, 170,
  176–7, 195n 47; and pleasure, 29, 94,
  97, 194n 40; as political tool, 37; and
  purgation, 4, 10, 40, 113, 160; in
  Renaissance criticism, 37–41; and
  reversal (*peripeteia*), 23, 52–3, 117–18,
  168; and the sublime, 15; and
  transgression, 50–2, 90, 97, 117, 118; as
  trauma, 7, 30, 33, 96, 98, 118

York cycle, 69, 188n 30, 190n 36; *Fall of
  Lucifer*, 14, 47–54, 187n 15, 188n 20;
  Transfiguration, 47, 54–8, 188n 26